Arthur M. Schlesinger, Jr., and the Ideological History of American Liberalism

STUDIES IN RHETORIC AND COMMUNICATION
General Editors:
E. Culpepper Clark
Raymie E. McKerrow
David Zarefsky

Stephen P. Depoe

Arthur M. Schlesinger, Jr., and the Ideological History of American Liberalism

The University of Alabama Press   Tuscaloosa and London

Library of Congress Cataloging-in-Publication Data

Depoe, Stephen P., 1959–
    Arthur M. Schlesinger, Jr., and the ideological history of
American liberalism / Stephen P. Depoe.
        p.   cm. — (Studies in rhetoric and communication)
    Includes bibliographical references and index.
    ISBN 0-8173-0718-4
    1. Schlesinger, Arthur Meier, 1917– . 2. United States—
Historiography.   3. Liberalism—United States—History—20th
century.   I. Title.   II. Series.
E175.5.S38D46   1994
320.5'13'0973—dc20   93-5806
                                                          CIP

British Library Cataloguing-in-Publication Data available

To my wife, Cindy, and
to my children, Aaron and Andrew

Contents

Preface

Historian John Higham has noted that "in almost every generation one or more historians have been among the leading lights of American culture, and their books have exemplified some of its most pronounced characteristics. The writing of American history has always had, therefore, an intimate relation to history in the making."[1] In the years since 1945, few American historians have had a more intimate relation to history in the making than Arthur M. Schlesinger, Jr. He has been influential in shaping our understanding of American political history and has written important treatises on Jacksonian America, the New Deal, the Kennedy administration, and the American presidency. He has also been active in partisan politics, has written articles espousing liberal positions on current issues, has championed liberal causes as cofounder of the Americans for Democratic Action, and has served as adviser to important political leaders such as Adlai Stevenson and John F. Kennedy.

Political commentators and historical scholars alike have long recognized the important role Schlesinger has played in shaping liberal political thought in America. For example, Henry Fairlie, never a Schlesinger ally, frankly admitted in 1978 that Schlesinger "is a significant writer who ought to engage our interest" because he "has made himself count in the middle years of our century in a way that has no parallel in any other career." Schlesinger, wrote Fairlie, is "perhaps the best representative figure of mid-twentieth century liberalism."[2] In a review of *The Cycles of American History* (1986), Alan

Brinkley noted that Schlesinger's work has been influential "because he possesses a rare ability to make history seem important, because he is willing to argue that the search for an understanding of the past is not simply an aesthetic exercise but a path to the understanding of our own time."[3] "The pen of Arthur Schlesinger, Jr.," concluded Thomas Axworthy in 1987, "may be American liberalism's most potent weapon." Throughout his career, Axworthy noted, the historian's work has been "animated by a coherent philosophy" that has placed him "at the vital center of his nation's life."[4]

Throughout his career, Schlesinger has attempted to use history to provide insight into contemporary issues and politics. In the foreword to *The Cycles of American History* (1986), Schlesinger wrote that the book's collection of essays "offers a historian's reflection on the past and the future of the American experiment." While history is not "the cure for all that ails us . . . ," he asserted, "knowledge of what Americans have been through in earlier times will do us no harm as we grope through the darkness of our own days."[5] Throughout his career, Schlesinger's accounts of the past have been shaped by his political viewpoint and activities in the present. As Arthur Mann once succinctly noted: "Professor Schlesinger writes history as he votes and votes as he writes."[6]

Central to Schlesinger's work has been the premise that American history has been characterized by recurring cycles of conservative and liberal dominance. Schlesinger derived this premise from a theory of American history advanced by his father, Arthur Schlesinger, Sr., entitled "the tides of national politics." Schlesinger, Jr., summarized the theory in his first important historical work, *The Age of Jackson*, which he completed in 1945 at the age of twenty-eight: "American history has been marked by recurrent swings of conservatism and liberalism. During periods of inaction, unsolved social problems pile up till demand for reform becomes overwhelming. Then a liberal government comes to power, the dam breaks, and a flood of change sweeps away a great deal in a short time. After fifteen or twenty years the liberal impulse is exhausted, the day of 'consolidation' arrives, and conservatism, once again, expresses the mood of the country, but generally on the terms of the liberalism it displaces."[7]

More than any of his other ideas, Schlesinger's cyclical view of history has influenced contemporary American political discourse. Wrong has claimed that the notion that "politics conform to . . . cyclical periodicity" has become "implicit in the most commonplace language of political journalism" and has at times dominated political debate and cultural life in the United States.[8] In his own work spanning over four decades, Schlesinger has used the tides of national politics to provide historical grounds and support material for arguments concerning the legitimacy and superiority of active liberal government and leadership.

This book examines the origin, elements, and evolving significance of the tides of national politics in the discourse of Arthur M. Schlesinger, Jr. I focus upon how the tides concept has functioned as the basis for both causal explanation in Schlesinger's historical scholarship and ideological justification in his partisan political discourse.

I analyze Schlesinger's tides concept from a *rhetorical* perspective, which defines the historian's discourse as arguments made to audiences. More specifically, I employ the rhetorical perspective of *dramatism* and the critical insights of Kenneth Burke. Broadly stated, dramatism is a critical stance that considers ways in which humans use symbols strategically to relate to one another in society.[9] The task of dramatistic criticism is to uncover purpose in human communication.[10]

Dramatistic criticism is based upon three assumptions. First, symbols shape human experience by directing our attention and influencing our intentions. Through the symbolic action of language, we define situations and adopt attitudes toward ideas and other people.[11] Second, human society is characterized by the constant merger and division of groups on the basis of the perception of shared interests and needs. As groups compete for resources and status within a society, they enact roles and interact in dramatic ways.[12] What William Rueckert calls the "drama of human relations" is the quest by individuals and groups for identity and autonomy in the larger social context, in which different motives create multiple and conflicting roles within people and organizations.[13] Third, individuals and groups use persuasion—rhetoric—as a primary means to produce cooperation leading to social action. Burke defines rhetoric as "the use of language as a symbolic means of inducing cooperation in beings that by nature respond to symbols."[14] In the paradox of merger and division that is human experience, we use words to try to persuade each other to identify common interests and to act together in response to situations.

I adopt a rhetorical perspective toward Schlesinger's discourse in order to accomplish three critical purposes. First, I attempt to illuminate the persuasive role Schlesinger's view of history has played in shaping liberal political thought in America since the end of World War II. Schlesinger's academic work has drawn both interest and criticism from fellow historians.[15] Other analysts have examined Schlesinger's political partisanship on specific issues ranging from McCarthyism to domestic policy to the Vietnam war.[16]

This study tries to discover how Schlesinger's conception of American history has served as an inventional principle guiding arguments he has made in various persuasive contexts throughout his career. Toward that end, the study applies Burke's concept of a *frame of acceptance* to Schlesinger's belief in the tides of national politics. Burke defines frame of acceptance as "the more or less organized system of meanings by which a thinking man gauges the historical situation and adopts a role with relation to it."[17] A frame of acceptance is an overall perspective or orientation toward the world taken by an individual or group. The perspective is symbolic, including both terms and propositions that identify positive and negative forces inhering in particular situations. In naming aspects of a situation as "friendly" or "unfriendly," Burke writes, we "form our characters, since the names embody attitudes; and implicit in the attitudes there are cues for behavior."[18]

This book considers the tides of national politics as the frame of acceptance that has provided Arthur Schlesinger with terms and propositions for defining his perspective toward his world. The book also explores the influence Schlesinger's frame of acceptance has had on the shape and substance of contemporary liberal discourse in America.

Second, this analysis of Schlesinger's work attempts to broaden understanding of how arguments about the past can influence political action in the present. All historians write history from a point of view and use rhetorical strategies to make a case for particular interpretations of past events. Most historians, who are interested primarily in persuading readers of the soundness or reasonability of their accounts of past events, construct conventional arguments *about* history.[19]

Other historians and many political advocates try to use history for more overtly partisan purposes. These advocates, who wish the past to provide "lessons which entail guidelines for directing future action," construct arguments *from* history. Such arguments synthesize "historical events into a perspective which could prescribe and direct a compelling course of action" in the present and future.[20]

When advocates construct and enact historical discourse for the purpose of persuading audiences to adopt policies or take actions in the present, they engage in what Michael McGee has called *ideological history.* In an ideological history, interpretations of past scenes, agents, motives, and actions are constructed to generate favorable or unfavorable perceptions of related circumstances in the present.[21] Such historical arguments can influence public discourse and decision by shaping the political values, presumptions, and priorities within a community.[22] I examine how Schlesinger not only utilized the concept of the tides of national politics as part of his academic arguments *about* American history but also applied the concept as the basis of ideological arguments *from* history in various persuasive contexts during his career as scholar and liberal political partisan.

Finally, this book hopes to contribute to ongoing attempts by rhetorical scholars to account for the way in which one symbolic choice we make may influence or constrain subsequent symbolic actions.[23] The dramatistic concept of *rhetorical trajectory* is used as a way of understanding Schlesinger's reliance on the tides of national politics as a means of coping with changing political situations throughout his career. Leland Griffin has defined rhetorical trajectory as "the salience and/or sequencing of god and devil terms in a body of discourse suggestive of the qualities, motivations, or state of mind of a speaker or writer, 'a state of mind in which another state of mind can appropriately follow.'" A rhetorical trajectory occurs when the choice of a symbolic term or perspective acts to direct or influence subsequent choices over time along a line of symbolic development suggested or implied in the initial choice.[24]

In a recent study of the rhetoric of Martin Luther King, Jr., Dionisopoulos, Gallagher, Goldzwig, and Zarefsky identified three aspects of the concept of rhetorical trajectory that are of importance to this book.[25] First, a rhetorical trajectory develops from an individual's orientation or frame of acceptance. As we respond to a situation confronting us, our "capacities and patterns of experience work together" to bring about a symbolic response "in one direction rather than another, to ensure emphasis of certain ideas and visions rather than others." We tend to construct responses that are compatible with our frame of acceptance not out of a determined logical necessity but because of what Burke calls "qualitative progression," a "feeling as to the rightness or destiny of a progression of events or words." Such a feeling of rightness or "poetic congruence" functions to motivate and direct our symbolic choices along a particular path of development.[26]

Second, the concept of rhetorical trajectory helps us to understand how "rhetoric designed to move others *also* works to propel the rhetor along a certain course of symbolic action." Dionisopoulos and his fellow scholars note that the context of a particular symbolic action "is heavily influenced by the progression of a speaker's rhetoric" in previous contexts or situations. Therefore, "tracing the strands that compose such a progression provides an understanding of the constraints as well as the possibilities for rhetorical invention" in a given situation.[27]

Finally, the concept of rhetorical trajectory can serve as "an effective critical construct for undertaking an analysis of a speaker's universe of discourse and of the limitations and constraints of certain types of discourse in a societal context."[28] In examining an individual's symbolic responses to situations over time as part of a rhetorical trajectory, a critic can consider how symbolic choices not only direct the rhetor and audience *toward* certain judgments or conclusions but also take attention *away* from other possible interpretations of the situation.[29]

This book examines how Arthur Schlesinger's notion of the tides of national politics generated a rhetorical trajectory that influenced subsequent symbolic choices made by Schlesinger in response to emerging challenges to his liberal perspective. My analysis also notes how the notion of the tides of national politics has directed Schlesinger throughout his career toward particular interpretations and judgments about situations and away from other interpretations and judgments about those situations.

The book has eight chapters. Chapters 1 and 2 trace the origin and development of the tides of national politics as Schlesinger's frame of acceptance and analyze its use by Schlesinger as the basis for historical explanation in his scholarly treatises *The Age of Jackson* and *The Age of Roosevelt*. In chapters 3 through 7, Schlesinger's applications of the tides concept as ideological history in his partisan political writings and speeches from the 1950s to the present are discussed. These chapters trace Schlesinger's rise to prominence as an influential liberal spokesman, explore his role in the presidential administration of John F. Kennedy, examine the influence of his historical perspective on the "new frontier" rhetoric of President Kennedy, and discuss his response to a series of challenges that have increasingly threatened his liberal perspective with obsolescence. Chapter 8 offers some concluding observations about Schlesinger's brand of liberalism and about the persuasive functions of ideological history.

This analysis of the works of Arthur M. Schlesinger, Jr., highlights the relationship between historical reasoning and public decision making. By studying the discourse of a man who has been both historical scholar and political advocate, we may gain a fuller appreciation of the ways in which arguments from history persuade audiences in the present.

Many people have helped me complete this book. I thank members of the Northwestern University Communication Studies faculty, especially Professors David Zarefsky, G. Thomas Goodnight, and Thomas B. Farrell, who guided my initial pursuit of this topic in graduate school; and Professor Emeritus Leland Griffin, who inspired me to continue my study and appreciation of Kenneth Burke.

Bonnie Dow, John Murphy, Scott Harris, Kathryn Olson, Edward Schiappa, and James Jasinski are all colleagues of mine who have offered advice, counsel, and friendship on the long path toward the finish line. I also thank Suzanne Prokup, Lisa Marie Luccioni, E. August King, Paul Ravetta, and Roger Wells for their research and proofreading assistance. The Department of Communication at the University of Cincinnati merits recognition for having provided me with financial support during the preparation of the manuscript. Finally, and most important, I want to thank my wife, Cindy, for her patience, kindness, and wisdom. I dedicate this work to all of you who made it possible.

Acknowledgments

I would like to thank the following for permission to quote from the published writings of Arthur M. Schlesinger, Jr.:

Harper's Magazine for quotations from "America, 1968: The Politics of Violence" (*Harper's*, August 1968, pp. 19–24). Copyright © 1968 by *Harper's Magazine*. All rights reserved. Reprinted from the August issue by special permission.

New Prospect, Inc., for quotations from "The Liberal Opportunity" (*The American Prospect*, Spring 1990, pp. 10–18). Copyright © 1990 by New Prospect, Inc.

New Statesman & Society for quotations from "The Administration and the Left" (*New Statesman*, February 8, 1963, pp. 185–86). Copyright © 1963 by New Statesman. Used by permission.

The New York Times Company for quotations from "The 'Threat' of the Radical Right" (*New York Times Magazine*, June 17, 1962, pp. 10, 55–58). Copyright © 1962 by the New York Times Company. Reprinted by permission.

In addition, I would like to thank Arthur M. Schlesinger, Jr., for permission to quote from his published and unpublished works. Professor Schlesinger has been prompt, courteous, and cooperative in his correspondence.

Arthur M. Schlesinger, Jr., and the
Ideological History of American
Liberalism

1

Origins of Schlesinger's Frame of Acceptance

Arthur Schlesinger, Jr., developed his political perspective in response to tensions and challenges that faced him and other liberals who came of age in America during the 1930s and 1940s. In his early years as an academic historian and political activist, Schlesinger would begin to develop and express his views on human nature, history, and ideology. Those views would find their most complete expression in a concept originated by Schlesinger's father, Arthur Schlesinger, Sr., entitled "the tides of national politics."

This chapter explores the emergence of the tides of national politics as the younger Schlesinger's *frame of acceptance*. According to Burke, human beings cope with the uncertainties of existence by symbolically defining "the problem of evil" in the world through a frame of acceptance. "In the face of anguish, injustice, disease, and death one adopts policies. One constructs his notion of the universe or history, and shapes attitudes in keeping."[1] A critical understanding of Schlesinger's developing frame of acceptance must begin with an examination of antecedent conditions, of the political influences, problems, and dilemmas that Schlesinger experienced in the early stages of his career.

Scholar and Political Activist

Arthur M. Schlesinger, Jr., was born in Columbus, Ohio, in 1917. He spent his formative years in Cambridge, Massachusetts, where his father, Arthur Schlesinger, Sr., was a member of the history faculty at Harvard University. Influenced by progressive historians such as Frederick Jackson Turner and Charles Beard, Schlesinger, Sr., taught courses and conducted research in intellectual and social history. In raising his son, Arthur, Sr., encouraged "Junior" to "hold the mirror up to everything, past and present, and to declare his judgment of what he saw."[2]

The product of this upbringing by the Schlesinger family was a bright, precocious young man "virtually bred" on "liberal history and politics"[3] who accomplished his education and early scholarship "on an accelerated time scale."[4] Arthur, Jr., graduated from Exeter prep school at the age of fifteen, completed his undergraduate degree at Harvard before he was twenty-one, and became a three-year Harvard Fellow in 1940 because of "promise of notable contribution to knowledge and thought."[5]

During these early years of academic apprenticeship, young Arthur completed a book-length study of Jacksonian religious reformer Orestes Brownson and a monograph, "The Problem of Richard Hildreth."[6] The son appeared destined at an early age to follow in his father's footsteps as scholar and pedagogue in American history.

But Arthur Schlesinger, Jr., was never content to remain in an intellectual's ivory tower. His father was a quiet political activist, more in keeping with his profession of academic historian.[7] As he explained in 1968, Arthur, Jr., felt "invariably less detached and judicious than my father, more eager for commitment and combat."[8] He wished to participate in transforming his ideas into concrete political actions.

So, for example, after returning from an eleven-month world trip in 1939, young Arthur "became an enthusiastic member and publicist for the preparedness organization, American Defense, Harvard Group" and "wrote articles for the *Boston Globe* opposing the student peace movement, urging conscription, [and] favoring American intervention following the fall of France."[9] After failing to qualify for combat status, Arthur served his country during the war in the Office of War Information in London, Paris, and Germany.[10] Reflecting on his experiences in 1949, Schlesinger claimed to have "gained more insight into history from being in the war and working for the government than I did from my academic training." In a stark rebuke of professional historiography, Schlesinger asserted: "The trouble is that American historians spend too much time writing about events which the whole nature of their lives prevents them from understanding. Their life is defined by universities, libraries, and seminars."[11]

Schlesinger returned to America to complete *The Age of Jackson*

(1945), a work that earned him a Pulitzer Prize and an appointment to the Harvard history department at the age of twenty-eight. Yet from the beginning of his academic career, the young historian longed to "smell the dust and sweat of battle," and to bring the perspective of historical understanding actively to bear on issues of the day.[12] He would feel the tension between intellectual detachment and political commitment throughout his career.

Postwar Liberalism in Crisis

In the years before World War II, most liberals in America subscribed to the progressive political tradition and philosophy embodied in the goals and policies of the New Deal and personified by Franklin Delano Roosevelt. To the progressive liberal, humankind had an essentially good nature. Human errors could be corrected and behavior improved through education and rational inquiry. History was therefore a comic journey through seasons of reform, revolution, and retrenchment toward a progressively better human society. The possibilities for public action to reform democratic institutions in America were bounded only by the ever-expanding limits of human ingenuity and reasoned democratic action at the grass roots level.[13]

These were sentiments found in the politics of Bryan and Wilson, the philosophy of Emerson and Dewey, and the historiography of Turner, Beard, and Becker. In *The American as Reformer*, Arthur Schlesinger, Sr., argued that progressive themes had uniquely dominated the American political tradition: "From the beginning, American democracy has been a method of evolution, a developing conception of human worth springing from Christianity and the doctrine of the rights of man. . . . Our national life has been healthy and virile because of the opportunity to criticize, protest and espouse unpopular causes. The reformer has always had his day in court, and if his case was good enough, he has won the verdict."[14] Writing in the *New Republic* in 1931, Benjamin Ginzburg characterized the progressive mind-set as "messianism, a religion which stakes everything on the hope of the future and which is compelled continually to read its hope into the future in order to support its faith in present action."[15]

The progressive faith in human nature and hopes for improving human society were confronted with the contradictory, harsh realities of deprivation, fascism, and totalitarianism culminating in the destruction of World War II. The horrors of Hitler and Stalin exposed the dark, brutal side of humankind, revealed history as tending not toward a better society but toward collective terror and violence, and confirmed the power of persuasion not for public interests but for the benefit of demagogues. Progressive idealism seemed to be significantly threatened by new technological, political, and spiritual powers of a new age of totalitarianism. Higham has asserted that for some liberals, "one of the principal casualties of the postwar world was the faith in progress itself."[16]

Events during and after World War II presented liberals in America not only with philosophical challenges to their progressive idealism but also with more concrete political problems and dilemmas. The sudden death of Franklin Roosevelt in 1945 created a vacuum of leadership not just for the nation but particularly for liberals, who had come to rely on the president to sort out the uncertain legacy of New Deal initiatives that had stalled before and during the war. The new president, Harry S. Truman, was not received favorably by liberals within the Democratic party, especially in the first few years of his administration. Without strong leadership, liberals fell to quarreling over emerging issues of the day, such as labor legislation, civil rights, and aid to Europe.[17] Yet, by 1948, many liberals chose to support Truman's electoral bid for the White House against the challenges of Republican Thomas Dewey and Henry Wallace, running as the nominee of the insurgent Progressive party.[18]

America's political Left was further fragmented by the rising tide of anticommunism. Cooperation on social issues among progressive liberals, trade unions, socialists, and Communists in America, which had begun in the 1930s and had been justified after 1941 as part of a united Popular Front against Nazi Germany, collapsed as tensions between the United States and the Soviet Union mounted after the war. By the end of the 1940s, liberals were forced to distinguish between genuine progressive reform impulses and what was often perceived as Communist infiltration into the progressive political movement. In 1947, a group of liberal intellectuals and politicians founded the Americans for Democratic Action (ADA) in an attempt to stake out a clear position for the "non-Communist Left" in American politics.[19]

In his book on the history of the ADA, Steven Gillon summarized the plight of liberals in postwar America: "ADA liberals, chastened by the harsh reality of the Great Depression and fascism, disenchanted with Marxist polemics, and skeptical of ideal solutions, placed a premium on bargaining and compromise. Yet, they also fancied themselves as reformers with a responsibility to promote social and economic justice." In the years after the war, liberals tried, often unsuccessfully, to "strike a balance between their commitment to abstract ideals of social justice and their sense of the politically possible." What Gillon described as the conflict between "politics and vision" would haunt liberals like Arthur Schlesinger, Jr., for more than a generation.[20]

In response to the "contradictions" of existence inherent in a situation, writes Burke, each of us "symbolically erects" a frame of acceptance or understanding by "overt or covert acts of 'transcendence'" that provide "solutions" to the puzzles of existence.[21] Early in his academic and political career, Arthur M. Schlesinger, Jr., began to construct a distinctive frame of acceptance in order to transcend the problems facing traditional liberalism in the frightening postwar world.

Sources of Schlesinger's Frame of Acceptance

During his first few years on the Harvard University faculty, Arthur Schlesinger, Jr., established himself not only as a scholar of American history but also as an advocate and defender of liberal political causes. He was a founding member of the Americans for Democratic Action and worked through that organization in the 1948 presidential campaign in support of Harry Truman. In 1949, he published *The Vital Center*, a book that was hailed as "the manifesto of postwar liberalism."[22]

The Vital Center contained Schlesinger's diagnosis of the troubled political times in America and around the world. In the opening pages, Schlesinger wrote, "Western man in the middle of the twentieth century is tense, uncertain, adrift. We look upon our epoch as a time of troubles, an age of anxiety. The grounds of our civilization, of our certitude, are breaking up under our feet, and familiar ideas and institutions vanish as we reach for them, like shadows in the falling dusk."[23]

For Schlesinger, the war and its aftermath forever "broke the bubble of false optimism" that had sustained progressive beliefs in the inevitability of liberal reform. "The Soviet experience, on top of the rise of fascism," continued the young historian, "reminded my generation rather forcibly that man was, indeed, imperfect, and that the corruptions of power could unleash great evil in the world."[24]

The dangers of naive optimism in an age of mass industrialization called for a new foundation for liberalism that could serve as a "fighting faith" for believers in democracy and reform.[25] As he began to put together a liberal philosophy in response to the uncertainties of the postwar world, Schlesinger was influenced by Reinhold Niebuhr's views on human nature, by the views of Arthur Schlesinger, Sr., on ideology and history, and by Franklin Roosevelt's views on the prospect for public action.

Initially, Schlesinger was guided by the critique of modern liberal culture found in the writings of Reinhold Niebuhr. Niebuhr, who had been influenced by both socialism and Christian existentialism, formulated a view of human nature based on "a secular interpretation of original sin."[26]

Searching for the essential characteristics of democratic societies, Niebuhr identified a tension between man's "essential freedom"—"the capacity for indeterminate transcendence over the processes and limitations of nature"—and the necessity for order in human communities. In response to the tension between freedom and order, man commits "original sin" by transforming the "will to live" into the "will to power" and by furthering self-interest at the expense of communal interests. Progressive optimists—the "children of light"—err in the sentimental belief that self-interest through felicitous reason alone can be made congruent with collective interests. Fascists—the "children of darkness"—err in the cynical belief that an individual interest can be imposed through terror and technological control on the entire community.[27]

Niebuhr believed that the morality of the "children of light" and the appreciation of power of the "children of darkness" must be combined into a collective wisdom expressing itself through constant and vigorous exercise of democracy. "Man's capacity for justice makes democracy possible," Niebuhr concluded in 1944, "but man's inclination to injustice makes democracy necessary."[28]

Arthur Schlesinger, Jr., who became associated with Niebuhr through their activity in the ADA, found in the theologian's work a healthy "skepticism about man" which, "far from leading to a rejection of democracy, established democracy on its firmest possible intellectual basis."[29] Niebuhr's views on human nature, Schlesinger wrote in retrospect, accomplished "in a single generation a revolution in the bases of American liberal political thought," an alternative explanation for "[a] culture which had staked too much on illusion" and had "found itself baffled and stricken in an age dominated by total government and total war."[30]

For Schlesinger, the Niebuhrian concept of original sin justified a renewed "fighting faith" in reform in the face of man's intrinsic evil. Niebuhr's contention that "there is a Hitler, a Stalin in every breast" held in check only through the power of majoritarian democracy provided both an explanation for the rise of totalitarianism in some parts of the world and justification for liberal government intervention into the economy and society to protect individual groups from themselves and from each other.[31]

Such a view of human nature magnified the importance of *struggle* and competition of interests in American society. In accepting Niebuhr's secular view of original sin based on power, Schlesinger accepted conflict as the essence of human experience. He wrote: "The choice we face is not between progress with conflict and progress without conflict. The choice is between conflict and stagnation. You cannot expel conflict from society any more than you can from the human mind. When you attempt it, the psychic costs in schizophrenia or torpor are the same."[32]

Schlesinger would resolve the contradictions between progressive and cynical views of human nature by adopting an attitude that "presumes a perpetual tension in our society, a doubtful equilibrium, constantly breeding strife and struggle" among individual groups refereed by a benign but activist liberal state.[33] The belief that conflict was inherent in human society was later reflected in the popular conception of "interest-group liberalism."[34]

Arthur Schlesinger's acceptance of a human nature based on conflict and struggle was tempered somewhat by his father's revulsion against radical extremism and devotion to empirical experience over ideology. Living through the ideological optimism and subsequent disillusionment of the progressive era, Arthur Schlesinger, Sr., counseled against adhering to absolutist creeds, which too often led to extremist violence (as in the case of Sacco and Vanzetti).[35]

The elder Schlesinger was convinced that democratic politics could be conducted only in the "middle zone" between radicalism and conservatism.[36] In this middle zone of political action, pragmatic, trial-and-error experimentation based on sound empiricism should take precedence over muddleheaded do-goodism. The historian sincerely believed that an empirical investigation of the facts could lead a trained mind to find appropriate means to accomplish desired ends.[37] Schlesinger, Sr., concluded that America, uniquely blessed by geography and lack of a feudal tradition, had the capability to accomplish progressive reforms that would lead to equal opportunity free from Old World ideological baggage.[38]

The younger Schlesinger shared his father's preference for flexible empiricism over ideology in the understanding of American history and politics. Wreszin writes that "what may set Schlesinger apart from a common stereotype is that, as a precocious undergraduate [at] . . . Harvard, he was not terribly interested in politics and 'had no patience with the turgid debates of the campus Marxists, finding their dogmatism downright silly.'"[39] Schlesinger explained in 1949 that his political generation grew up as Soviet communism was being exposed not as the fulfillment of a utopian ideal but as a harsh brutal regime of terror. Never having had the dream of collectivism to lose, Schlesinger, Jr., had neither the aspirations nor the disappointments of the ideologue. He wrote: "We were simply the children of a new atmosphere—history had spared us any emotional involvement in the Soviet mirage" of Marxist ideology.[40] The younger Schlesinger would retain an unbending opposition to communism throughout his career.

In constructing a new liberal frame of acceptance, Schlesinger, Jr., denied the desirability of ideology altogether. Reflecting his father's historical understanding, Schlesinger, Jr., contended that in America "our philosophical heritage—empirical, pragmatic, ironic, pluralistic, competitive—has happily inoculated us against rigid, all-encompassing, absolute systems of historical interpretation."[41] "Ideology" became a devil term in Schlesinger's vocabulary, a term of reprobation applied to the enemies of liberalism. Ideology took many forms; Schlesinger denounced equally both the crass materialism and greed of conservatism and the cruel doctrines of Marxian determinism.[42]

It is interesting to note that in *The Vital Center*, Schlesinger especially chastised the utopian sentimentality of "doughface progressivism." In this work, Schlesinger equated progressivism with a kind of political idealism represented by wrongheaded politicians such as Henry Wallace:

For its persistent and sentimental optimism has endowed Doughface progressivism with what in the middle of the twentieth century are fatal weaknesses: a weakness for impotence, because progressivism believes that history will make up for human error; a weakness for rhetoric, because it believes man can be reformed through argument; a weakness for economic fetishism, because it believes that the good in man will be liberated by a change in economic institutions; a weakness for political myth, because Doughface optimism requires somewhere an act of faith in order to survive the contradictions of history.[43]

"Progressivism was not prepared for Hitler," continued Schlesinger, "because the pervading belief in human perfectibility" had "disarmed progressivism in too many of its encounters with actuality."[44] The "fatuity of Progressive presumptions" made them "if not an accomplice of totalitarianism, at least an accessory before the fact."[45] By the end of the 1940s, Schlesinger had dismissed the vision of progressive philosophy as at best naive and at worst politically dangerous.

Schlesinger believed that while America had "had the good fortune not to be an ideological society," progress had been made through "innovation and experiment," the rejection of abstraction when it collided with "reality."[46] In *The Age of Jackson*, he cited George Bancroft's formulation of the perpetual conflict in American society as that between empiricism ("good") and ideology ("evil"):

"The feud between the capitalist and the laborer, the house of Have and the house of Want, is as old as social union, and can never be entirely quieted; but he who will act with moderation, prefer fact to theory, and remember that everything in this world is relative and not absolute, will see that the violence of this contest may be stilled."[47] Contrasts between "fact" and "theory," between reality and appearance, would show up again and again in Schlesinger's historiographical works, and formed a key building block for his emerging frame of acceptance.

If Schlesinger, Jr., redefined human nature through Niebuhr and gained an appreciation for empirical history from his father, he found a role model for democratic public activism in Franklin Delano Roosevelt. Arthur Schlesinger, Sr., was a big Roosevelt supporter and was acquainted with some of the cast of New Deal reformers. Young Arthur was fascinated with power and attracted to the strength of leadership of the resolute president of the United States during the years of depression and world war.[48]

In the first pages of *The Vital Center*, Schlesinger paid homage to the liberal leader and revealed his attitude concerning the need for dynamic leadership in a democracy:

I was born in 1917. I heard Franklin Roosevelt's first inaugural address as a boy at school, fifteen years old. Since that March day in 1933, one has been able to feel that liberal ideas had access to power in the United States, that liberal purposes, in general, were dominating our national policy. For one's own generation, then, American liberalism has had a positive and confident ring. It has stood for responsibility and achievement, not for frustration and sentimentalism; it has been the instrument of social change, not of private neurosis. During most of my political consciousness this has been a New Deal country. I expect that it will continue to be a New Deal country.[49]

From Schlesinger's association of liberal reform with his own hero Franklin Roosevelt came the belief that ideas gained access to power "from the top down," from strong leadership. In this view, public action became possible only through a process of education from above that would lead the masses toward beneficial policies of the moment.[50]

The example of Roosevelt led Schlesinger, Jr., to assert that a realistic liberalism would be sustained against modern challenges only so long as strong leaders were able to resolve conflicts and regulate human nature through governmental experimentation. "Every great crisis thus far in American history has produced a leader adequate to the occasion from the ranks of those who believe vigorously and seriously in liberty, democracy, and the common man," Schlesinger asserted in *The Age of Jackson*. "The sense of public responsibility, the ability to inspire national confidence, the capacity to face imperative issues, seem in this country to have been largely the property of the great democratic leaders."[51] Only leadership could salvage the possibility of public action in the postprogressive age.

Drawing upon the ideas of Niebuhr, Arthur Schlesinger, Sr., and Roosevelt, young Arthur, Jr., began to develop a set of terms and assumptions that would both influence his interpretation of American history and help him to define and address challenges to liberalism in the coming years. The concept that most completely incorporated his beliefs about human nature, history, and public action was a theory of American politics he inherited from his father entitled "the tides of national politics." This theory would function to organize Schlesinger's emerging political thought into a frame of acceptance.

Components of Schlesinger's Frame of Acceptance

According to Burke, a frame of acceptance is the attempt to resolve or round off contradictions of existence through symbolic action. It is the summation of an attitude into a formula of terms, a symbolic orientation that prepares individuals for combat in the world.[52]

The tides of national politics, a theory that posits a cyclical alternation between conservative and liberal epochs in American history, was first articulated by Arthur Schlesinger, Sr., in a speech in 1924 and was later developed into an article for the *Yale Review* in 1939.[53] Beginning in the early stages of his career, Schlesinger adapted his father's theory to a broader political perspective or frame of acceptance. The younger Schlesinger's perspective included three parts: a comparison between the liberal and the conservative, the predictable alternation of liberal and conservative eras in American society, and the need for strong leadership.

The first element is the comparison between liberals and conservatives. Both Schlesingers have asserted that fundamental differences in temperament and interest divide people into liberal and conservative camps. Schlesinger, Sr., quoted Thomas Jefferson's belief that individuals, "according to their constitutions, and the circumstances in which they are placed," either "fear the people, and wish to transfer all power to the higher classes of society," or "consider the people as the safest depository of power in the last resort."[54] Schlesinger, Jr., paraphrased Emerson's decree that mankind is "divided between the Party of Conservatism and the Party of

Innovation, between the Past and the Future, between Memory and Hope." While neither Memory nor Hope "provides by itself an entirely persuasive basis for political action," Schlesinger, Jr., explained in 1963, "the distinction expresses a deep contrast in temperament and purpose."[55]

In Schlesinger's definitional scheme, a liberal is distinguished from a conservative on the basis of attitudes held toward human nature, history, the desirability of change, the public good, and the state. The modern liberal, influenced by Niebuhr and hardened by the experience of totalitarianism, views humanity as inherently flawed but potentially controllable through empirical reason. The conservative, influenced by Andrew Carnegie and other robber barons, views humanity as an instrument to serve the ends of efficiency and profit.[56] Schlesinger's liberal sees history as an unfinished, inscrutable continuum of human choice. The conservative sees history as a finished work that serves as intractable precedent.[57] Toward change, the liberal believes that society can and should be improved through the application of pragmatic solutions to meet particular circumstances. The conservative "opposes efforts at purposeful change because he believes that things are about as good as they can be reasonably expected to be, and that change . . . is . . . likely to be for the worse."[58] To the liberal, the public good lies in protecting a diversity of interests among the "humble members of society." To the conservative, the public good lies in protecting the enterprising interest of business and industry.[59] Finally, the liberal conceives of the state as a positive means to promote ends of economic distribution and social justice. The conservative conceives of the state as an evil mechanism that intrudes without warrant into the free marketplace.[60]

It is essential to note that Schlesinger sees a positive role for a responsible conservatism based on a "belief in the organic character of society" consisting of "common trust and mutual obligation."[61] Schlesinger has characterized American society as a perpetual struggle between conservatives and liberals that takes place within a common framework of shared values, a "vital center" based on faith in democratic processes and civil liberties and opposition to communism and other forms of totalitarianism.[62] In this "vital center," each camp (conservatism and liberalism) serves a function in "preserving the health of the body politic" by checking the excesses of the other.[63]

Schlesinger has argued that the American political system functions best when members of the public, liberals and conservatives alike, engage in reasoned discourse and gradualism rather than in utopian idealism or radical protest. He has consistently asserted "the basic liberal proposition that complicated problems can be solved only by thoughtful analysis."[64] As long as the American people maintain belief in a rationally derived vital center of values, American politics will not fluctuate wildly from one ideology to another.[65]

The second element in the frame of acceptance concerns the predictable alternation between liberal and conservative epochs. Both Schlesingers have conceived of American history as a continuing conflict for power between liberals and conservatives within a consensual framework of values. While believing that the liberal position is superior, they have recognized that conservatives have often gained the upper hand in the struggle for popular support and public office during America's lifetime. Schlesinger, Sr., explained that throughout American history "[a] period of concern for the rights of the few has been followed by one of concern for the wrongs of the many. Emphasis on the welfare of property has given way to emphasis on human welfare."[66]

Schlesinger, Jr., has focused on three aspects of the alternations of liberal and conservative dominance first identified by his father. First, the alternation between liberal and conservative eras has been attributed to psychological rather than economic or political causes. In 1949, Schlesinger, Sr., based the causal explanation of the American political system on an "interplay of subjective influences . . . springing from something basic in human nature." The elder Schlesinger adopted as causal law Thomas Jefferson's observations that individuals act in political contexts "according to their constitutions" and that "human beings in the mass . . . respond to psychological impulses" of activity and rest.[67] The younger Schlesinger has traced the source of the ebb and flow of liberal and conservative dominance to roots which "lie deep in the natural life of humanity." American history has conformed to a cyclical pattern much like those found "in organic nature—in the tides, in the seasons, in night and day, in the systole and diastole of the heart."[68] Much of politics is thus a "physiological process" for Schlesinger. After "seasons of action, passion, idealism, reform" presided over by liberalism, Schlesinger explains, people naturally "long for respite" offered by conservative retrenchment.[69]

Second, the alternation between conservatism and liberalism is regular and can be predicted. Using "not preconceived theory but pragmatism" as his "guiding star," Schlesinger, Sr., surveyed American history and discovered eleven periods of liberal or conservative dominance averaging 16.6 years in duration.[70] On the basis of that survey, the elder Schlesinger confidently predicted in a 1949 revision of "Tides of American Politics" that the latest conservative epoch, which had "begun" during the 1946 congressional elections, would end in 1962, at which time America would enter a new liberal era.[71] Finding predictable patterns of electoral behavior was apparently of significant interest to America's leaders. In his memoirs, Schlesinger the elder asserted that he heard from a White House aide that President Roosevelt had read the original 1939 essay, "and the prospect it held out of a liberal era lasting till 1947 or 1948 helped him decide to run for a third term."[72] Schlesinger, Jr., has also subscribed to the predictive nature of America's political tides, recently adding "generational experience" as a regulator of historical movements from liberalism to conservatism.[73]

Third, the alternation between liberalism and conservatism gradually moves American political thinking to the left with each completion of the cycle. Schlesinger, Sr., posited that as each new liberal generation of government activity becomes entrenched in established institutions, conservatives tend to begin defending the liberal reform as part of the status quo. The liberalization of the American body politic has been confirmed, according to the elder Schlesinger, by the conservative support for some progressive legislation during the 1920s and 1950s. The progressive movement leftward led the father of the theory to speak of a liberal "spiral" in American life, and the son in 1980 to assert the "inevitability" of liberalism.[74]

The final major component of the younger Schlesinger's frame of acceptance has been the argument that heroic political leaders are necessary in a democratic society. Strong leadership is needed for a democracy, Schlesinger has maintained, for *functional* and *moral* reasons.[75]

The functional justification for heroic leadership stems from a discrepancy between the progressive ideal of an informed, active electorate and the actual American public, which harbors strains of antiintellectualism and is limited by the structural nature of representative government. Heroic leadership is needed to "offset the centrifugal effects of the dispersion of political power" to mass voting populations. Schlesinger has posited that democratic publics have been able to "focus their aspirations only as strong individuals embodied and clarified the tendencies of their people."[76]

The historian has borrowed from the writings of Emerson, Carlyle, and William James to support his belief in the functional need for heroic leadership in a democracy. In a 1958 article in the *Saturday Evening Post*, Schlesinger cited the following to define the functional aspects of a hero: " 'The appearance of a great man,' Emerson wrote, 'draws a circle outside our largest orbits and surprises and commands us.' . . . Carlyle [said], 'The great man, with his free force direct out of God's own hand, is the lightning. . . . The rest of the men waited for him like fuel, and then they too would flame.' . . . 'In picking out from history our heroes,' said William James, 'each one of us may best fortify and inspire what creative energy may lie in his own soul.'"[77]

The diverse interests of the liberal coalition have been combined only by leaders who could innovate, teach, and persuade. And in a crisis, only liberal heroes like Jackson, Lincoln, and Roosevelt have been able to guide the entire American people toward their best interests.[78]

The moral justification for heroic leadership stems from the belief that the personal virtues of heroes serve as exemplars to restore faith in the potency of human choice. "The heroic leader," Schlesinger has written, "has the Promethean responsibility to affirm human freedom against the supposed inevitabilities of history. As he does this, he combats the infection of fatalism which might otherwise paralyze mass democracy."[79] In response to the "increasing velocity of history" that threatens man with technological depersonalization, heroes serve as examples of human potentialities.[80] Only heroic leadership can infuse the vital center of American values with a "fighting faith."[81] Without the hero, Schlesinger has concluded, a democratic society would tend to "acquiesce in the drift of history" and would succumb to totalitarian demagoguery.[82]

Thus, the hero figure has served as the catalyst for each new epoch of liberalism. The hero is the symbolic device in Schlesinger's frame of acceptance that bridges remaining gulfs, contradictions, or shortcomings in historical understanding.

Possibilities for Transcendence

The tides of national politics provided Arthur Schlesinger, Jr., with a basis for defending his conception of liberalism in the postwar world. The theory helped Schlesinger to develop both a historical rationale for liberalism and a public vocabulary through which he would sustain liberal causes and candidates for the next five decades. In that vocabulary, Schlesinger began to assign a positive status to terms such as "fact," "empirical," "pragmatic," "experiment," "liberal," "action," "leadership," and "vital center." In contrast, terms such as "ideology," "radical," "idealism," "conservative," and "communism" were cast in a negative light.

In the coming years, Schlesinger would attempt to apply the terms and assumptions of the tides of national politics in a variety of ways in order to transcend the problems and contradictions that threatened liberalism in America.[83] The notion of a cyclical alternation between conservatism and liberalism seemed to offer Arthur M. Schlesinger, Jr., ways of symbolically resolving continuing conflicts between progressive liberal conceptions about human nature, history, and the prospects for public action and contradictory facts of the modern postwar situation.

Schlesinger could use his frame of acceptance to reconcile progressive beliefs that humanity was good with Niebuhrian assumptions about original sin by positing that people contained potential for both good *and* evil, depending on tendencies toward liberalism or conservatism in individual character. He could reconcile progressive optimism concerning the telos of human history with the harsh brutalities of the current age by asserting that American political thought gradually drifted to the left even during times of apparent retrenchment. He could adjust the endpoints of the conservative and liberal epochs at a given point in American history in order to rationalize yesterday's liberal defeats or to predict tomorrow's liberal victories. Finally, he could confirm the potency of public action in the face of totalitarian demagoguery and control by posing the liberal hero as the catalyst and symbol of liberal state action on behalf of the "forgotten men and women" in American society.

Arthur Schlesinger's academic and political discourse was shaped by his historical understanding of the tides of national politics. Schlesinger would rely on the tides of national politics as a symbolic frame of acceptance through which he attempted to deal with dilemmas between politics and vision that confronted liberalism throughout his career.

The remainder of this book examines Schlesinger's strategic uses of the terms and assumptions of tides of national politics to defend and extend his conception of postwar American liberalism. Chapter 2 analyzes the way in which Schlesinger used the tides of national politics as the basis of historical explanation in his scholarly treatments of the ages of Jackson and Roosevelt, works that laid the foundation for Schlesinger's ideological history of American liberalism.

2

The Age of Jackson and *The Age of Roosevelt:* A Foundation for Ideological History

Arthur Schlesinger, Jr., quickly climbed the academic ladder in his chosen profession as practicing historian. From the beginning of his years at Harvard as graduate fellow and later as professor of history, his work in the field of American history was prolific and popular. His first major book, *The Age of Jackson* (1945), won him the Pulitzer Prize at the age of twenty-eight. During the 1950s, he turned his attention to writing a history of the New Deal era and produced three volumes: *The Crisis of the Old Order* (1957), which won the 1957 Bancroft Prize for literary distinction; *The Coming of the New Deal* (1959); and *The Politics of Upheaval* (1960).

In these studies of American liberal politics from Jackson to Roosevelt, Schlesinger engaged in conventional arguments *about* history, drawing upon the tides of national politics as a basis for causal explanation of past events and trends. These works would also provide ammunition for Schlesinger's political advocacy in behalf of contemporary liberalism, serving as grounds for partisan arguments *from* history in which Schlesinger engaged throughout his career.[1]

This chapter analyzes Schlesinger's treatises on the Jackson and Roosevelt eras as the foundation of his "ideological history" of American liberalism. The analysis proceeds by providing a fuller definition of ideological history, summarizing Schlesinger's views toward history, examining Schlesinger's historical treatments of the "ages" of Andrew Jackson and Franklin Delano Roosevelt (FDR), and reviewing critical responses to Schlesinger's historical discourse.

What Is Ideological History?

The classical educational tradition attempted to distinguish rhetoric from historiography according to subject matter and purpose.[2] The classical view, which held that rhetoric was concerned with choice and avoidance of policy while history was concerned with verisimilitude to the reality of past events, dominated centuries of pedagogical and professional practice.[3]

In recent years, however, scholars have begun to reexamine classical distinctions between rhetoric and history.[4] The consensus of historians now views historical discourse as the result of an inventional process involving both the interpreter's point of view and the unprocessed historical record. In an important address before the American Historical Association in 1933, Charles Beard declared that "every written history . . . is a selection and arrangement of facts, or recorded fragments of past actuality," an operation that is "an act of choice, conviction, and interpretation respecting values, is an act of thought."[5]

Rhetorical critics have also noted that arguments about history have a distinctly persuasive dimension. Drawing from distinct points of view and using different kinds of analysis, historians present causal and explanatory claims concerning past events to audiences of popular readers and scholarly critics, with the purpose of demonstrating the soundness or reasonability of a particular interpretation of the past.[6] In dramatistic terms, all arguments about the past are responses of the historian's frame of acceptance to a situation in need of definition. Historical discourse may thus be viewed as symbolic action that provides a strategic "answer" to "questions" posed about the past.[7]

An advocate who makes arguments concerning events from the past with the purpose of guiding prudential conduct in the present and future is engaging in *ideological history.* McGee defines ideological history as accounts of the past written by advocates "to 'prove' the superiority of one political system over another and thereby justify reform or revolution."[8] "As advocates make the 'presentist' arguments," McGee continues, "events . . . are overly romanticized, social movements are simplified, and individuals become 'paradigms rather than people.'" Rather than dismissing such discourse as "bad history," McGee insists that critics view such arguments *from* history in terms of their effects on the given political discourse and praxes of their time.[9]

An ideological history includes three rhetorical moves. First, the advocate develops an explicit or implicit view of time and history, including variables that may influence motives, behaviors, and events.[10] These general attitudes toward history make up the advocate's orientation or frame of acceptance.[11] Second, the advocate applies her general orientation toward time to a narrative account of particular events. This involves the transformation of data and information based on a causal hypothesis or lawlike explanation sketch with varying degrees of persuasive force.[12] Finally, the advocate projects elements of the explanation sketch into the present and future in order to generate popular support for particular policies or political leaders. Judgments about the present or predictions about the future are made on the basis of lawlike properties of the original historical explanation.

Ideological history differs from conventional historical discourse in several respects. In conventional history, statements about the past function as the claim or conclusion in the argument. Conventional history involves arguments *about* history. In ideological history, statements about the past function as the grounds or support material for other claims dealing with the present and future. Ideological history involves arguments *from* history.[13]

In addition, in conventional history, the contextual relationship between author/speaker and reader/audience may be described as academic and technical in nature. Here, the author and reader have a shared purpose of discovering accounts of past events that have a degree of explanatory soundness or reasonability. In ideological history, the relationship between author/speaker and reader/audience is more partisan and public in nature. Here the author attempts to move the audience toward acceptance of a particular political viewpoint, platform, or candidate on the basis of parallels drawn between the present and the past.[14]

Advocates employ ideological history in order to influence the shape of political *presumptions* within a community. Presumption is connected with what is normal or likely.[15] Goodnight explains that in a political controversy, advocates attempt to gain presumption for their positions by making their positions appear safer, less risky, less out of the ordinary. Presumption constitutes the argumentative authority to determine a hierarchy of values for decision making.[16] A significant source of presumption within a community or society rests in an understanding of its history. According to McGee, "the first principles of all public argument appear to lie in society's collective judgment of its past."[17]

Our understanding of the past, shaped by ideological arguments from history, provides us with the symbolic tools to accept—or transform—the principles underlying communal action in a society. As a repository of a community's values, the past can help to establish the presumptive legitimacy of ideas and policies in the present. Carpenter has asserted that arguments from history are "the rhetorical vehicle" by which members of a society "arrive at their acceptance of the concrete world of human fulfillment."[18]

Arthur M. Schlesinger, Jr., shared the view that historical understanding can make a difference in the political life of a community. Throughout his career, Schlesinger has considered his academic scholarship in American history as a prime inventional resource for his more overtly partisan writing and speaking on behalf of contemporary liberal causes and candidates. He has made connections between scholarship and politics because of his ideas about the nature of history and historical discourse.

Schlesinger's Attitudes Toward History

For all of his interest in contributing historical works to American arts and letters, Schlesinger has always been more concerned with the ways in which the past influences the present. "I have long been fascinated and perplexed," he wrote in 1966, "by the interaction between history and public decision: fascinated because, by this process, past history becomes an active partner in the making of new history; perplexed because the role of history in this partnership remains both elusive and tricky."[19]

Schlesinger believes that both policymakers and ordinary citizens can gain corrective insight from the past as they act to construct social policy in the present. As a result, he has never considered his historical works in a narrow academic context, intended to be read and studied only by practitioners of his discipline. He has defined himself and his audience more broadly, as participants not just in the pursuit of knowledge about the past, but in the struggle for political power in the present.

The historian asserted his views on the relevance of the past for political action in the present in the foreword to *The Age of Jackson:* "If democracy is indeed to be the hope of the future, we know now that we must have its lineaments clearly in mind, so that we may the more surely recognize it and the more responsibly act upon it." The key to survival of American democracy, he continued, was the recognition that "its moods, methods, and purposes . . . bear a vital relation to its attack on similar (if less intense) crises of the past."

Understanding the "clash of ideas" revealed in studies of the past "may help perhaps in building up a conception of the peaceable 'revolution' by which our democracy has . . . thus far avoided the terror of violent revolution."[20]

Schlesinger's interest in the relationship between academic arguments *about* history and political advocacy based on arguments *from* history also reflects the underlying tensions and paradoxes between progressive idealism and the harsh postwar realities discussed earlier. Despite his criticisms of progressive philosophy, Schlesinger shared the progressive belief that the past can influence the present because past, present, and future share tendencies toward a common liberal telos, or end. At the same time, the historian's disillusionment with progressive hyperoptimism based on his experience of economic depression, world war, and totalitarianism led him to distrust mechanistic formulas or models for historical explanation. Schlesinger abhorred Marxism and other manifestations of historical determinism that were both inaccurate empirically and immoral politically because they eliminated the notions of free will and individual responsibility.[21]

Reliance on gross overgeneralization or crude analogies between present and past transformed "historical understanding" (a positive term in Schlesinger's lexicon) into "ideology" (a negative term). "Indeed, history written according to deterministic conceptions ceases to be history," Schlesinger asserted. "It becomes a form of myth, which abandons testable propositions, moves beyond tangible evidence, and commits itself to the notion that the past has a single, unique structure in terms of which the apparent diversity and chaos of the human story can find place and resolution."[22]

Schlesinger resolved the tension between his progressive belief that history has a liberal teleology and the rejection of rigid historical pattern by adopting a middle way between historical determinism and historical anarchy. Neither historians nor policymakers, Schlesinger contended, should conceive of history according to a "positive model," in which a mechanistic theory "prescribes not only for the long but for the short run, not only strategy but tactics—the immediate policies to be favoured, courses pursued, action taken."[23] Instead, policymakers should derive "historical insight" from the past, "a sense of what is possible and probable in human affairs, derived from a feeling for the continuities and discontinuities of existence." Historical discourse should be akin to the "diagnostic judgments of the doctor" that generate both the pragmatic wisdom of statecraft[24] and a "vision of the broad direction in which the world is moving."[25]

Schlesinger's views on historical generalizations can be understood as what Hempel calls an "explanation sketch," which "consists of a more or less vague indication of the laws and initial conditions considered as relevant" in the description of historical events or trends. An explanation sketch "needs 'filling out,'" or "further empirical research," in order "to turn it into a full-fledged explanation [or law]."[26]

The explanation sketch used most frequently in Schlesinger's historical discourse was, in his words, "a thesis of my father's which I inherited—a discernible rhythm in American national affairs which swings at fairly regular intervals from affirmative to negative government, from periods of activism in public policy to periods of consolidation or lull."[27] The tides of national politics provided a way of understanding the past that overcame Schlesinger's own objections to a positive model of history. It provided a general explanation of the ebb and flow of American political history without succumbing to the "fantasy" of determinism.[28] It was also flexible enough to allow some room for free will and responsibility while at the same time allowing for a leftward drift in the American political consensus over time.

Employing the tides of national politics as the basis for historical explanation sketches preserved Schlesinger's beliefs in the predictive function of historical understanding *and* in the "intractable and uncontainable diversity" of "an open and unfinished universe."[29] The simplicity and flexibility of the concept also provided Schlesinger with a foundational rationale that allowed him to engage in both scholarly arguments *about* history and political arguments *from* history while maintaining the insistence that his work was empirical rather than ideological.[30]

The Tides of National Politics as Explanation Sketch

The tides of national politics served as both the basis of Schlesinger's general frame of acceptance and the generating principle for explanation sketches he developed in academic works concerning events and trends during the Jackson and Roosevelt eras of American history. In these discourses, Schlesinger adapted the three components of his frame of acceptance—definition of liberal/conservative, predictable alternation of liberal/conservative epochs, and need for heroic leadership—to construct causal arguments concerning past decisions, actions, and trends in American politics.

In Schlesinger's arguments about history, American policy actions were described as extensions of the personalities of statesmen and bureaucrats. Individual characters—good and evil—did not merely aid or reflect trends and events; they *caused* trends and events. In *The Age of Jackson*, Schlesinger conceived of America's liberal political history as one in which the character of certain select individuals determined the course of events. Men such as Biddle, Calhoun, Van Buren, and members of Jackson's "Kitchen Cabinet" fought over differences between Hamiltonian and Jeffersonian philosophies of government. Conservatives such as Biddle represented the business community, while liberals such as Jackson represented the rest of society. In the struggles of early America, liberals prevailed *because* of their character and the way it reflected a genuine American heritage of ideas. Thus, Biddle lost the Bank War *because* he was "drunk with power"; Jackson's men succeeded *because* they valued fact over theory in true American fashion.[31]

Central to Schlesinger's mode of reasoning was his remarkable gift for portraiture. For example, here was Schlesinger's unendearing synopsis of Daniel Webster in *The Age of Jackson:*

Daniel Webster lacked precisely that talent for stirring the popular imagination. He was an awe-inspiring figure, solid as granite, with strong shoulders and an iron frame. His dark, craggy head was unforgettable; strangers always recognized the jet-black hair, the jutting brow, the large smoldering eyes, and the "mastiff mouth," as Carlyle saw it, "accurately closed." Yet, he inclined to be taciturn in public, except when he worked up, with the aid of brandy, a heavy geniality for social purposes. He loved his comfort too much: liquor and rest, duck-shooting at Marshfield, and adulation in Boston.[32]

Upon labeling Webster an acquisitive sot, Schlesinger went on to assert that while "Clay fought for Biddle and the Bank because it fitted in with his superb vision of America, Webster fought for it in great part because it was a dependable source of revenue."[33] Webster thus became a conservative blackguard in a world where personalities greatly influenced the shape of social policy.

In Schlesinger's version of America's liberal lineage, ideology was the last refuge of the scoundrels from the Right and Left. Radical viewpoints on material equity either were praised by Schlesinger when their spokesmen converted to advocating Jacksonian pragmatism or were condemned as utopian sentimentality. Emerson, for example, was criticized for having little concern for practical policy.[34] Liberal American thought, concluded Schlesinger, arose from a mixture of personalities and pragmatism.[35]

In his account of the New Deal in the three-volume *Age of Roosevelt*, Schlesinger developed a similar causal relationship between character and policy outcomes. The New Deal was a success, according to Schlesinger, because of the personalities within an interested bureaucracy living in Washington, D.C. The New Deal, wrote Schlesinger, was for many intellectuals "the happiest time and the deepest fulfillment they would ever know," because they were given a chance to put ideas to work. A large degree of Schlesinger's causal explanation rested upon his depictions of the "endless stream of bright young men" who brought to Washington "an alertness, an excitement, and appetite for power, an instinct for crisis and a dedication to public service" that was the essence of the New Deal.[36]

Schlesinger posited two reasons for the importance of individual character to the New Deal. First, the ambiguous nature of the New Deal mandates made success dependent upon the personalities of the administrators of New Deal programs. Schlesinger's narrative of program after program was informed by the persistent pattern of creation and resolution of legislative ambiguity by individual bureaucrats. So, for example, the success of the Securities and Exchange Commission rested on the talents of Kennedy; the mixed results of Roosevelt's farm program were due to struggles among Wallace, Peek, Tugwell, Davis, and Frank over interpreting the missions and priorities of the Agricultural Adjustment Act (AAA); the rhetorical excesses of the Blue Eagle program of the National Recovery Administration (NRA) were outgrowths of the mercurial personality of Colonel Johnson.[37] Eschewing any detailed explanation as to *why* the New Deal mandates were vague in the first place, Schlesinger asserted that Roosevelt fell back upon people as the means of coordination because of a belief that the execution of a government policy depended more on the "liveliness, vitality, and vision" of "the right people" than on a sound, precise legislative program.[38]

Second, the emergent organization of the Roosevelt bureaucratic structure made success dependent upon the intellectual resources of the members of the bureaucracy. Schlesinger argued that creative government *depends* on overlapping jurisdictions within bureaucracy. Roosevelt thus favored the "competitive theory of administration," which kept "grants of authority incomplete, jurisdictions uncertain, charters overlapping" precisely because the president wanted access to diverse ideas and opinions. Such a bureaucracy "made public service attractive to men of certain boldness and imagination" because they knew that good ideas would have access to power.[39] Schlesinger relegated the explanation as to *why* the organizational structure of the bureaucracy rested more on personality than function to the realm of Roosevelt's personality itself.

Thus, in both *The Age of Jackson* and *The Age of Roosevelt*, the importance of liberal and conservative character in Schlesinger's frame of acceptance was elevated to the status of cause in his explanation sketches of American political history. The emphasis on character reflects the central importance of definitions of "liberal" and "conservative" in Schlesinger's accounts of American politics.

Predictable Alternation Between Liberalism and Conservatism

Schlesinger used the notion of alternating periods of conservative and liberal dominance both to rationalize the decaying popularity of Jacksonian policies by 1840 and to proclaim a new era of liberal activism during the 1930s. Jacksonian democracy, argued Schlesinger in *The Age of Jackson*, had "satisfied the popular desire for change" by the end of the 1830s. The Whigs, led by able younger men such as Seward, Lincoln, and Thaddeus Stevens, combined an appreciation for the public's desire for rest with a campaign of borrowed Jacksonian phrases for electoral victory in 1840. William Henry Harrison ousted Martin Van Buren as president of the United States, and the age of Jackson ended.[40]

However, Schlesinger continued, while defeat in 1840 dealt "a terrific blow to Democratic morale" and set the stage for the eventual sectional disintegration of the Democratic party in the 1850s, the election was "the most conclusive evidence of the triumph" of liberal populism over the business interests.[41] "Conservatism had carried the election," the historian declared, "but it had to assume the manner of the popular party in order to do it." The "Jacksonian triumph" of the 1820s and 1830s, which established the liberal presumption for an affirmative state aiding the humble members of society, meant that "the struggle would be renewed on Jackson's terms, and not on those of Daniel Webster or Nicholas Biddle."[42] The predictable alternation of the tides of national politics allowed Schlesinger to explain the temporary conservative victory of 1840 as part of the overall establishment of liberalism as the prevailing presumption in American political life.[43]

The tides of national politics also led Schlesinger to explain the New Deal as mass psychological therapy for the troubled public of the 1930s. Schlesinger viewed the Great Depression as much as a depressant on the American psyche as a reflection of underlying material inequity within a moribund capitalist economy.[44] The American public was described as a "great mass" of "baffled and despairing" folks who had lost faith in a free system.[45] Society "seemed confronted by the specter of dissolution" that had been scared up during the Hoover years by a frightened business class that lacked imagination, understanding, and compassion. The economic travails of the 1920s and 1930s threatened America not only with starvation but also with "clouds of inertia and selfishness" that could lead to a totalitarian solution to the growing vacuum of leadership.[46]

In Schlesinger's view, the public apathy and disillusionment of the early 1930s were *natural* products of the political cycle of reform and inactivity. Only a return to the bold activism of the liberal side of the American political cycle could snap the country out of its malaise and fear. The New Deal offered just the tonic for a depressed America, argued Schlesinger. Beginning with the First Hundred Days of the Roosevelt administration and continuing throughout the 1930s, the country regained confidence in itself. The New Deal provided not so much solutions as sheer activity that buoyed the sagging nation.

Schlesinger contended that while programs like the National Recovery Administration and the Agricultural Adjustment Act and policies like tinkering with the gold standard may not have substantially alleviated physical hardship in America, they also quickened popular interest in public affairs and acted as "a great schoolhouse, compelling Americans to a greater knowledge of their country and its problems."[47] The New Deal thus signaled the beginning of a new era of liberal activism in accordance with the cyclical alternation of liberalism and conservatism in American politics.

The Need for Heroic Leadership

Schlesinger saw Andrew Jackson and Franklin Roosevelt as both necessary instruments and popular embodiments of America's liberal heritage. During the 1820s and 1830s, only a pragmatist such as Andrew Jackson saw that Hamiltonian means (active government intervention) were required to meet Jeffersonian ends (free competition in the economic marketplace). A leader who knew "the difference between firmness and obstinacy"[48] in his political beliefs, Andrew Jackson served as an eternal reminder that "if social catastrophe is to be avoided, it can only be by an earnest, tough-minded, pragmatic attempt to wrestle with new problems as they come, without being enslaved by a theory of the past, or a theory of the future."[49]

Jackson combined a pragmatic approach to governance with a deep, abiding popularity that won him access to democratic power. The "secret of his strength," wrote Schlesinger, was "his deep understanding of the people" combined with "the intuitive grasp of the necessities of change." Andrew Jackson was one of a handful of men of liberal character who were called upon by "the urgencies of the moment" to lead.[50]

As a summary of his description of Andrew Jackson, Schlesinger quoted Martin Van Buren's belief in "the production of great men by great events, developing and calling into action upon a large scale intellects the power of which, but for their application to great transactions, might have remained unknown alike to their possessors and to the world."[51] "The people called him," Schlesinger concluded, "and he came, like the great folk heroes, to lead them out of captivity and bondage."[52]

In his history of the New Deal era, Schlesinger developed an account of national government action that depended upon the creative and rhetorical talents of one man to keep the tempest of conflicting ideas and competing programs going. Franklin Delano Roosevelt was "the essential ganglion for reception, transmission, and realization" of the reform impulses of the nation, and served "as the substitute for a structure of coordination."[53]

Roosevelt's employment of the political "low road" (manipulation of Congress, bureaucrats, and the press) in his management of government was "offset," according to Schlesinger, by the political "high road" of personal courage and idealism. Schlesinger argued that while the deepest recesses of Roosevelt's personality remained inaccessible even to his close friends, he was able to exhibit a "passionate affirmation" of human possibility that allowed him to fulfill both the functional and moral potential of the heroic leader.[54]

Throughout the series of works on Roosevelt, Schlesinger portrayed the dynamism of the president's multidimensional personality as a causal force in the bureaucratic reaching out and the therapeutic healing of the New Deal. He wrote of Roosevelt: "His patience, his personal solicitude, his fantastic grasp of detail, his instinct for timing, his jocose and evasive humor, his lightheartedness, his disingenuousness, his reserve, his serenity, his occasional and formidable severity, his sense of his office, his sense of history—these were the *means* by which he ordered and dominated the crises of his administration" [emphasis added].[55]

The "essence" of the liberal presidency, wrote Schlesinger, depended upon "something like the Rooseveltian sleight-of-hand at the center." Schlesinger located the origins of New Deal liberalism within the "bewildering personality" of Franklin Roosevelt, whose various roles within his office were unreflectively guided by his "instinct for the future" and his love for "adventure and experiment."[56] By basing the bulk of historical explanation upon the inner qualities of Roosevelt's psyche, Schlesinger seemed to make Rooseveltian personality a *necessary condition* for modern liberal government.

It is crucial to note that the tides concept placed the locus of political action at the top, not the bottom, of the social structure. Schlesinger tended to focus on the character and temperament, whether liberal and conservative, of key political figures of the age. He placed great responsibility upon heroic liberal leaders who had "a sense, at once, of short-run variables and long-run tendencies, and an instinct for the complexity of their intermingling." Schlesinger believed his understanding of history came from "people, not from doctrine."[57] Yet the general public was defined as a broad mass responding to psychological impulses alternating in a cyclical fashion between activity and rest, between private and public interests. Schlesinger's historical understanding of the relationship between political leaders and the public would lead to difficulties when he tried to apply that understanding to the increasingly complex problems of his own time.

Critical Responses to Schlesinger's Historical Discourse

The evaluation of Schlesinger's work has varied, depending on how critics have viewed the nature of the relationship between Schlesinger and his readers. As mentioned earlier, in conventional historical discourse, the author focuses on making claims about past events with the purpose of producing an explanatory account that critical readers may judge as sound or reasonable. Evaluating Schlesinger's accounts of the eras of Jackson and Roosevelt just as scholarly arguments about history yields a mixed critical response.

Many within the academic discipline of history believe that Schlesinger's views on America's past have influenced a generation of historical scholarship. Pessen has written that "critics have paid indirect tribute to *The Age of Jackson* by dealing with the era largely in terms of the issues and questions posed by its author."[58] Sellers has noted that Schlesinger's histories of American liberalism have "not only provided a sharper definition of the democratic movement and a clearer explanation of its origins" but have "also stirred up a warm debate which prompted other historians to offer alternative definitions."[59]

At the same time, other scholars with doubts about Schlesinger's objectivity toward the subject matter have questioned the soundness of Schlesinger's historical explanations. Two examples illustrate this kind of critique. In a widely cited negative review of *The Age of Jackson*, Bray Hammond charged that Schlesinger's political one-sidedness, combined with "a fumbling treatment of economic matters and particularly of the Bank of the United States," made for bad history. Hammond concluded that Schlesinger's work "represents the age of Jackson as one of triumphant liberalism when it was as much or more an age of triumphant exploitation; . . . fosters a simplistic notion of continuing problems of human welfare; and . . . thickens the myths around a political leader who had more capacity for action than for accomplishment."[60]

Assessing Schlesinger's scholarship concerning the Roosevelt era as part of a revisionist review of historical treatments of Calvin Coolidge, T. B. Silver accused Schlesinger of setting up Coolidge as a "straw man" target for broadside attacks on conservatism during the 1920s. "Coolidge is interesting to Schlesinger less in himself than as a symbol of American conservatism more generally," wrote Silver. Silver went on to demonstrate several instances in which Schlesinger wrenched statements from Coolidge and others out of context to make a partisan point. "Professor Schlesinger's selectivity," charged Silver, "puts him in the role of a prosecutor who wrenches one damaging remark out of a witness' mouth and then shuts him up before he can say anything else." In a final rebuke, Silver asserted that "Schlesinger, not content merely to set forth Coolidge's political opinions, proceeded from the issues to a [slanted] presentation of Coolidge's character." Such practices, Silver concluded, are inappropriate for a historian, whose "high duty" is "to eschew caricature in the name of truth" by taking care "to draw his heroes and villains true to life."[61]

Others have considered Schlesinger's historical accounts of the ages of Jackson and Roosevelt in a different light, defining Schlesinger's relationship to his readers from a broader political perspective rather than the perspective of academic historiography. For example, *Time* magazine's review of *The Age of Jackson* identified an implicit partisan purpose in the book. In addition to producing a work of scholarship, the reviewer found that Schlesinger was attempting "to establish these [Jacksonian] ideas as the missing link between the somewhat contradictory body of theory and practice known as Jeffersonianism and the somewhat contradictory body of theory and practice called the New Deal." In that context, the review praised the work as "an unusually readable history about one of the most opaque episodes in the American past."[62] In a similar fashion, Esmond Wright hailed *The Crisis of the Old Order* as "vital, vivid, revealing history" in which "the people come alive on the page and the tensions mount." The work "has the atmosphere of a contemporary chronicle, so detailed is the research, so sharp the insight." Wright concluded by asserting that Schlesinger's work should be read not only as history but also as parable.[63]

Gerald W. Johnson, in a review of *The Crisis of the Old Order*, suggested a reason for the disparate views toward Schlesinger's historical scholarship. "As a historian, Schlesinger is bold, opinionated, somewhat arrogant, and occasionally wrong," argued Johnson. "But Schlesinger has the enormous merit of saying something; he is committed to the old-fashioned and perhaps illiberal theory that there is not only a difference, but a perceptible difference between a scoundrel and an honest man, and he never ends a discussion with the arid recommendation that the subject deserves further study."[64]

What emerges from this second critical perspective is the conclusion that Schlesinger's scholarship on the ages of Jackson and Roosevelt served as the foundation and starting point for his ideological history of American liberalism. In these works, Schlesinger presented arguments *about* history that could then function as grounds for arguments *from* history concerning contemporary political questions. Schlesinger constructed accounts of the ages of Jackson and Roosevelt in order to help shape public presumption concerning the character and desirability of liberalism and conservatism in the present. His explanations of the Jackson and Roosevelt eras in American history, drawing upon definitions of liberals and conservatives, the regular ebb and flow of public activism, and the necessary emergence of a liberal leader, established a pattern of analysis that would also characterize his diagnoses of the political issues of his own time.

Viewing Schlesinger's writings on American political history as part of a broader persuasive campaign on behalf of liberalism helps account for the historian's influence in shaping political attitudes in his own time. Nuechterlein has asserted that in tracing liberal political thought in America from the 1800s to the New Deal, Schlesinger attempted to accomplish one of his own "primary political purposes—the legitimizing of the New Deal through the establishment of suitable historical antecedents." In so doing, Schlesinger produced grounds for the claim that his liberal frame of acceptance is "*the* legitimate tradition of American liberal democracy."[65] According to Cunliffe, Schlesinger made a strong case for his liberal political viewpoint by drawing implicit parallels between past and present.[66]

Historian John Higham has noted that "the alleged 'lessons' of history have often made themselves powerfully felt in public affairs."[67] The remainder of this study examines the relationship between Schlesinger's historical understanding, summarized in the "tides of national politics," and American history in the making. We begin with Schlesinger's attempts to bring history to the aid of politics in reshaping the definition of liberalism in the 1950s.

3

From the New Deal to Camelot: Ideological History in Action

By the beginning of the 1950s, according to Michael Wreszin, Arthur Schlesinger, Jr., "was admired across the entire spectrum of the culture." "The world was his oyster," writes Wreszin, "and Washington his favorite city."[1] Never satisfied with being an academician, Schlesinger took unmistakable steps to leave the ivory tower during the next decade. As cofounder of the Americans for Democratic Action, a group identifying itself with the noncommunist Left in American politics, Schlesinger became increasingly involved in agenda setting and platform writing for liberal political candidates.[2]

As he became more politically active, Schlesinger wrote and spoke more frequently for popular audiences in popular media. During the 1950s, the contexts, purposes, and substance of his discourse became more overtly partisan in nature. In the wake of his successful book-length historical works, Schlesinger began to "capitalize on the journalistic contracts that came flooding in from *Life*, *Fortune*, *Collier's*, *The Saturday Evening Post*, *Atlantic Monthly*, as well as *The New Republic*, *The Nation*, and *Partisan Review*."[3] Working as a speech writer for Democratic presidential candidate Adlai Stevenson in 1952 and 1956, Schlesinger "experienced the exhilaration of taking his ideas and talents out of the academy and moving into the world of power politics."[4] By 1953, even conservative critics like Ralph de Toledano conceded that Schlesinger's ideas had "exerted a remarkable influence on the body politic."[5]

Yet the 1950s were troubled times for Schlesinger and for all

American liberals. Schlesinger attempted to use historical under-standing to answer challenges to contemporary liberalism during the 1950s. In so doing, the historian employed aspects of the tides of national politics as ideological history. His comparisons between past and present functioned to help Schlesinger to rationalize past liberal failures, shift the focus of liberalism from quantitative to qualitative, and predict future liberal triumphs. By 1960, Schlesinger found in Democratic presidential candidate John F. Kennedy some-one who embodied the qualities of liberal leadership called for in his frame of acceptance. Schlesinger's adoption of the tides of national politics as a means of diagnosing American politics during the 1950s also produced the beginnings of a rhetorical trajectory, a path of symbolic development that influenced and constrained Schlesinger's rhetorical choices in the years that followed.

As I will show in this chapter, Arthur Schlesinger, Jr., used the tides of national politics to answer challenges to contemporary liberal thought during the 1950s. This chapter will also examine Schlesinger's support of Democrat John F. Kennedy during the 1960 presidential campaign. I begin by describing the rhetorical problems that confronted liberalism throughout the decade.

The Troublesome Rhetorical Climate of the 1950s

Matusow asserts that by the end of the 1950s "proponents of liberalism had experimented with so many intellectual reformula-tions that liberalism seemed less a creature of the past than of mere mood."[6] Schlesinger himself admitted in 1957 that "liberalism in America has not for thirty years been so homeless, baffled, irrele-vant, and impotent as it is today."[7] The bewilderment of the Ameri-can liberal during the 1950s was caused by three interrelated rhetorical problems during the decade.

The first challenge to liberalism was the problem of *consensus.* Arthur Schlesinger, Jr., viewed American society in terms of struggle and conflict between groups for political hegemony. In *The Age of Jackson,* Schlesinger characterized America's past as a "feud be-tween the capitalist and the laborer, the house of Have and the house of Want," that "is as old as social union" and "can never be entirely quieted."[8] In *The Vital Center,* Schlesinger applied the theme of struggle to America's battle against communism. The international system, he wrote, is "essentially in a state of tension"; and "if we believe in free society hard enough to keep on fighting for it, we are pledged to a permanent crisis which will test the moral, political, and very possibly the military strength of each side."[9] Schlesinger's liberalism was primed by temperament and necessity for active struggle against the foes of conservative greed and communist totalitarianism.[10]

Such a contentious view of American society was not suited to America in the 1950s. During the 1950s, America was characterized much more by *consensus* than by conflict. Liberal critique of social institutions was drowned out by the steady cold war drum beat of anticommunism, and liberal critique of big business was eroded by the growing material prosperity of the age.[11] Throughout much of the decade, both conservatives and liberals agreed on the ends of American life: anticommunism and economic growth.

In a time of an "extraordinary degree of commonality of purposes, values, and assumptions among most Americans throughout the national experience," writes Nuechterlein, Schlesinger's call for a "fighting" liberalism sounded out of place.[12] Schlesinger's differentiation between conservatives and liberals appeared to be ideological in a period hailed by Daniel Bell as "the end of ideology." "The tendency to convert concrete issues into ideological problems, to color them with moral fervor and high emotional charge," wrote Bell in a passage aimed straight at Schlesinger's vital center, "is to invite conflicts which can only damage a society."[13] Schlesinger's assumptions that change was good and that ideological competition was the sign of a healthy society seemed to be empirically refuted by the growing sense of agreement and good feeling that characterized politics and culture in the 1950s.

The second challenge to liberalism was the problem of *affluence*. A major premise of Schlesinger's theory of the cyclical alternation of conservative and liberal epochs was that liberals would regain power from the conservatives as the result of some major social problems left unaddressed during conservative administrations. These social problems, which would "pile up till demand for reform becomes overwhelming," had always been characterized by Schlesinger as being *economic* in nature. The "age of Jackson" was ushered in as a result of a monetary crisis involving availability of currency and the Bank of the United States. The "age of Roosevelt" began in the depths of a depression exacerbated by conservative Republican neglect.[14]

Schlesinger's scenario for a liberal comeback generated by an unsolved economic crisis seemed unlikely during the 1950s, which were characterized not by another crisis of capitalism but by general growth and prosperity. Despite periodic recessions, Matusow asserts, the "character of the era" was "decisively determined" by the "growing amount of discretionary income" enjoyed by the mass of Americans.[15] It was in the context of increasing affluence that Louis

Hartz wrote, "The age of purely domestic crisis is apparently over."[16] Liberals like Schlesinger who based their political fortunes on the economic cycle were told to "quit worrying about contemporary capitalism."[17]

Schlesinger's belief that liberalism would become popular in response to crisis depended on the *existence* of a crisis. In a time both of widespread agreement on the goals of free enterprise and economic growth and of general economic stability, liberal policies modeled after the New Deal seemed to have little ideological justification. Schlesinger's liberal viewpoint was saddled with the charge that it would take another Great Depression to make liberalism rise again.[18] "The politics of the vital center, flourishing in conditions of Depression, appeared to flounder in the midst of prosperity," asserts Nuechterlein.[19]

The final challenge involved the problem of *power.* Schlesinger's belief in the need for heroic liberal leadership was also refuted by the experiences of the Eisenhower years. Schlesinger believed that democracy had a functional and moral need for heroic leadership to keep America moving toward progressive ends of freedom and prosperity. In Schlesinger's interpretation of American history, the heroes responding to crises had always been liberals. The temperament and sympathies necessary for heroic leadership had always belonged to liberals such as Jackson and Roosevelt, not to conservatives such as Webster, Biddle, Coolidge, and Hoover.

During the 1950s, Schlesinger's constellation of liberal heroes and conservative villains was confronted with the stark anomaly of Dwight D. Eisenhower, the popular *conservative* leader of the nation. Eisenhower, the military-hero-turned-president, created "an atmosphere of greater serenity and mutual confidence" during his tenure that rivaled Roosevelt's New Deal years. The "celebration of life" in America during the Eisenhower administration was the product not of calls for heroic sacrifice in response to crisis but of calm stewardship of the state.[20] "It was typical of President Eisenhower," writes O'Neill, "that his greatest achievements were negative. He ended the Korean War, entered into no new ones, and kept military spending down."[21]

Eisenhower seemed to break the liberal monopoly on heroic political figures. In Eisenhower, America found a hero cast in the image not of bold crusader or reformer but of a grandfather. Schlesinger was forced to confront the reality that conservatism could maintain popularity through the manipulation of heroic images. As the 1950s waned, liberals such as Schlesinger grew increasingly restless out of power and came to realize that national electoral victory was an essential precondition to effective political action.[22]

Schlesinger applied his conception of the past to deal with political problems liberals faced in the present. Before examining his campaign to revive liberalism, we should discuss two specific rhetorical strategies Schlesinger would use to transform his arguments about history into arguments from history.

Analogy, Dissociation, and Ideological History

Analogy and dissociation are powerful persuasive strategies that can assist advocates engaging in ideological history in linking their claims about the present to their views of the past. The drawing of direct correspondences between past and present events through historical analogy often serves as the persuasive foundation for ideological history.[23] Gronbeck explains that an analytical approach to history, "which seeks out and abstracts causal patterns in human events, can be used to warrant propositions concerning contemporary social affairs." The key assumption in such arguments is "the commensurability of human actions across stretches of time." Advocates who ground claims in this assumption attempt to abstract or loosen configurations of behaviors in a past situation "so as to help us understand other events in other situations 'in the same way.'" Such analogical arguments, Gronbeck concludes, "not only make sense out of today's events" but also "add moral overtones to those understandings."[24]

The strategic use of definition, particularly through the technique of dissociation, is another important persuasive resource available to an advocate engaging in ideological history.[25] According to Perelman and Olbrechts-Tyteca, dissociation is the splitting of a seemingly unitary concept into two parts by linking each part to a philosophical pair of terms, the first of which has a negative connotation and the other a positive connotation (such as "appearance/reality" pair). At the conclusion of the dissociation, a previously single term has been divided into a favorable and an unfavorable term.[26]

The strategy of dissociation contributes to the advocacy of ideological history by providing a rationale for making distinctions between what is "apparent," or false, and what is "real," or true, concerning events, terms, and individuals from the past.[27] The advocate divides a historical term or concept into its "apparent" and "real" aspects in order to fit the demands of changing political situations. Based on the dissociation, interpretations of the past are constructed to generate favorable or unfavorable perceptions of related circumstances in the present.

Terms such as "liberal" and "conservative," which are often important aspects of a political controversy, are susceptible to strategic definition as part of an argument based on ideological history. McGee refers to such one-term summaries of political orientations as *ideographs*. Ideographs contain both contextual (synchronic) and historical (diachronic) dimensions of meaning. Through dissociation, advocates can distinguish between "apparent" and "real" historical meanings of ideographs such as "liberal" and "conservative" in order to influence the configuration of communal values and policies. Relations drawn between particular definitions of "liberal" or "conservative" and past situations can influence an audience's positive or negative interpretations of such ideographs in present or future usages.[28]

Drawing upon elements of the "tides of national politics," Schlesinger would respond to attacks upon liberalism by presenting both analogical and dissociational arguments which related present situations to the past. In applying the tides of national politics to the contemporary political scene, Schlesinger engaged in the third rhetorical move associated with ideological history: the utilization of historical explanation as support for arguments concerning the present and future.

Schlesinger's Move to "Qualitative Liberalism"

During the 1950s, Schlesinger used his growing political visibility to articulate new ends and means for liberalism in response to the problems that confronted his liberal viewpoint. Through the persuasive powers of historical analogy and definition through dissociation, Schlesinger hoped to "recover" the "central place" of liberalism in American life.[29]

His attempt to revive liberalism would be drawn from his understanding of history. For Schlesinger believed that the tides of national politics could explain and transcend the rhetorical problems of the times. "The battlefield of American politics," wrote Schlesinger in 1954, "is often dark and confused, with shouts and sighs and blood-curdling screams echoing through the night." The problems confronting liberalism were nothing more than "occasional flares, rockets, and bombs bursting in air to provide brief and delusive impressions of light and action." While manifestations of the liberals' rhetorical problems often appeared to be "the pivots of our whole political equilibrium," in the longer view of historical perspective they would soon "come to seem almost irrelevant."[30]

Schlesinger found explanation and solace by turning to his cyclical view of America's political past. "Underneath the sound and the fury," he continued, "there remains a persistent deeper logic in American political life" that, "in the long run," may be "more important in political behavior than all the clamor of the moment."[31]

This central assumption provided the foundation for Schlesinger's persuasive use of history. Throughout his career, he drew clear connections between past and present based on the cyclical inevitability of the "tides of national politics." During the 1950s, Schlesinger adjusted all three components of the "tides of national politics" to respond to the challenges of consensus, affluence, and power.

Adjusting Definitions of Liberal and Conservative

The defeat of liberal presidential candidate Adlai Stevenson in 1952 convinced Schlesinger that the "liberal program" of the New Deal "had bogged down in the ruts of old issues and old debates" and had been subsumed by the growing conservative consensus among the American people. What was needed, Schlesinger concluded, was a revamped liberal philosophy that would seek "to abolish the liberal banalities and move beyond the liberal dogmas."[32] To reshape his conceptions of liberalism and conservatism, Schlesinger used a series of dissociations between the "apparent" and "real" aspects of liberalism. His arguments included an identification of the "true" American political consensus, a refined analogy between past and present conservatism and liberalism based on interests, and a call for a new liberal agenda.

First, Schlesinger attempted to identify the "true" American political consensus by labeling it a *liberal* consensus. "In a sense," Schlesinger wrote in 1956, "all of America is liberalism." Americans "assume liberalism as one of the presuppositions of life."[33] Schlesinger equated liberalism as it appeared throughout American history with "the philosophy of a free society," based on "the faith that the purpose of society is to foster the growth of the individual in freedom, dignity, and responsibility."[34]

Schlesinger created the broadest possible definition of liberalism in response to the writings of "New Conservatism," a "counterrevolution in political philosophy" based on the belief that "liberalism had its chance and failed."[35] Instead of being the foundation for a conservative American consensus, "New Conservatism" was "the wrong doctrine in the wrong country directed against the wrong enemies," charged Schlesinger.[36] Schlesinger tried to place Eisenhower and his "New Conservative" supporters *outside* the range of consensual American values. In America, Schlesinger concluded, the *liberal* values of realism, gradualism, and empiricism had always been the true expressions of the national experience. The views of the "New Conservatives" constituted only the apparent mainstream of American public opinion; the real consensus was a liberal consensus.

Second, Schlesinger attempted to redirect the focus of the conflict between liberals and conservatives away from the economic theme of Haves versus Have-Nots. Recognizing that during the affluent years of the 1950s many Americans believed that what was good for General Motors was good for the country, Schlesinger began to differentiate between liberals and conservatives less on the basis of economic class and more on the basis of general *interests.*

Schlesinger accomplished this move by drawing upon a specific interpretation of America's past. "Political parties," Schlesinger wrote in 1956, "acquire identities, like people; and history has endowed each of our national parties with a distinctive personality and philosophy." The "character" of conservatives and liberals has been derived "in great part" from the relationship each group has had "with the interest it represents."[37] From the beginning of American history, Schlesinger argued, liberal Democrats have been a *multiinterest* party, a "receptacle for . . . miscellaneous lesser interests of the nation."[38] Conservative Republicans have been a *single-interest* party, identifying "the general welfare with the welfare of the most powerful group in our society—the business community."[39]

Based on this adjusted reading of the past, Schlesinger addressed the present political situation. Insisting that his characterization was "not a partisan thesis" but a historical truth based on the soundness of the analogy between past and present, he charged that the significance of the Eisenhower administration lay in "the consequences of a change from a government by a multi-interest to a government by a single-interest party."[40] Eisenhower had "given us a copybook demonstration of the meaning of a single-interest government" by deluding himself with "the belief that successful businessmen have cornered the wisdom necessary" to run a diverse nation. By believing "that what is good for one's own private interest is good for all," Eisenhower had neglected larger public interests in national security and the maintenance of cultural diversity.[41]

It is crucial to understand that Schlesinger's redefinition of "liberal" and "conservative" based on interests was not meant to be a new broadside attack on American business. In fact, Schlesinger took great pains to distance his new description of liberalism from a larger critique of capitalist institutions. "I should point out,"

Schlesinger commented in 1960, "that the basic trouble is *not* that the Republican Party represents the business community. The trouble is that it represents a *single* interest." Schlesinger then discredited previous distinctions between political orientations based on Haves versus Have-Nots by adding: "I would object just as strongly to a party who addressed itself exclusively to the welfare of labor or farmers (or, for that matter, college professors)."[42] The "miscellaneous lesser interests" making up the liberal coalition during American history have had "very little else in common except their opposition to rule by the first interest."[43] In short, Schlesinger reframed the basic issue of American politics during the 1950s from the regulation of economic power to the management of interests generated by "the inexhaustible variety of a multi-interest country."[44]

Third, and finally, Schlesinger reshaped the liberal agenda in order to answer the conservative charge that economic depression must precede a new wave of liberal reform. Schlesinger began this move by again differentiating between a real and an apparent understanding of America's past, making the startling claim that the New Deal was *not* typical of liberalism in American history. "The New Deal experience" left "a misleading legacy to the present generation of liberals" by bequeathing "the notion that the essential problem of liberalism was the fight against poverty, that the essential method was economic reform, and that the essential stimulus was a depression."[45] Previous liberal eras—including Jeffersonian democracy, the antislavery movement, and the Progressive movement—had been spurred on not by the fight against poverty but by a more "original concern" for "the status and growth of the free individual in the mass society."[46]

The historian concluded that "there is nothing more inaccurate than to suppose a depression to be the necessary condition for a new period of liberal reform."[47] With this claim, Schlesinger dissociated the periodic rise of liberalism from economic depression and enlarged the scope of social and material concerns that could spark a revival of liberalism in America.

The separation of the term "liberal" from economic depression allowed Schlesinger to admit the relative prosperity of the postwar age and to claim it as proof of liberalism's *success*.[48] "Poverty has receded from the forefront of our national life," Schlesinger boasted in 1956. Largely because of the "brilliant success" of New Deal programs, Americans now dwelled in an "economy of abundance" in which "the central problems" were no longer "want and privation."[49] While there are "pools of poverty which have to be mopped up," Schlesinger optimistically concluded in 1960, the robust American economy "has made possible for the first time the democratization of human comfort."[50]

In an age of abundance, American liberals would have to seek a new agenda. The new agenda would have to begin by addressing the "widespread anxiety and discomfort" in middle-class society caused by stifling pressures toward conformity and rising frustration at the tradeoff between the benefits of a mass economy and the dullness of a mass culture. It was time, Schlesinger announced in 1957, for liberalism to "shift its focus from economics and politics to the general style and quality of our civilization."[51]

Schlesinger derived the new liberal agenda from a key distinction between quantity and quality regarding social issues. What was required, Schlesinger contended, was a *qualitative* liberalism "dedicated to bettering the quality of people's lives and opportunities." This new liberalism would "move on from the quantitative problems" of economic policy "to the more elusive and complicated task of fighting for individual dignity, identity, and fulfillment in a mass society."[52] The issues to be placed on the new liberal agenda would include "those of education, health, equal opportunity, [and] community planning" and the refurbishing of the nation's physical plant in the national interest.[53]

It is important to note that Schlesinger's shift to qualitative liberalism was based on the premise that the "fight" to secure general economic prosperity had been won by the 1950s. The assumption that economic growth would remain high led Schlesinger to conclude in 1959 that "we should be able to give the public sector what it needs without substantial increases in taxation" and without inflation. Schlesinger saw potential limits to growth as merely "technical problems, far more manageable once the national will has decided in favor of definite goals than in the current state of public confusion and apathy."[54]

Thus, Schlesinger attempted to alter both historical and contextual dimensions of the term "liberal" by widening the circumference of the liberal agenda from economic matters to matters of culture, lifestyle, and opportunity for individual fulfillment.[55]

Adjusting the Definition of Alternating Political Eras

As liberals suffered electoral defeats and witnessed the popularity of the conservative hero Eisenhower in the halls of American political power during the 1950s, they grew anxious about the prospects for a turn in fortune in their favor. To combat liberal ennui,

Schlesinger persuasively extended his conception of alternating eras of liberal and conservative dominance to include a predictive claim that forecasted the coming of a new political era of liberal reform in the 1960s.

This predictive claim was supported by two assertions. First, Schlesinger distinguished between apparent and real explanations for liberal electoral defeats during the 1950s. Schlesinger saw conservative triumphs not as proof of liberal failure but as natural products of the larger tides of national politics.

Liberal Democrats lost the reins of presidential power in 1952, according to Schlesinger, simply because "the tides were running too deep . . . for any candidate—even Adlai Stevenson—to reverse them."[56] Using physiological terminology, Schlesinger repeated the explanation after the 1956 reelection of President Eisenhower: "Americans, after a generation's buffeting by depression and war, had to have a breathing spell. . . . Even by 1956, they had not had their fill of inertia."[57]

What accounted for the condition of the American public during the 1950s? Schlesinger believed that the "fundamental factor" contributing to "the swing to conservatism during the late forties and early fifties" was "the condition of national weariness produced by two decades of unrelenting crises."[58] During those years, Presidents Roosevelt and Truman "kept demanding from us a lively interest in public policy and kept confronting us with tough problems of national decision." The implicit consensus of American values was securely *liberal*. Yet, by the early 1950s, Schlesinger continued, "the American people had had it."[59] Consequently, the decade was dominated by "the politics of fatigue."[60]

Schlesinger assured liberals that they need not panic during times of public weariness. The Eisenhower administration of the 1950s was merely playing a part "in the larger rhythm of our politics."[61] Eisenhower's tenure was not the sign of a permanent conservative majority in America but a "wholly natural and predictable expression" of the tides of American politics.[62]

After interpreting liberal defeats as natural results of political tides, Schlesinger then began to forecast in more detail the coming of the new liberal era. This forecast represented the fullest extension of Schlesinger's original explanation sketch. "The Eisenhower epoch is drawing to a natural end," Schlesinger wrote in 1959.[63] The Eisenhower administration "no longer interprets our desires and needs as a people," Schlesinger continued in 1960. "New forces, new energies, new values are straining for expression and release."[64] Cultural and political signs during the late 1950s indicated a "more general turning of the tide" back toward support for liberal activism in government.[65]

To reinforce his opinion about changing political tides in America, Schlesinger employed historical analogy. The historian found striking parallels between the contemporary public mood and the "mounting spiritual and psychological discontent" during the years preceding the era of New Deal liberal activism. While economic trends during the two periods were admittedly different, Schlesinger cited "the defection of writers, educators, newspapermen, [and] editors" who saw "the increasingly visible discrepancy" in the Coolidge-Hoover era "between what was and what might be in America." The activity occurring beneath "the official crust of self-congratulation" during both the 1920s and 1950s led Schlesinger to conclude that "a period of acute intellectual revolt is likely to foreshadow a period of political revolt."[66]

"The crust is breaking up," Schlesinger concluded in a 1959 political memorandum entitled "The Shape of National Politics to Come." "The sixties await, and they promise to be one of the great decades in our history."[67] Although Schlesinger was reluctant to say when "these new sentiments will become dominant," he did argue for the virtual inevitability of a new liberal era.[68] "There is no reason to suppose," Schlesinger wrote in 1960, "that this pendular motion [toward liberalism] has suddenly come to a stop."[69] What was needed to complete the "cyclical overturn" was a detonating issue with "some larger national purpose" and "the revival of public leadership." Once the liberals found an issue and "a national voice (like Theodore Roosevelt in 1901 and Franklin Roosevelt in 1933)," then "there will be a breakthrough into a new political epoch."[70]

Adjusting the Definition of Heroic Leadership

Schlesinger completed the ideological application of his historical understanding by guiding liberals toward a choice of a capable presidential candidate in 1960 through a call for a different kind of heroic leadership. According to Schlesinger, new heroic leadership was needed to move America into the 1960s for two reasons: to manage interests and to call for sacrifice.

First, a heroic leader was needed to manage interests. As explained earlier, Schlesinger's reformulation of the term "liberal" was based on the idea that "government by a single interest is bad, whatever the nature of the interest." A liberal platform representing a multitude of lesser interests in society could form the basis for a successful government only if "a positive philosophy of the public interest" was developed "to be asserted against the parochial interests of any single group."[71] A multiinterest liberal government demanded strong leadership to manage the diversity of interests just as "the driver with a team of fractious horses must learn to impose his will if he is to stay on the road."[72] Without strong leadership, Schlesinger continued in 1959, "the idea of the welfare state will degenerate into what Robert M. Hutchins referred to as 'the pressure group state, which cares only for those who are well enough organized to put on the pressure.'"[73]

Managing a modern liberal government requires a "willingness to take on the private interests whose aggressive pursuit of their own advantages imperils the general welfare." Taking on the interests was a heroic act, Schlesinger asserted, because "the price of being right in such matters has always been a bad press and some outrage in the business community." "No liberal statesman in American history," Schlesinger concluded, "has ever been admired at the time by the respectable elements in society."[74]

While recognizing the functional necessity of heroic leadership in an interest-based society, Schlesinger assumed that turmoil and crisis would *produce* strong leaders. "The experience of controlling these tendencies," he remarked in 1954, "only further develops capacities for national leadership." Pragmatic experimentation, combined with a firm sense of direction and purpose, would be sufficient to overcome the dangers of basing a social philosophy on competition among interests.[75]

Second, a heroic leader was needed to call for sacrifice. The "trick of political greatness," Schlesinger wrote in 1954, "is to develop an ardent sense of the national interests which includes and transcends special interests."[76] While the previous liberal era had been triggered by the Great Depression, which demanded national attention, the coming of the new liberal era in the 1960s would not be triggered by a clear, tangible precipitating event. Instead, the qualitative issues Schlesinger identified as heading the new liberal agenda concerned "the discrepancy between our national potential and our national performance."[77] In order to convince the American people that society should resume a forward motion toward liberal goals, a heroic leader was required with a "personal vision of the future."[78]

The heroic vision could be conveyed not only by what a leader did but by how he did it. To improve the quality of our lives at home and to regain our superiority over communism abroad would take an immense effort that could be aroused only by a charismatic *style* of leadership capable of compelling sacrifice of individual interest in favor of the national interest.[79]

Once a leader stepped up to demand individual sacrifice, Schlesinger concluded, a new liberal era would begin "like the breaking of a dam." "Thus the 1960s," the historian predicted, "will probably be spirited, articulate, inventive, incoherent, turbulent, with energy shooting off wildly in all directions."[80] Above all, the emergence of a liberal hero for the 1960s would provide liberals with "a sense of motion, of leadership, and of hope."[81]

Summarizing Schlesinger's Persuasive Campaign

Arthur Schlesinger's campaign to redefine liberalism was an attempt to address the rhetorical problems of consensus, affluence, and power that confronted liberals during the 1950s. Through ideological arguments from history based largely on techniques of analogy and dissociation, Schlesinger adjusted historical and contextual dimensions of meaning concerning the term "liberal," and reconfigured conceptions of liberal presumption. Schlesinger hoped that the results of the 1960 presidential election would vindicate his efforts to reinvigorate liberals as a powerful group within the American political spectrum.

The Tides of National Politics and the 1960 Election

Arthur Schlesinger's discourse in support of Democratic candidate John F. Kennedy during the 1960 presidential campaign may be analyzed as a representative anecdote, the culmination of a period of symbolic adjustments made in Schlesinger's frame of acceptance during the 1950s.[82] To analyze Schlesinger's discourse, one must begin by summarizing Schlesinger's association with Kennedy and the Kennedy campaign.

Arthur M. Schlesinger's association with the Kennedy family began in the 1930s, when young Arthur and the eldest Kennedy son, Joe, Jr., were classmates at Harvard. During the 1940s and 1950s, Schlesinger and John Kennedy knew each other only as casual acquaintances in the large circles of fellowship in Washington, D.C., and Cambridge, Massachusetts.[83]

Schlesinger supported and worked for Adlai Stevenson's presidential campaigns during the 1950s. But he appreciated the potential winning appeal of young Democrats such as John Kennedy and supported Kennedy's unsuccessful bid for the vice presidential nomination to the Stevenson ticket in 1956. Schlesinger brought his appreciation of the need to change to his work with liberal political platforms. His political memorandum, "The Shape of National Politics to Come," came in 1959 to the attention of Kennedy, now a presidential hopeful. During the summer of 1959, Kennedy discussed the importance of the memorandum with its author and eventually decided to incorporate some of Schlesinger's ideas concerning the need for forward motion and strong leadership into his campaign for president in 1960.[84]

As it became clear that Adlai Stevenson did not want to seek the Democratic presidential nomination in an active way in 1960, Stevenson's supporters were faced with the decision of whether or not to back another candidate. During the spring of 1960, Schlesinger began to ease himself away from Stevenson toward the Kennedy camp. On June 17, Schlesinger was one of a number of liberal intellectuals who officially endorsed Kennedy's candidacy for president. In the weeks immediately before and the months after the nominating convention, Schlesinger served as a liaison between Kennedy and a remaining cadre of intransigent Stevenson supporters who opposed Kennedy's election.[85]

During the fall campaign, Schlesinger gave several speeches in support of Kennedy in which he attempted to describe a Kennedy style distinct from and superior to the style of Kennedy's opponent, Vice President Richard Nixon. Convinced that John Kennedy was the embodiment of the hero liberalism so desperately needed, Schlesinger agreed to publish a campaign document designed to widen distinctions between Kennedy and Nixon. The fifty-page book, entitled *Kennedy or Nixon: Does It Make Any Difference?*, was published in September 1960, on the eve of the first televised debate between the two candidates. The conjunction of the book's release and the first debate was marked by Schlesinger as a "turning point" in the campaign. By the beginning of October, "the atmosphere had changed," and the once hostile intellectual community was "now showing enthusiasm and commitment" toward young John F. Kennedy.[86]

Kennedy or Nixon: Does It Make Any Difference? was a document that summarized the symbolic adjustments made in Schlesinger's frame of acceptance during the 1950s. Schlesinger's objective in writing the book was to dispel "the favorite cliché of 1960," which was "that the two candidates, John F. Kennedy and Richard M. Nixon, are essentially the same sort of men, stamped from the same mold, dedicated to the same objectives," and that "there is very little to choose [from] between their parties either."[87] Typical of this sentiment was the contention of columnist Eric Sevareid that "the managerial revolution has come to politics and Nixon and Kennedy are its first packaged products."[88] Schlesinger set out to prove that Kennedy and Nixon were "vastly different in their interests, their skills, and their motivations."[89]

Schlesinger's analysis of the two candidates reflected an interest more in style than in substance. While the latter third of the book provided a cursory treatment of each man's stand on the issues

(Nixon believes we are strong, Kennedy believes we are slipping; Nixon supports the single interest of business, Kennedy supports many interests combined into the national interest), most of the book delved into the personalities of the two candidates.[90]

Frankly, it was true that Nixon and Kennedy differed little on the substantive issues. What Schlesinger was doing in *Kennedy or Nixon* was letting the American people know that John Kennedy fit Schlesinger's script for the emergence of a liberal hero better than Richard Nixon. Only Kennedy had the character and style befitting a hero. Schlesinger's discussion of the different styles of the candidates was a direct outgrowth of his recognition that leadership style was a crucial part of the moral function of a hero to compel sacrifice. According to Nuechterlein, Schlesinger's concentration on style represented the culmination of "an evolution in liberal emphasis from content to process" that had occurred during the 1950s.[91]

How were the two men different? Richard Nixon was described in Riesman's terms as an outer-directed man who stood for nothing, who had no coherent public philosophy. Because Nixon was totally responsive to his outer environment, his strengths lay in his absence of political viewpoint and his ability to flip-flop on issues without loss of public standing. Nixon had no sense of history to check his contradictory positions on issues and was concerned with his image only as it was reflected in the opinions of others. What was even worse, Nixon had no taste and demeaned public discourse by constantly referring to his wife and to his humble roots. In short, Nixon was a hollow man, a perfect product of the materialistic 1950s, a man who would not be able to manage interests or call for sacrifice. His so-called experience would only serve as a hindrance, for it derived solely from the exercise of simplistic stereotypes to complex situations.[92]

John Kennedy, in sharp contrast, was an inner-directed man whose positions on issues reflected dispassionate rational analysis instead of political expediency. He cared more about being right than about being popular, and his sense of history told him that leaders can affect events by anticipating problems and educating the public about those problems. Kennedy was committed to liberal ideas based on intellect rather than emotion and shared Adlai Stevenson's vision of a need for sacrifice in a time of national renewal. Whereas Nixon lacked taste, Kennedy behaved in a serious and objective manner, unconcerned with image or self-gratification. Kennedy had the proper character and style to manage interests and compel sacrifice, for he had adapted to and grown into every political office he had undertaken. He was, by all accounts, "the heir and executor of the Stevenson revolution."[93]

For Schlesinger, it did make a difference whether Kennedy or Nixon became president in 1960 because the election represented an opportunity for Americans to fulfill the promise of a new liberal epoch. Schlesinger feared that Nixon's personality created "the expectation of a static government dominated by the forces in our society most opposed to change." On the other hand, Kennedy's personality created "the expectation of an affirmative government dominated by intelligence and dedicated to abolishing the terrifying discrepancy between the American performance and the American possibility." The 1960 election presented two alternatives: "to muddle along as we have done for a decade, watching our power and influence decline in the world and our own country sink into mediocrity and cant and boredom," or "to recover control over our own national destiny and resume the movement to fulfill the real promise of American life."[94]

For Schlesinger, the electoral choice between Kennedy and Nixon represented much more than a reaffirmation of the prevailing cold war consensus in favor of economic growth and against communism. In many respects, the election was also a referendum on his own frame of acceptance. By electing Kennedy, the American public could confirm Schlesinger's interest-based definition of liberalism and conservatism, his prediction for a new liberal era, and his call for a heroic liberal leader. John F. Kennedy represented much promise and potential to Arthur Schlesinger, Jr.

The Birth of a Rhetorical Trajectory

Democratic candidate John F. Kennedy narrowly won the presidential election of 1960, as Arthur Schlesinger, Jr., hoped and predicted he would. The success of Kennedy's campaign rhetoric, from his calls for sacrifice to his general charge that the country must "get moving again," seemed to confirm Schlesinger's prediction of a renewed public desire for government activism.[95] In addition, Kennedy's promises to move in areas affecting the quality of life— especially in the area of civil rights—offered hope that the agenda of qualitative liberalism might begin to be addressed.[96]

While Schlesinger cautioned against hyperoptimism, he maintained serene confidence that "vital center empiricism" would temper the idealism of the new day. The new president represented "the perfect equilibrium between fact and theory, realism and idealism" to Schlesinger.[97] Kennedy was seen as a "man of action who could pass easily over to the realm of ideas and confront intellectuals with perfect confidence in his capacity to hold his own."[98] The presidency of John F. Kennedy promised to be one that a new generation of liberal historians might chronicle.

John Kennedy's victory in 1960 was a turning point both in Schlesinger's professional career and in the evolution of his public discourse. For a decade, Schlesinger had applied elements of the "tides of national politics" to diagnose the political troubles of liberalism. Now Kennedy's victory seemed to represent the ultimate vindication of Schlesinger's frame of acceptance. Shortly after the election, Schlesinger wrote this note of mock self-congratulation: "My father and I are both indebted to John F. Kennedy for vindicating a cyclical theory of American politics."[99]

The outcome of the 1960 presidential election produced what Burke would call a moment of "qualitative progression," a "feeling as to the rightness or destiny of a progression of events or words." This feeling of rightness or "poetic congruence" served to magnify the salience of the tides of national politics in subsequent symbolic choices Schlesinger would make in the years ahead.[100]

The 1960 election marked the culminating event of a decade in which Schlesinger's discourse moved along a rhetorical trajectory or path of symbolic development suggested by his theory of the tides of national politics. Griffin has argued that once a symbolic path is taken to define situations, we tend to follow that path in order to cope with other contexts or situations we may face. As symbolic choices are made over time along a path of development, a rhetorical trajectory may develop in the discourse of an individual or group. "We are moved by our rhetoric as our rhetoric is designed to move others," Leland Griffin has written in describing the nature of rhetorical trajectory. "By the tracing of the terminological trajectories in the rhetoric of an individual or collectivity we may gain understanding as to how a particular state of readiness is achieved."[101] As Schlesinger was confronted with new and more complex challenges to liberalism in the 1960s and beyond, he would increasingly rely on the components of his frame of acceptance as a way of answering situations. For Schlesinger, the "tides of national politics" became a firm pattern of symbolic adjustment to changing political realities.[102]

In the early moments of the Kennedy administration, all was well for liberals and for Arthur Schlesinger, Jr. He described the mood of those early days in his memoir of the Kennedy administration, *A Thousand Days:* "Meetings were continuous. The evenings too were lively and full. The glow of the White House was lighting up the whole city. Washington seemed engaged in a collective effort to make itself brighter, more intellectual, more resolute. It was a golden interlude."[103]

4

The Tides of National Politics and the Rhetoric of Dawnism

John Kenneth Galbraith coined the term "dawnism" to describe the "Democratic style of hyperbole" practiced by John Kennedy and others during the 1960s. According to Galbraith, the rhetoric of dawnism held out the "natural if adolescent . . . hope that some new leader, some new policy, will bring the dawn of a new day."[1] John F. Kennedy's discourse represented perhaps the paradigm case of the rhetoric of dawnism. In his speech accepting the 1960 Democratic nomination for president, Kennedy stated, "We stand today on the edge of a new frontier—the frontier of the 1960s—a frontier of unknown opportunities and perils—a frontier of unfulfilled hopes and threats." The "new frontier" was "here, whether we seek it or not," he continued. "Beyond that frontier are uncharted areas of science and space, unsolved problems of peace and war, unconquered pockets of ignorance and prejudice, unanswered questions of poverty and surplus."[2] Jamieson has noted that the "new frontier" was a theme that reverberated throughout the campaign and presidency of John Kennedy.[3] Matusow has claimed that Kennedy's frontier rhetoric provided the optimistic premises that supported liberalism throughout the decade of the 1960s.[4]

Englehardt has asserted that Arthur Schlesinger, Jr., "played an important role in shaping the new liberalism" during the 1950s and 1960s, "an especially critical time for American liberals."[5] One way to understand the influence of Schlesinger's thinking on the liberalism of his time is to explore similarities between John Kennedy's political message, including his calls for sacrifice and his general charge that the country must "get moving again," and the historian's views on liberalism and the necessity of active liberal leadership. This chapter analyzes the relationship between the rhetoric of dawnism and the conception of liberalism popularized by Arthur Schlesinger, Jr., during the late 1950s.

Kennedy, Schlesinger, and the Tides of National Politics

Arthur Schlesinger's notion of the tides of national politics provided a supporting rationale for the new frontier rhetoric developed by John F. Kennedy during his presidential campaign and subsequent term in the White House. Before the beginning of the 1960 campaign, Schlesinger and Kennedy met to discuss campaign themes and strategies. In *A Thousand Days*, Schlesinger reported, somewhat immodestly, that Kennedy had told the historian about a need to "give his campaign identity." The candidate had been "stimulated" by reading Schlesinger's memorandum "The Shape of National Politics to Come," which contained ideas that "evidently corresponded to things that Kennedy had for some time felt himself." Among those ideas were "the belief that we stood on the threshold of a new political era, and that vigorous public leadership would be the essence of the next phase" of American history.[6]

Schlesinger was not alone in noting the significance of the concept of historical tides in Kennedy's thinking about the 1960 campaign. Fairlie observed that Schlesinger's cyclical theory of history attracted Kennedy and a host of intellectuals and journalists. As a result of that influence, coupled with publicity over President Eisenhower's Commission on National Goals, the early months of 1960 saw a frantic search for "national purpose" among the intelligentsia. The mood described in Schlesinger's theory "could not have better suited a young and vigorous candidate" like Kennedy, who would come to base his campaign on the "need to move again" after "eight years of quietude."[7]

Kennedy consistently applied Schlesinger's theory about the coming liberal era in his campaign speeches during the fall of 1960. On September 19, in Atlantic City, New Jersey, Kennedy first mentioned the notion of a political cycle of action and inertia: "I do not believe that the period of the 1960s is a period in which we can conserve, in which we stand still, in which we gather ourselves for renewed effort. We have done that in the 1950s. I think the 1960s are the time for a new effort. This election is not 1900. This election is 1912 and 1932 and 1948. This is a time for a new go-ahead for this country and the American people."[8] Two weeks later, in Terre Haute, Indiana, Kennedy repeated the cyclical theme: "I believe the issue is very clear, and the issue is whether the American people are satisfied with things as they are, whether they feel that the 1960s are a time to really conserve and stand still and gather our energy, or whether the 1960s are a time to move forward again as 1932 was, as 1912 was."[9]

In some respects, Kennedy's call for renewal was drawn from standard liberal rhetorical stock.[10] But Kennedy seemed to fix upon Schlesinger's idea of political tides as a way of explaining the need for a new era of active leadership. A more direct citation of Schlesinger's concept came in a speech in Bowling Green, Kentucky, on October 8: "The history of this country moves in rhythms, back and forth, between progress and standing still, between liberalism and conservatism, and I believe in 1960 the choice for the United States is forward."[11] Kennedy recapitulated the theory seven days later in Kittaning, Pennsylvania: "I think the reason they [the voters] choose one party at one time and another party at another time is because history and events and the mood of history swings like a pendulum back and forth."[12] Many of Kennedy's speeches closed with Benjamin Franklin's line, "It is a rising sun and the beginning of a new day."[13]

It is apparent that Schlesinger's concept of the tides of national politics provided Kennedy with many of the themes of his 1960 presidential campaign, including optimistic contrasts between activity and inertia, verbs such as "move," and metaphors such as "pendulum" and "tide." Closer examination of Kennedy's discourse reveals additional symbolic linkages between the tides of national politics and the rhetoric of dawnism.

Elements of Kennedy's Rhetoric

"If there is one certain thing in a world of change," John Kennedy stated in 1960, "it is that the coming years will bring new problems, undreamed-of challenges, unanticipated opportunities."[14] 1960 was "a time, in short, for a new generation of leadership—new men to cope with new problems and new opportunities" that constituted the new frontier.[15] "Problems" and "opportunities" were the twin pillars that served as the foundation for liberal rhetoric during the 1960s. The rhetoric of dawnism as practiced by President Kennedy was composed of two parts: the call for sacrifice and the promise of transcendence.

"And so, my fellow Americans," President Kennedy announced in his memorable inaugural address, "ask not what your country can do for you—ask what you can do for your country."[16] The first part of a liberal rhetoric proclaiming the dawn of a new day was a call for the American people to sacrifice private comfort for public interest so that the "challenges" and "problems" of the coming era could be transformed into fulfilled "opportunities."

Kennedy's call for sacrifice followed a three-step process that would serve as a pattern for subsequent liberal rhetoric during the decade. First came the *proclamation of a crisis*. During the early years of the decade, Kennedy sought to label all sorts of domestic and foreign policy concerns as "crises." On the domestic side, Kennedy the presidential candidate awkwardly attempted to transform the general ennui in American society into a "crisis" of mediocrity. "This is a great country," Kennedy repeated constantly during the 1960 campaign, "but I think it can be better."[17] During his administration, President Kennedy would apply the notion of crisis to concerns of lagging economic growth, civil rights turmoil, and deteriorating public education.[18]

Kennedy also elevated foreign policy to a state of perpetual crisis, particularly in his characterization of U.S.-Soviet relations. Kennedy often compared the freedom-versus-communism issue to the slavery issue that had engulfed America a century earlier. "The great question confronting the country today is can the world exist half slave and half free," he said in 1960. The world rested on the "razor edge of decision," and the United States occupied a "conspicuous stage," where the rest of mankind watched us for signs of weakness.[19]

In his first State of the Union address, President Kennedy echoed the crisis mentality of the New Frontier foreign policy: "I speak today in an hour of national peril and national opportunity."[20] "No other generation of free men in any country has ever faced so many and such difficult challenges," Kennedy reported at the end of 1961, a year of turbulence in Latin America and Europe. "But more than any other people on earth, we bear burdens and accept risks unprecedented in size and duration, not for ourselves but for all who wish to be free."[21] The president proclaimed that the "hour of maximum danger" was at hand in both his 1961 *and* 1962 State of the Union addresses.[22] Ultimately, Kennedy characterized the genuinely threatening events in Cuba in October 1962 as yet another "new crisis" that he was compelled to report to the public "in fullest detail."[23]

Proclamation of crisis was symbolically consistent with Arthur

Schlesinger's concept of the tides of national politics. In *The Age of Jackson,* Schlesinger had argued that in any new period of liberal activism, in which "the dam breaks and a flood of change sweeps away a great deal in a short time," chaos, confusion, and even crisis were to be expected in American life.[24] More specifically, Schlesinger had predicted that the 1960s would be a time when new forces, new energies, and new values would be straining for expression and release. Schlesinger and other liberals, including President Kennedy, believed that strong executive leadership could transform crises into triumphs of liberal ingenuity and planning for "higher splendors in the future."[25]

Second in Kennedy's three-step call for sacrifice was the *identification of the present as a turning point* in American history. The year "1960, whether we wish it or not, whether there were an election or not, is a turning point in our history," Kennedy claimed during the 1960 presidential race. "Either we move with new leadership, new programs, and a new spirit of education, or we stand still and therefore we fall back. This is the call of the New Frontier."[26] The choice between Kennedy and Nixon was really a choice between different outlooks on the future, "one of whom says 'Yes' to the next 10 years and the other [who] says 'No.'"[27] The decade ahead would be the critical period during which "we must prove all over again whether this nation—or any other nation so conceived—can long endure" and "compete with the single-minded advance of Communism."[28]

Above all, Kennedy did not want "historians writing in 1970 to say that the balance of power in the 1950s and 1960s began to turn against the United States and against the cause of freedom."[29] By highlighting the importance of the decision in the 1960 election, Kennedy hoped to separate himself from his opponent in an election year when pundits were labeling Kennedy and Nixon as the "Gold Dust Twins" of American politics.[30]

After being elected president, Kennedy continued to argue that the years he was in office were to be momentous ones. "The torch is passed to a new generation of Americans" who realized that "the world is very different now," full of new dangers and opportunities, Kennedy stated in his inaugural address.[31] "Before my term has ended," the new president stressed in his first State of the Union message, "we shall have to test anew whether a nation organized and governed such as ours can endure. The outcome is by no means certain."[32]

Identifying the 1960s as a turning point in history was also consistent with Arthur Schlesinger's belief in periodic alternations between conservative and liberal epochs. Schlesinger's theory focused attention on key moments in history, such as 1932, when the locus of power shifted from one ideological pole to the other. President Kennedy's rhetoric echoed statements from Schlesinger such as "The sixties await, and they promise to be one of the great decades in our history," and seemed to confirm the historian's predictions concerning the importance of 1960 as another key moment in American political life.[33]

The third and final step in Kennedy's call for sacrifice was the *actual request for commitment*. For Kennedy the candidate in 1960, the term "new frontier" summed up "not only what I intend to offer the American people, but what I intend to ask of them." His administration would "hold out the promise of more sacrifice instead of more security."[34] Kennedy claimed to run not on the promise that "if I am elected . . . , life will be easy and the problems will be solved," but on the premise that the 1960s would be "among the most difficult years in our history," requiring us to give "the best of us all" to survive and triumph.[35]

The burden Americans faced was competition with the Soviet Union on all fronts. "In the next 10 years," Kennedy asserted, "this globe around us is going to move in the direction of freedom or in the direction of slavery."[36] "This country is going to have to build an image around the world of a strong and vital and progressive society," Kennedy stated in October 1960, "and convince a watching world . . . that we represent the way of the future."[37]

To "convince the watching world" of America's superiority required beating the Soviet Union. It meant being "first" at home and abroad. "I do not mean first, *but*," Kennedy repeated during the campaign. "I do not mean first, *when*. I don't mean first, *if*. I mean first, *period*."[38] Defining the issues of the 1960s in the context of a competition or race with the Russians led Kennedy to conclude that it was necessary for Americans to "dedicate ourselves again" to being the best we could be.[39] The "responsibility of this generation of Americans" was to "devote ourselves to the public interest." The "burdens which go with self-government and the maintenance of freedom" included providing "a defense second to none," building an economy that could be "the No. 1 productive power in the world" and providing "equality of opportunity" for all citizens.[40] Private interest had to be subordinated to national purpose because America faced "an adversary who mobilizes all of the resources of the state for the services of the state."[41]

As president, Kennedy continued to call for sacrifice in the name of American superiority over the Soviet Union. "Let every nation know . . . ," Kennedy declared in his inaugural address, "that we shall pay any price, bear any burden, meet any hardship, support any friend, oppose any foe to assure the survival and the success of liberty."[42] In the 1962 State of the Union speech, President Kennedy claimed that America's "role of being the great defender of freedom" was both "the greatest adventure of our century" and "the fate of this generation . . . , to live with a struggle we did not start, in a world we did not make."[43] America's efforts in "defense of alliances and countries around the globe," Kennedy stated on the morning of his death in 1963, required "sacrifice by the people of the United States," in order to remain "the keystone in the arch of freedom."[44]

Kennedy attempted to transfer the call for commitment from foreign policy rhetoric to his discourse concerning domestic policy. For example, in his television address in response to the steel "crisis" of 1962, Kennedy chided the steel executives with the following comment: "In this serious hour in our nation's history, when we are confronted with grave crises in Berlin and Southeast Asia . . . [and are] asking reservists to leave their homes and families for months on end and servicemen to risk their lives . . . , the American public will find it hard, as I do, to accept a situation in which a tiny handful of steel executives whose pursuit of *private* power and profit exceeds their sense of *public* responsibility can show such utter contempt for the interests of 185 million Americans."[45]

The call for self-denial and commitment was also congruent with Arthur Schlesinger's frame of acceptance. Schlesinger had warned in 1960 that "the cyclical rhythm we have identified in our national affairs offers no guarantee of salvation." A new liberal era would come only if "men and women rise to a towering challenge." In particular, noted the historian, people must realize "that private interests and the public interest often come into harsh conflict." "In a sane society," Schlesinger asserted, private indulgence "can no longer be unlimited." Sacrifice would be required "to make possible the allocation of resources to necessary public purposes."[46] The rhetoric of dawnism generalized the need to sacrifice to all realms of political action.

The Promise of Transcendence

The second part of Kennedy's rhetoric of dawnism included the promise to transcend the problems of the day.[47] Kennedy's discourse contained not only a warning of impending crisis but also a promise that the problems of the coming decade could be resolved only by redefining government responses to those problems in a new and broader context. The "frontier of the 1960s" included both "perils" *and* "opportunities," "threats" *and* "hopes." According to Kennedy in the 1960 campaign, a vote for "public interest" over "private comfort" meant that Americans would once again breathe "the fresh air of progress" and experience "national greatness" in years to come.[48]

Kennedy's promise to transcend the problems of war and peace, economic growth and equal opportunity, took three forms during his presidential campaign and subsequent administration. First, Kennedy promised transcendence through *movement*. Throughout the 1960 campaign, Kennedy contrasted himself to Nixon on the basis of a distinction between his own liberal desire for motion and his opponent's conservative inertia. The 1960 election was "really a choice . . . between a party who wishes to act, between a party which wishes to move ahead to a new frontier, and a party which believes in the status quo," Kennedy said on September 3. "The theme of this campaign is going to be action, action here at home to keep pace with the growing needs of an expanding country, action abroad to meet the challenge of adversaries."[49] "Those who share a feeling that we can do better, that we must do better, that we must move ahead, that things are not perfect the way they are," Kennedy continued on September 7, "I want them to join with us in this crusade to make this country *move* again."[50]

Through daring action, Kennedy asserted, America *could* meet her "rendezvous with destiny" in the 1960s.[51] "If we mobilize ourselves for the public interest," Kennedy predicted on September 21, "I believe this country will not only endure, but prevail. I think the future can be bright."[52] "Do you feel the tide of history is moving with us?" Kennedy asked on October 17, in a direct reference to Schlesinger's temporal metaphor. "I hold the view that the tide and history *can* move with us."[53]

During the early months of his term, President Kennedy's administration generated enough sheer activity to cause the *New Republic* to report that "Washington is crackling, rocking, jumping."[54] In the trial-and-error method of the early administration, action seemed to have intrinsic value.[55] "I believe that we are going to fail as well as succeed," Kennedy admitted in a speech a few days after the botched Bay of Pigs invasion attempt, "but I believe that we are at least going to make the effort. I believe that we are going to try, and we will take our setbacks as well as our successes, and we will continue to move here, and around the world."[56]

The second form of transcendence Kennedy promised was transcendence through *technique*. As he proceeded in his administration, Kennedy gained an ever greater appreciation for technical expertise in foreign and domestic affairs. Over time, themes of movement and activity were accompanied by and eventually supplanted by themes of complexity and management in Kennedy's rhetoric.

In foreign affairs, Kennedy began to introduce the idea that the world was a complicated place where problems could be solved only through expert military and diplomatic techniques. The Bay of Pigs taught Kennedy the lesson that the global struggle with communism "goes far beyond the clash of armies or even nuclear armaments." The United States, Kennedy reported in 1961, would have to "reexamine and reorient our forces" and "grasp the new concepts and new tools" of warfare, including "subversion, infiltration, and a host of other tactics." Unless we adopted a more "realistic" approach to the menace of international communism, "our security may be lost piece by piece, country by country, without the firing of a single missile or the crossing of a single border."[57]

Because "the world relations of this country have become tangled and complex," Kennedy continued in late 1961, ". . . we must face problems which do not lend themselves to easy or quick or permanent solutions." Foreign policy action would have to be made within "carefully defined limits" that neither appeased nor antagonized the enemy.[58] While there was "an understandable effort to recover an old feeling of simplicity," Kennedy argued in 1963, ". . . in world affairs, as in all other aspects of our lives, the days of the quiet past are gone forever." Fortunately, through technical management, America could hope to continue to "shape real events in a real world."[59]

Kennedy's advocacy of domestic policies also began to include the theme of technical management. The president stated in 1962 that most of the country's economic problems "are technical problems, are administrative problems" requiring "sophisticated judgments which do not lend themselves to the great sort of 'passionate movements' which have stirred this country so often in the past." Modern domestic issues "deal with questions which are beyond the comprehension of most men."[60] "The central domestic issues of our time," Kennedy continued in his Yale University commencement address in 1962, ". . . relate not to the basic clashes of philosophy but to ways and means of reaching common goals—to research for sophisticated solutions to complex and obstinate issues." What the country needed was "not labels and clichés but more basic discussion of the sophisticated and technical questions involved in keeping a great economic machinery moving ahead."[61]

The third and final form of promised transcendence was transcendence through *personality*. Throughout the 1960 campaign, John Kennedy focused attention on the importance of the office of president. The president was "the only one who can speak for the people of the United States," Kennedy said on September 3. The next president would be required "to set before the American people the unfinished business of our society, our national goals, what we must hope to achieve in the next 10 years."[62] The presidency was a "key office" because only the president could "mobilize the resources of this country so that we begin to move again."[63]

Equally as important as the office of president was the character of the man who held that office. During the campaign against Nixon, Kennedy asserted that the personality of the chief executive should match the tempo of the times. The man who occupied the White House had to "give an impression around the world of force and vitality."[64] "In the final analysis," Kennedy argued on October 3, "whatever we do depends on the President of the United States, depends on his vigor, depends on his concept of what needs to be done to make this a stronger and better country."[65] Above all, the president had to be an individual "who believes in the national interest—who serves no other master—who takes no instructions but those of his conscience—who puts no personal interest, no public pressure, no political hopes, and no private obligation of any kind above his oath to promote the national interest."[66]

In the rhetoric of his administration, President Kennedy continued to point to the capacity within his own character to accept challenges and to act boldly. "In the long history of the world, only a few generations have been granted the role of defending freedom in its hour of maximum danger," the president stated in his inaugural address. "I do not shrink from this responsibility—I welcome it."[67] After noting in a speech following the Bay of Pigs invasion that "history will record the fact that this bitter struggle [against communism] reached its climax in the late 1950s and early 1960s," Kennedy concluded, "I am determined upon our system's survival and success, regardless of the cost and regardless of the peril."[68]

In addition, Kennedy's public and private lives were orchestrated to convey an image of the president as a youthful, vigorous, and courageous leader.[69] Throughout his term, Kennedy sought to communicate the notion that a president led his people by personal examples of courage and self-sacrifice.

All three promises of transcendence—movement, technique, and personality—were consistent with the liberal frame of acceptance advocated by Arthur Schlesinger, Jr. Schlesinger's theory of the tides of national politics offered the promise that activity and motion were intrinsically beneficial as part of an era of liberal reform. Schlesinger's shift from "quantitative" to "qualitative" liberalism offered the promise that most of America's problems could be solved through technical fine-tuning of the society. And Schlesinger's emphasis on the need for heroic leadership offered the promise that a strong individual would emerge from the realm of politics to shape and tame the multitudinous private interests in America and make them conform to a sense of national purpose and a public interest.[70] In many respects, Schlesinger's campaign to redefine liberalism during the 1950s sowed the rhetorical seeds for the dawnism of the 1960s.

The Rhetorical Legacy of Dawnism

Elements of dawnism characterized conventional liberal rhetoric throughout the 1960s.[71] In many ways, President Lyndon Johnson continued along the symbolic path initiated by his predecessor. In both domestic and foreign policy rhetoric, Johnson followed the pattern of pronouncing a crisis, calling for sacrifice, and promising technical solutions.[72] Johnson's ability to maintain a liberal consensus, however, dwindled during the course of his administration as economic realities blunted his drive to win a war abroad while conquering social problems at home.[73]

Galbraith claimed that Johnson was the "greatest practitioner" of the rhetoric of dawnism and that Vice President Humphrey was Johnson's "apt and energetic pupil." "The promises of the Book of Revelation are modest, on the whole," continued Galbraith, "compared with what these two men have pictured for this planet." As evidence for his claim, Galbraith cited Johnson's promise to "extirpate poverty" as the result of declaring "unconditional war," the boundless vision Johnson promoted in his "Great Society speeches," and the optimistic call for the development of a "new Marshall plan for Asia."[74]

By the end of the 1960s, the rhetoric of dawnism would lead to political problems for the liberal perspective. The contradictions between the promises of transcendence and the increasing complexity of the problems of the decade stretched conventional liberal thought to its breaking point. The tensions in the rhetoric of dawnism between defining issues as crises and then promising to overcome the crises through techniques of social governance became more and more evident as conventional liberal approaches of gradualism and experimentation became less able to cope with the salient issues of the era—Vietnam, civil rights, the environment, resource scarcity.

For example, in his study of the War on Poverty, Zarefsky explains that liberals too often defended a tenuous middle ground on the poverty issue between conservatives who opposed all change and radicals who wanted to overthrow the system. Zarefsky concludes that liberal argument in contemporary American politics has now reached an "impasse" because of promises made during the 1960s to tackle complex issues such as income and social inequality through incremental reform rather than through more systemic policies of wealth redistribution. The optimistic assumptions of qualitative liberalism led liberals to "clothe incrementalist programs in an absolutist rhetoric," which in turn produced unrealistic expectations for positive social change.[75] The rhetoric of dawnism made promises that liberalism could not keep.[76]

Inflated expectations may have contributed to a schism within the liberal political community during the late 1960s and 1970s. Burner and West assert that the Kennedy style of highlighting the urgency of the times led to a split between those liberals who favored the politics of incremental change and those who grew disillusioned with conventional political instrumentalities and sought the politics of immediacy and emotion. The increasing tendency in liberal rhetoric to rely on promised expertise and technique to solve foreign and domestic problems also contradicted the calls for movement, mass activism, and witness made by the growing New Left rhetoric in the late 1960s.[77]

As we shall see, Arthur Schlesinger, Jr., would be forced to confront the growing challenges to his frame of acceptance and to the liberal rhetoric of dawnism throughout the 1960s. At the beginning of the decade, he served as a loyal member of the presidential administration of John F. Kennedy. By the end of the decade, he would become an increasingly strident critic of a liberal president and of American society itself.

5

In the Halls of Power, 1961–1965

After years of supporting liberal candidates and causes, Arthur Schlesinger, Jr., anxiously awaited the arrival in the White House of John F. Kennedy, someone whom he believed had the character to be the "right man for the big job."[1] There was hope that the conservative tide in America had turned and that a new liberal agenda would be undertaken. As Kennedy took office in early 1961, Schlesinger found himself in a new position: as adviser, spokesperson, and official member of a liberal presidential administration. This new title led Schlesinger to adopt and defend a new rhetorical stance as an academician working within government.

During the three years of the Kennedy regime, Schlesinger attempted to defend the administration against attacks from what he viewed as the "Radical Right" and the "New Left" elements of the American political spectrum. Sadly, the assassination of President Kennedy in 1963 would thrust Schlesinger into the unwelcome role of premature biographer and defender of the Kennedy record and legacy. *A Thousand Days*, Schlesinger's memorial account of the Kennedy presidency published in 1965, functioned both as a tribute to a fallen leader and as an extended defense of Schlesinger's own frame of acceptance. This chapter explores the role of Arthur Schlesinger, Jr., as a member of the presidential administration of John F. Kennedy from 1961 to 1963 and surveys his writings concerning those years of triumph and tragedy.

Defining a New Rhetorical Stance

Shortly before John Kennedy was sworn into office as president, his brother Robert asked Arthur Schlesinger, Jr., to "come down" to Washington "as a Special Assistant to the President and serve as sort of roving reporter and trouble-shooter." Delighted at the prospect, Schlesinger took an extended leave of absence from Harvard to join the New Frontier team. For Schlesinger, these would be the best of times. "There was the excitement" in Washington, he wrote later, "which comes from an injection of new men and new ideas, the release of energy which occurs when men with new ideas have a chance to put them to work."[2]

Schlesinger entered public life uncertain about his function in the new administration. The historian later recalled a conversation with President-elect Kennedy about their new assignments in the executive branch: "The President elect . . . asked whether I was ready to work at the White House. I said, 'I am not sure what I would be doing as Special Assistant, but, if you think I can help, I would like very much to come.' He said, 'Well, I am not sure what I will be doing as President either, but I am sure there will be enough at the White House to keep us both busy.'"[3] Schlesinger wound up participating in a wide range of activities, including several trips abroad promoting the Alliance for Progress and foreign aid, some speech writing and consulting, and general resource work on historical concerns of the Kennedy White House.

During his stay in Washington, Schlesinger was viewed as everything from irrelevant to dangerous.[4] As he left the realm of academia for the realm of government service, Schlesinger was forced to justify his new position as an intellectual and historian working *within* the establishment. Schlesinger went about this task with relish, publishing several articles over the next decade on the theme of "historian-as-participant."[5] In these articles, Schlesinger attempted to adopt a new rhetorical stance that would preserve and strengthen his own objective ethos or credibility as an academic historian. Schlesinger argued that his new role allowed him a unique perspective on and access to the corridors of political power.

His new rhetorical stance reflected two premises. The first was that an intellectual could be an effective bureaucratic actor. Arthur Schlesinger's life and career served as evidence that intellectuals have the opportunity and responsibility to serve their society in arenas of pragmatic collective activity. Schlesinger's role model was not Walter Lippmann, who preached detachment and once proclaimed, "We must not expect society to be guided by its professors." Instead, Schlesinger revered men like Reinhold Niebuhr and Bernard DeVoto, who coupled the ability to critique society with the commitment to act through political channels to improve society.[6]

Schlesinger believed that the intellectual could serve society at the intersection between ideas and power. "It seemed to me," he wrote in 1965, "that there was also a strong case for intellectuals so inclined to take part in government if only to provide a link between the political and intellectual communities." The process of mediation "might well give the intellectual community more impact on the political process than if it remained in solid opposition." Schlesinger went to work for Kennedy convinced of the new president's "desire to bring the world of power and the world of ideas together in alliance," and warned fellow intellectuals that if they "decided to abandon government to nonintellectuals, they would have only themselves to blame for the result."[7]

The argument justifying the intellectual's place in government service was part of Schlesinger's attempt to construct a position or stance from which he could advocate partisan political viewpoints while retaining the ethos of intellectual detachment. Advocating the legitimacy of the intellectual-as-bureaucrat was a new and more precarious move by Schlesinger to both sit in the hall of establishment power and sit in judgment on it.[8]

The second premise supporting Schlesinger's new position was the belief that a historian could provide a unique and important chronicle of contemporary events. In serving as in-house historian for a president, Schlesinger confounded traditional preferences within the field of academic history that the chronicler should be an uninvolved observer of events that occurred in the somewhat distant past. Defending his position "on the inside" of policymaking, Schlesinger was quick to point out that many of the great historians in times before "the professionalization of the craft" were "men for whom the history they wrote was a derivation from the experiences they enjoyed or endured." Having "the opportunity to watch history in the making," Schlesinger claimed that "involvement" with the subjects of historical record "has its benefits." "To take part in public affairs, to smell the dust and sweat of battle," he concluded in 1963, "is surely to stimulate and amplify the historical imagination."[9]

Perhaps more important to Schlesinger was his conviction that historical understanding was a crucial ingredient in effective leadership of a nation. This view was consistent with the persuasive uses of history found in his own political advocacy. Every great leader, he asserted, has had both "a feeling for the direction in which the world was moving" and "his own conception of the nature of the historical process" that combined to form a "vision which connects the past and future and gives his decisions a setting and a point." Schlesinger hoped that his reporting of events from the vantage point of those who made policy would contribute to "the intellectual climate which shapes the actual unfolding of history in the future."[10]

While interpreting events from "the inside," Schlesinger recognized that partisanship could affect historical analysis and judgment. He wrote in 1963: "The dangers of involvement are self-evident. To act is, in many cases, to give hostages—to parties, to policies, to persons. Participation spins a web of commitments which may imprison the chronicler in invisible fetters." Yet, the historian concluded, the compensations outweighed the hazards. He became determined to retain academic respectability by redefining the boundaries of legitimate historical inquiry, which he characterized as "a collective exercise of thinking aloud."[11]

The argument justifying the chronicling of the present as ongoing history was the second part of Schlesinger's new rhetorical stance. By advocating the legitimacy of "insider" history, Schlesinger completed his adjustment to his new position as an adviser to the president of the United States. Armed with the belief that political participation would benefit both his country and his own scholarship, Schlesinger proceeded with the business of government service.

Defending the Kennedy Administration

During the 1960 presidential campaign Arthur Schlesinger, Jr., had predicted that with the coming of a new decade, Americans would "cross the threshold into what promises to be one of the exciting and creative epochs in our history." In accordance with a "larger rhythm of our politics," the administration of John Kennedy would be one of intense activity and societal reform.[12] As we have seen, the rhetoric of the new president, which stressed sacrifice and commitment, also heralded the dawn of a new era.

As much was promised, much was expected of the Kennedy administration. The New Frontier honeymoon period soon waned and was replaced by foreign policy debacles, sluggish economic performance, and disappointment. Conservatives, heeding Kennedy's rhetoric, felt that Kennedy was moving too quickly. Liberals, judging the actual legislation passed, believed that Kennedy was not accomplishing enough. The civil rights issue, part of the "qualitative" liberal social agenda, exemplified the problems of the new president. Conservatives charged that Kennedy was intervening in sensitive matters involving state's rights and social gentility. Liberals felt that Kennedy was only paying lip service to the growing movement in favor of legal protections of racial equality.[13]

In addition, the early 1960s saw the emergence of organized right- and left-wing opposition groups. Critics of Kennedy from the "Radical Right" and the "New Left" challenged the liberal mainstream assumptions of the New Frontier.[14] A major portion of Schlesinger's writings published while he worked in the Kennedy White House was devoted to assessing radical opposition to the president.

Schlesinger's defense of Kennedy was in keeping with his own frame of acceptance and provides another illustration of his ideological use of history. His arguments against rightist and leftist critique followed a discernible pattern. First, Schlesinger defined each critique as a natural part of the cyclical ebb and flow of American politics. Second, he presented reasons why each critique or movement against administration politics was weak or inconsistent. Finally, he reassured his readers that a liberal-reform consensus was still in place in American society.

Answering the Radical Right

Schlesinger followed the three-step attack in his review of the so-called "'threat' of the radical Right." First, he tried to put the conservative movement in historical perspective. The traditional American temperament, Schlesinger concluded, was "combativeness." What passed for calm consensus during the 1950s was "really one of those moments of national exhaustion which, throughout our history, have regularly followed periods of intense national exertion." In the predictable ebb and flow of America's political physiology, "the historian must regard the revival of controversy [from the Radical Right] not as a worrying aberration, but as a return to normality." "This latest eruption of republic-saving," Schlesinger concluded, "is entirely consistent with the rhythm of our national history."[15]

Second, Schlesinger sought to prove that "the United States was not threatened by an internal counter-revolution" from the Radical Right. To minimize the strength of the reactionary movement, Schlesinger referred to the past, citing differences between the current radicals and the conservative opposition to the administration of President Franklin Roosevelt. The 1930s movement "had genuinely formidable leadership" from men like Huey Long and Father Coughlin. In addition, "conditions of national disaster enabled these leaders to make contact with large and baffled masses in the electorate" during the depression era. In contrast, the 1960s movement "lacks . . . impressive leadership," "lacks a major calamity to drive masses of people into angry despair," and "remains in chronic organizational disarray." Given the differences between radical protest then and now, Schlesinger concluded that "the nation is surely still a long distance from a Right-Wing counter-revolution."[16]

Third, and finally, Schlesinger reassured his readers that the liberal consensus on values and policies was still in place. In fact, the stirrings of the Radical Right merely offered *proof* that the American political pendulum was swinging in a liberal direction. "It was wholly expected," Schlesinger asserted, "that the extremists of the Right would raise their voices precisely when the national mood is moving in a progressive direction." For "the election of a progressive Administration," whether it be led by Roosevelt or Kennedy, "has a galvanizing effect" on the Right, making reactionaries grow "desperate" with the belief "that the nation is in mortal danger, that there is only a short time left to save the American way of life." Schlesinger was confident in 1962 that "the grumbles and growls on the Right" were "normal by-products of our process of democratic change."[17]

In a burst of New Frontier optimism, Schlesinger concluded his diagnosis of the Radical Right with the following summary of his own frame of acceptance: "The great underlying movement in our country is once again toward the assurance of equal opportunity for all, toward fulfillment for as many of our citizens as possible of the promise of American life."[18]

Answering the New Left

Schlesinger defended the Kennedy administration from the critique of the New Left with a similar three-step refutation. First, he placed the difference between mainstream liberals and the New Left in perspective through the use of historical analogy. "From the beginning of the republic," he wrote in 1963, "there have been two strains . . . in American progressivism." Schlesinger labeled these strains "pragmatic" and "utopian." The pragmatic liberal "accepts, without approving, the given structure of society and strives to change it from within." The pragmatic liberal is "practical" and "tough-minded," viewing history as a continuity of progress and power as a responsibility for civic action. In contrast, the utopian liberal "rejects the given structure of society, root and branch, and strives to change it by exhortation and example from without." The utopian liberal is "prophetic" and "tender-minded," viewing history as a "sequence of catastrophe and salvation" and power as inherently corrupting.[19]

The historian traced the clash between the two strains of liberal thought from the dispute during the age of Jackson between pragmatists such as George Bancroft and utopians such as Emerson, through the clash during the 1920s and 1930s between Dewey's pragmatism and Steffens's collectivism, and into the age of Kennedy. Placing the New Frontier squarely in the pragmatist camp, Schlesinger asserted that "the left-wing critique of the Kennedy Administration in the United States is, in great part, a new expression of an old complaint by those [utopians] who find satisfaction in large gestures of rejection against those [pragmatists] who find satisfaction in small measures of improvement." "To understand the present situation of the Left in the United States," Schlesinger concluded, one need merely view the contemporary conflict as part of the ongoing "nature of the democratic movement."[20] The dichotomy Schlesinger drew between utopian and pragmatic liberals echoed the critique of doughface progressivism he had developed in *The Vital Center* several years earlier.

Second, Schlesinger attempted to minimize the importance of the New Left by belittling or trivializing the movement's positions on foreign and domestic policy. On foreign policy, Schlesinger upheld the cold war consensus view of hostility toward communism and support of peace through strength. He refuted the leftist view that some form of communism was the inevitable end state of human society with the claim that "history suggests that communism appeals to countries in the preliminary rather than the concluding stages of economic development; that the modernization process carries nations not toward Marx, but away from Marx." Suggestions of disarmament were dismissed as "premature." Rather than promoting unilateral moves toward arms reduction and neutralism, Schlesinger asserted, "it would seem that the best way of persuading communist states to accept international arms control is to convince them that, if they do not, the democracies can stay in the arms race as long as they can."[21]

On domestic policy, Schlesinger upheld the consensus view of the primacy of economic growth and the need for a mixed economy. Making an exception for the issue of civil rights, Schlesinger derided "the contribution of the utopian left to the discussion of domestic issues" as "unimpressive" and "divided within itself." Those on the left who still advocated "the supersession of the mixed economy by state ownership of the means of production" were "committed to a gospel which is politically irrelevant and intellectually obsolete." Those who merely wanted to buck the "suffocating consensus blanketing American life" were not taking matters seriously enough.[22] On the "relevant" issues of "a high technology society," Schlesinger concluded in 1963, "the American Left (with the exception of Mr. Michael Harrington) has made almost no contribution at all."[23]

Third, and finally, Schlesinger reassured his audience that the rise of the New Left was a sign not of confusion but of health for liberalism. Society needs the utopians, Schlesinger argued. At their best, utopian liberals "could offset pressures from the Right for inaction and thus enlarge the range of political alternatives." The utopian Left contributed to American society its "bracing criticism of irreverence, satire and wit, emerging from a contempt for compromise and a passion to measure American society by its highest possibilities." "There is no more valuable American tradition," Schlesinger continued, "than that of not permitting anyone to get away with anything." Pragmatic and utopian leaders "will continue in their accustomed state of symbiosis tempered by mutual disdain," the historian concluded.[24]

In his answers to the challenges from the Right and the Left, Schlesinger was defending not only the Kennedy administration, but also a pragmatic liberalism that lay at the core of his own frame of acceptance. Schlesinger's refutation of radicalism was based on the assumption that the liberal consensus formed by the swinging pendulum of political history would be strong enough to absorb the growing diversity of viewpoints in America. "A nation of 186 million people," Schlesinger mused in 1962, "ought to have its quota of eccentrics and extremists. If it did not, then something would be badly wrong with our free society."[25]

Schlesinger thus accounted for extremist protest by placing it within the bounds of acceptable social conflict that was moving America toward a better life. The question remained whether or not the nation's political equilibrium as described by Schlesinger would survive the turbulent years ahead.

A Thousand Days: Tribute to a Fallen Leader

An assassin's bullet brought the administration of President John F. Kennedy to a premature end in November 1963. In an emotional eulogy to the fallen leader, Arthur Schlesinger, Jr., called the death of John Kennedy "grotesque and unbelievable." Summing up the feelings of a nation, Schlesinger wrote: "John Kennedy's death has greater pathos, because he had barely begun—because he had so much to do, so much to give to his family, his nation, his world. His was a life of incalculable and now of unfulfilled possibility."[26]

Writing in 1983, Tom Shactman described the assassination of Kennedy as a moment of severe trauma for America: "Apart from the detonation of the atomic bomb at Hiroshima, the murder of President Kennedy was the single most shocking event of our time. Reverberations from the act are still being felt today. The assassination shattered the time of complacency that had existed in the United States since the close of World War II and ushered in an era of uncertainty and anguish."[27] Even after the country seemed to rally around the new president, Lyndon B. Johnson, in the weeks and months following Kennedy's death, Shactman argued, "some psychic damage remained in part of the body politic, covered up but still potent, a load of unfinished emotional business."[28]

Millions of Americans eagerly awaited the results of the Warren Commission report on the events in Dallas in hopes that the report could assuage some of the horrible uncertainty about the assassination. Some of the individuals close to the fallen president chose to work out their grief by writing memoirs or other accounts of their days in the White House.

To Arthur Schlesinger, the sudden death of the president was undoubtably a severe personal loss. In addition, the assassination dealt a considerable "shock" or blow to Schlesinger's liberal political philosophy. His frame of acceptance had reconciled contradictory social impulses of the times in large part through the belief that heroic liberal leadership had always emerged at key moments in American history to lead society into the next era of progressive reform. In Schlesinger's conception of American history, liberal heroes such as Jackson and Roosevelt had been the catalysts that periodically urged the nation toward liberal values and policies. Symbolically, these heroic leaders had functioned as a salvation device for Schlesinger, a way of combining the ideal of progressive reform with the pragmatic necessity of political power. Heroic leadership had been both a necessary and an inevitable part of the political cycle. Now John Kennedy, the latest in the series of liberal heroes elected to lead the country through another period of change and growth, was gone.

Arthur Schlesinger, Jr., did not make up his mind to write a book about the Kennedy administration until weeks after the assassination—only after members of the Kennedy family urged him to use his writing acumen and heartfelt commitment to record his years in Washington.[29] At the request of the president, Schlesinger had compiled volumes of notes about the events and decisions during the years Kennedy was in office. The historian had intended to leave his notes at Kennedy's disposal when the president departed.[30] But "after Dallas," Schlesinger said in 1965, "I came to realize that I had the good fortune to have been the only professional historian for a long time to see history from the vantage point of the White House. I felt I owed it both to the memory of the President and the profession to put it all down."[31]

Once he decided to write about John F. Kennedy, Schlesinger worked with feverish dispatch. The result of his efforts, a nine-hundred-page memoir entitled *A Thousand Days: John F. Kennedy in the White House*, was completed in just over a year. The book achieved instant notoriety and controversy when three advance excerpts were published by *Life* magazine in the summer of 1965. The finished product, characterized by Schlesinger as a "personal memoir," not a "comprehensive history," of the Kennedy presidency, won for its author a Pulitzer Prize.[32]

A Thousand Days *as a Defense of Liberalism*

To cope with the Kennedy assassination, Americans tended toward two behaviors common to situations in which individuals respond to shock. Shactman refers to these behaviors as "preserve and search modes." For some people, actions were motivated by "the desire to preserve and defend" what was left to them after the shock. For others, actions were motivated by the desire to "search to find the causes" of their misfortune, to understand what happened and why it happened.[33]

A Thousand Days was a skillfully crafted account of the Kennedy White House, written in what Shactman would call the "preserve mode" of posttrauma behavioral style. Schlesinger believed that his book would demonstrate the ultimate greatness of John F. Kennedy as a leader of the nation. In the foreword, Schlesinger stated the objective of his efforts: "But I hope it will suggest something of the way in which [Kennedy] quickened the heart and mind of the nation, inspired the young, met great crises, led our society to new possibilities of justice and our world to new possibilities of peace, and left behind so glowing and imperishable a memory."[34] Consequently, much of the book was devoted to defending Kennedy's controversial foreign policy decisions in the Bay of Pigs incident, the Berlin Wall and Cuban missile crises, and Southeast Asia.

In addition, *A Thousand Days* can be analyzed as Schlesinger's attempt to preserve and defend his own liberal perspective. The historian saw John Kennedy as the personification of his own frame of acceptance.[35] In his memoir, Schlesinger explored Kennedy's brief tenure as president in light of each of the three main components of Schlesinger's frame of acceptance: the definition of conservative/liberal, the predictable alternation between conservative and liberal epochs, and the need for heroic leadership. In applying of the tides of national politics to understand the Kennedy administration and legacy, Schlesinger attempted both to reinforce the political supremacy of liberalism and to elevate the fallen president into the pantheon of liberal heroes of the past.

First, Schlesinger characterized Kennedy as representative of the definition of a liberal. While he could not point to a long list of liberal legislation passed during Kennedy's tenure, Schlesinger intimated that Kennedy possessed a liberal temperament and style of leadership. "His approach to economic and social policy" was "that of an experimentalist and activist, restrained by politics and prudence and unfettered by doctrinal fetish or taboo." In his manner and speech, Kennedy communicated "a deeply critical attitude toward the ideas and institutions which American society had come in the fifties to regard with such enormous satisfaction." Kennedy was a pragmatic, not a utopian, liberal.[36]

In the process of naming Kennedy a pragmatic liberal, Schlesinger inevitably drew upon historical analogy. Part of Schlesinger's case was a comparison of Kennedy to another pragmatic liberal of the past—Franklin Roosevelt. That the title of the memoir—*A Thousand Days*—invoked the spirit of FDR's "Hundred Days" was no accident. Throughout the book, Schlesinger viewed the New Frontier as a reincarnation of the New Deal.

Kennedy and Roosevelt were said to share views concerning a strong presidency and fluid administrative methods.[37] Both men were "natural Presidents" whose temperament and background were alike in many ways. Both men "were patrician, urbane, cultivated, inquisitive, gallant; both were detached from the business ethos, both skeptical of the received wisdom, both devoted to politics but never enslaved by it, both serene in the exercise of power, both committed to the use of power for the ends of human welfare and freedom; both too had more than their share of physical suffering."[38]

Both Kennedy and Roosevelt also attracted bright men and women into public service. The staffs of the New Frontier and the New Deal shared "ideas of national reconstruction and reform," an aspiration "to the world of ideas as well as to the world of power," and a versatility and vitality that "flowed throughout the government and created a sense of vast possibility." Kennedy, like his predecessor Roosevelt, imbued the nation's capital with "an unquenchable spirit of sardonic liberalism and an unceasing drive to get things done."[39]

Schlesinger also declared Kennedy's record exemplary of the accomplishments of a liberal administration during a progressive epoch in the cyclical alternation of American political consensus. The historian portrayed Kennedy as a president who accomplished much in a brief time despite the many obstacles inherent in a modern presidency.

Surveying the early years of Kennedy's term, Schlesinger asserted that the president had amassed "a legislative record unmatched in some respects since the days of Roosevelt." The assassination "robbed" Kennedy of what typically are the most productive years of a liberal administration.[40]

Even more central in Schlesinger's explanation than Kennedy's concrete accomplishments was a description of the obstacles that impeded the president. In discussing these impediments, the historian now drew distinctions between Kennedy's "thousand days" and Roosevelt's prolific "Hundred Days." Unlike the Roosevelt administration, which passed significant legislation establishing social service institutions in a time of national crisis, Kennedy was forced to do battle with a slow-moving bureaucracy and a hostile Congress in order to pass controversial legislation in a time of relative prosperity. Throughout the work, Schlesinger wrote of the "bureaucratosclerosis" that pervaded the Pentagon, the State Department, and agencies charged to carry out domestic policies. A "central frustration" of Kennedy's New Frontier was the collision between "new ideas" and "the feudal barons of the permanent government," a collision not experienced in the early years of the New Deal.[41]

The frustration was compounded by frequent confrontations between Kennedy's liberal agenda and a conservative, predominantly southern congressional leadership that was wary of rapid change in areas such as civil rights and was willing to use tactics of delay to defeat reform legislation.[42] In addition, Kennedy had neither a clear electoral mandate nor a national emergency to justify going beyond Congress to take his case to the American people. In short, Schlesinger concluded, Kennedy accomplished as much as could be expected in a time of "extraordinary transformation of national values and purposes" that proceeded at a rate faster than the machinery of government was willing to go.[43]

Finally, Schlesinger portrayed Kennedy as a true American liberal hero with the potential to lead his people toward progressive goals even after his untimely death. Kennedy fulfilled both the functional and moral requirements of a heroic leader as outlined in Schlesinger's frame of acceptance.

Kennedy's heroism was functional in that he "educated" the public about modern trends in domestic and foreign policy. Schlesinger answered criticism that Kennedy "never really exploited his considerable gifts as a public educator" by pointing to the president's speeches and policies that demonstrated an "impatience with the postures and pieties of other days" and "an open mind toward the unknown future."[44]

In domestic affairs, Kennedy informed his audiences that "most of the problems, or at least many of them, that we now face are technical problems, are administrative problems" that will demand the ability to "look at things as they are, not through party labels." The key to moving the economy ahead was to ignore "the clichés of our forbears" and to generate new ideas in fiscal and monetary policy.[45]

In foreign affairs, especially in 1963, Kennedy moved beyond "the rhetoric of the cold war," which featured "self-serving platitudes about the total virtues of one side and the total evil of the other," to emphasizing the need for peace and the recognition of diversity and universal commonalities. By the end of Kennedy's shortened tenure, Schlesinger concluded, he was teaching the American people a new vocabulary to use in understanding foreign relations.[46]

Kennedy's heroism was moral in that he exhibited qualities of courage above and beyond the ordinary quotient of selflessness in pursuit of accomplishing his political objectives. Schlesinger filled *A Thousand Days* with tales of Kennedy's courage in overcoming physical pain and, more importantly, Kennedy's willingness to stand up to "systematic and foul vilification" by his enemies from the Radical Right and the Left. The historian foreshadowed Kennedy's eventual fate throughout the narrative and intimated that the president had a sense of tragic fatalism, an understanding that his personal safety was on the line whenever he went out among the people. Kennedy was willing "to attest by example his faith in American rationality and decency" and to "define 'the nature of our reality for us by his actions.'" The president "never hesitated to define America by his presence and courage in the heart of the enemy's country."[47]

So it was that Kennedy went to Dallas, a "city of violence and hysteria," in November of 1963 as part of a statewide trip to patch up feelings among feuding Texas Democrats. To highlight the courageous quality of Kennedy's trip, Schlesinger reported the apprehension of Adlai Stevenson, who had been in Dallas shortly before the president. Stevenson had warned Schlesinger: "But, you know, there was something very ugly and frightening about the atmosphere. Later I talked with some of the leading people out there. They wondered whether the President should go to Dallas, and so do I."[48] Schlesinger then told of Kennedy's unfearing attitude toward the possibility of assassination. "'It didn't bother him at all,' according to aide Kenneth O'Donnell." "No one expects that our life will be easy," Kennedy had said in a speech in Fort Worth on the morning of November 22. "History will not permit it."[49] Later that afternoon, President Kennedy was killed.

"'Is there some principle of nature,'" Schlesinger wrote, quoting Richard Hofstadter, "'which requires that we never know the quality of what we have had until it is gone?'"[50] Schlesinger asserted that Kennedy's life and the manner of his death were heroic exemplars of the best qualities of humanity. "Lifting us beyond our capacities," the historian wrote, "he gave his country back its best self, wiping away the world's impression of an old nation of weary men, played out, fearful of ideas, change, and the future."[51]

In all ways, in death as in life, John Kennedy epitomized Schlesinger's conception of a liberal hero enacting a liberal frame of acceptance. Kennedy's functional pragmatism and moral fortitude exhibited in substance and style what liberalism could be. The vacuum created by Kennedy's death reinforced for Schlesinger the necessity of heroic action for the successful fulfillment of his liberal frame of acceptance.

Schlesinger ended *A Thousand Days* on a note of grim faith in his own liberal perspective. He hoped that John Kennedy's personal courage and vision would influence events after his death. "The energies he released, the standards he set, the purposes he inspired, the goals he established," Schlesinger concluded, "would guide the land for years to come."[52]

Critical Responses and New Directions

Critical responses to *A Thousand Days* were as diverse as they were numerous. Most viewed the book as a partisan defense of a beloved president with little historical objectivity.[53] Some objected to the harsh treatment of Secretary of State Dean Rusk and the inclusion of overly intimate details of the president's personal life. From the floor of the House of Representatives, Congressman Widnall criticized Schlesinger's view of Rusk with the following rebuke: "I always thought that the mark of a truly liberal mind was supposed to be fairness to the individual, respect for office, dislike for kicking a man when he is unable to answer because of his office, and distaste for commercial profit at the expense of others."[54]

In contrast, Senator George McGovern came to Schlesinger's defense by inserting Max Freedman's review of *A Thousand Days* into the *Congressional Record*. Freedman argued that the risks involved in an "instant history" like Schlesinger's were "worth taking, for it is one of [Schlesinger's] majestic endowments as a historian that he never is depressed into solemnity by an accumulation of documents."[55]

An important by-product of the critical scrutiny (and ultimate Pulitzer Prize–winning acclaim) of *A Thousand Days* was that it served to complete the transformation of Arthur Schlesinger's public persona from an academic historian to a liberal spokesman and defender of the New Frontier. Schlesinger's biography appeared in extensive articles in *Time* and *New York Times Magazine*. He was hailed by William Shannon as "America's most controversial historian."[56]

Equipped with the experience and ethos of the New Frontier, Schlesinger left the Kennedy years as an influential intellectual and rhetorician with a persuasive conception of American history at his disposal. He was able through the "preserve mode" of posttrauma behavior to weather the shock of Kennedy's assassination with his own frame of acceptance apparently intact. His adaptation of the tides of national politics to defend the Kennedy administration illustrates the rhetorical trajectory that continued to lead Schlesinger to define and interpret situations in particular ways.

Yet Schlesinger's accounting for bureaucratic and congressional opposition to the agenda of the New Frontier covered over a potential limitation in his cyclical explanation of American politics. The simplicity of the tides metaphor, which promised that a new wave of liberal reform would periodically occur as if a dam had burst, could not easily accommodate the growing complexities of American society and institutions of power. Schlesinger's conception of heroic leadership that could manage the diverse interests of society seemed to underestimate the difficulty of achieving social consensus on divisive issues such as civil rights. Ironically, issues like civil rights had been identified by Schlesinger as forming the core of "qualitative liberalism." Even the heroic leadership of a John Kennedy did not produce the kind of liberal legislative record that Schlesinger's theory had forecast. The continued reliance on the tides of national politics as a means of optimistic explanation and prediction would contribute to an emerging gap between liberal rhetoric and legislative reality in the 1960s and 1970s, a gap illustrated by the rhetoric of dawnism.

In addition, the logic of the tides metaphor, a simple physiological cycle of movement and rest, provided no underlying material basis upon which a thorough critique of American life could be sustained, other than a vague contrast between liberal calls for change and conservative defense of stability. Schlesinger's faith that social conflict could be contained within a "vital center" of American political values, a faith exemplified in his earlier defenses of the Kennedy administration against attacks from the political Left and the Right, was shaken by the tragedy in Dallas. *A Thousand Days* demonstrated, however, that that faith had not been destroyed. If anything, Schlesinger's account of the Kennedy administration only reinforced the symbolic function of heroic liberal leadership as a salvation device in his frame of acceptance.

What lay ahead for Schlesinger during the next several years was a series of stark new challenges to his liberal perspective. The components of Schlesinger's frame of acceptance were to be stretched to the breaking point in the years after 1963 by the challenges of Vietnam and political violence and by the threatened delegitimation of the term "liberal" in American political discourse. These challenges would severely test the tides of national politics as a generating principle for liberal rhetoric in contemporary American society.

6

Vietnam and Violence, 1965–1972

After the assassination of President John F. Kennedy, Arthur Schlesinger, Jr., stayed on as assistant to the new Johnson administration for only a few months, then left the executive branch to work on *A Thousand Days*. His memoir of the Kennedy White House earned him the Pulitzer Prize for biography in 1965. After the book's completion, Schlesinger took some time off for travel and study, then accepted an endowed position as Albert Schweitzer Professor of the Humanities at the City University of New York beginning in the fall of 1966.[1] While he returned to an academic position, Schlesinger remained politically active, supporting liberal causes and candidates in speeches and in articles published in popular magazines such as *Harper's* and *Saturday Evening Post*. During the latter half of the 1960s, Schlesinger was seen as an important defender of the legacy of President Kennedy's New Frontier.[2]

The next several years were marked by two divisive and interrelated issues, the war in Vietnam and the growing amount of social unrest and violence at home. These two issues challenged Schlesinger's definition of liberalism and cyclical conception of American history. Schlesinger's response to the war in Vietnam and domestic social upheaval was influenced by and contained within the rhetorical trajectory produced by his belief in the tides of national politics. As when responding to earlier challenges, Schlesinger called upon his frame of acceptance to perform persuasive functions of defense, explanation, and prediction in order to adjust to dramatic changes in the American political scene. In these turbulent years, Schlesinger's liberal perspective would be stretched to the breaking point.

The Challenge of Vietnam, 1965–1968

Throughout 1964 and early 1965, Arthur Schlesinger, Jr., did not perceive Vietnam as an important issue and trusted President Johnson's ability to draw American military involvement to a satisfactory conclusion. On May 15, 1965, during the National Teach-In on Vietnam, prompted by emerging public awareness of U.S. military involvement, Schlesinger participated in the Washington, D.C., teach-in as a defender of administration policy.[3]

For Schlesinger, the National Teach-In was an unmistakable sign that Americans were eager for a rational discussion on the Vietnam question. The apparent cooperation by the Johnson administration was interpreted by Schlesinger to mean that the president must want to set everyone straight on Vietnam.[4]

During 1965 and 1966, however, as American bombing of North Vietnam continued to escalate, Schlesinger came to believe that U.S. involvement in Southeast Asia had gone too far and was in need of moderation. As with other political issues that had confronted the nation, Schlesinger came to view his role as one of a teacher and diagnostician concerning American foreign policy. The historian believed that America's deepening involvement in Vietnam was due to ignorance about the "real" situation in Southeast Asia and that his intended audiences—the Johnson administration and the intellectual community—would be as pupils attentive to the lessons of a schoolmaster's insight.[5]

From 1965 to 1968, Arthur Schlesinger, Jr., spoke and wrote extensively on the Vietnam issue. In radio interviews and talk shows, in television news programs, panel discussions, speeches, newspaper editorials, popular magazine articles, and speech writing, Schlesinger proclaimed his desire for a "middle way out of Vietnam." Perhaps no single intellectual commanded more popular attention and produced more messages in more media during those years than Schlesinger.[6]

While the basic arguments remained constant throughout the rhetorical campaign, the target of Schlesinger's criticism gradually shifted from the general public's ignorance about Vietnam to the wrongheadedness of President Johnson's advisers and ultimately to President Johnson himself. The shifting focus of blame reflected Schlesinger's growing understanding that what was at stake in the Vietnam debate was not only the credibility of a president but the viability of Schlesinger's own frame of acceptance as it applied to foreign policy.

Threats to Schlesinger's Liberal Frame

The growing public concern about U.S. military involvement in Southeast Asia created rhetorical problems for Arthur Schlesinger's liberal frame of acceptance. All three components of Schlesinger's perspective—definitions of liberal/conservative, predictable alternations of liberal and conservative political dominance, and the call for heroic leadership—were called into question in the Vietnam debate.

Criticism of U.S. involvement in Southeast Asia soon grew into criticism of the cold war anticommunist worldview, one of the premises supporting Schlesinger's "vital center" and accompanying definitions of liberal and conservative political philosophies. Although Schlesinger left the impression in *A Thousand Days* that John Kennedy would probably have wound down American involvement in Vietnam, he remained in favor of containment of communism through means of counterinsurgency. For Schlesinger, at least from 1961 to 1963, South Vietnam seemed to be an ideal place to test new methods for achieving cold war foreign policy objectives. In the emerging Vietnam debate, Schlesinger would be forced to reconcile his cold war worldview with more radical critiques of U.S. foreign policy.[7]

As protest against U.S. involvement in Southeast Asia became more radical and pronounced, particularly on college campuses, Schlesinger's conception of an orderly, cyclical progression of liberal and conservative epochs operating within a framework of rationality was also jeopardized. While Schlesinger conceived of the 1960s as a progressive era in which pragmatic liberals could find appropriate means to accomplish desired ends, dissent over Vietnam threatened to discredit liberal pragmatism by labeling it as a *cause* of America's problematic escalation of military force in Southeast Asia.

Finally, criticism of U.S. involvement in Southeast Asia threatened the untarnished martyrdom of Schlesinger's favorite liberal leader, John F. Kennedy. As President Johnson escalated the war effort, critics within Congress, the intellectual community, and the cadre of journalists reporting from Vietnam began to question the success of U.S. action and to attack Johnson *and* his predecessor for leading the country into the Vietnam "quagmire."[8] In the Vietnam debate, Schlesinger would be faced with the alternatives of repudiating the principles of containment and activist "flexible response" that were followed by Kennedy or coming up with a different line of attack against Johnson's policy.

Dissociation in Vietnam Dissent

In defense of his frame of acceptance, Schlesinger again employed the strategy of dissociation in a critique both of Johnson administration policy and of extremist antiwar protest. He then carefully constructed an alternative "middle way out of Vietnam" that he hoped would unite liberals in support of a pragmatic solution to the Vietnam problem in keeping with the tenets of his own liberal philosophy. The historian justified his dissociations on the grounds that it was essential that advocates in the Vietnam debate discard "slogans and bright phrases" and carefully distinguish between appearance and reality in foreign policy.[9] By the mid-1960s, the attempt to distinguish between appearance and reality had become a standard rhetorical strategy for Schlesinger, part of a well-worn symbolic path of development he was following in conjunction with his frame of acceptance.

In the discussion about Vietnam, Schlesinger gave two new reasons for the importance of separating appearance from reality in foreign affairs. First, he argued that history was "inscrutable." Denouncing adherence to ideological creeds, Schlesinger contended that history was too unpredictable, too dependent on accident, to be explained by absolute theories. In debate over foreign policy, the tendency was strong to predict how nations would behave on the basis of crude historical analogies. Particularly during wartime, Americans often oversimplified issues and degraded debate with emotionalism. The repression and demagoguery of McCarthyism, Schlesinger argued (ironically using his own analogy) were the result of the public's inability to separate appearance from reality in the debate over the Korean War. Schlesinger wished to maintain the supremacy of reason over emotion, of reality over illusion, in the Vietnam debate.[10]

Second, Schlesinger argued that history was "moving faster." The "increasing velocity of history" made it necessary to base judgments on the circumstances of the present rather than on the stereotypes of the past, Schlesinger asserted. Because the "transformations wrought by science and technology" had accelerated the rate of change in the world "exponentially," perceptions of reality had become obsolete "with disconcerting rapidity." The failure to update notions such as communism, containment, and flexible response constantly had been "the underlying source of our troubles in foreign policy," Schlesinger reasoned.[11] American leaders needed to "recover our cool and try to see the situation as it is" in order to avoid the dangers of misperception and anachronism that could lead us to blunder into nuclear war.[12] By the end of the decade, this concept of history moving faster would also become a central feature of Schlesinger's diagnosis of American society as well as American foreign policy.

DISSOCIATION IN THE CRITIQUE OF ADMINISTRATION POLICY.   From the general premise that appearance must be distinguished from reality, Schlesinger moved to a critique of the three most important arguments for U.S. involvement offered by the Johnson administration. With each argument, Schlesinger dissociated the key idea into its apparent and real components and asserted that Johnson's positions were based on illusion rather than fact.

The first administration argument Schlesinger critiqued was that the United States is committed to defending Southeast Asia. Schlesinger dissociated the idea of "commitment" into illusory and real obligations that the United States had in Vietnam by stating that none of the claims by the Johnson administration described the realities of the situation.[13] The insistence by Secretary of State Rusk that the South East Asia Treaty Organization (SEATO) established a legal mandate for U.S. military action could "only be regarded as an exercise in historical and legal distortion."[14] Any commitment America had was a *political* commitment not to leave the region suddenly for fear that a hasty U.S. withdrawal would "have ominous repercussions throughout Asia."[15]

In addition, no historical precedent for commitment existed. The history of U.S. involvement from 1954 to 1965 revealed that America had become entangled in Vietnam through a "series of small decisions" that represented more the "triumph of the politics of inadvertence" than a precedent for future action. The legacy of the Kennedy administration was ambiguous, Schlesinger stated. While Kennedy had followed the "policy of 'one more step'" advocated by his military advisers, by the fall of 1963 he had realized that ultimately "it is their [the South Vietnamese] war" to win or lose.[16] President Johnson, like all presidents, had to "expect to be accountable" for his own real choices.[17]

Finally, although the American goal of containing communism was laudable in Schlesinger's opinion, Johnson's Vietnam policy would have to be judged on its execution and not its ideals.[18] "Why we are in Vietnam," Schlesinger asserted in the key opening lines of his book-length critique *The Bitter Heritage*, "is a question of mainly historical interest. We *are* there, for better or worse, and we must deal with the situation as it exists."[19] By defining American commitment as a question of real practice rather than apparent principle, Schlesinger hoped to convince his audience that different practices could fulfill basically the same principles.

The second argument Schlesinger critiqued was that the threat of communism in Southeast Asia requires U.S. military involvement. Schlesinger dissociated the idea of "communist threat" into illusory and real threats to American interests by again claiming that the administration's claims concerning the monolithic threat posed by communism in North Vietnam did not square with the realities of the situation.[20] Those who viewed communism in Asia as a monolith were guilty of "obsessive anti-communism," which, according to Schlesinger, "blinds its victims to the realities of a changing world."[21] The split between Russia and China had created a polycentrist world in which nationalism was more pervasive than communism.[22] And although Hanoi and Peking shared many interests, Schlesinger posited, they also had divergent purposes that were stronger than their affinities.[23]

The administration's belief that the Vietcong uprising was a North Vietnamese product was also an "illusion" and a "misperception" of "not only the political but even the military character of the problem."[24] A look at the facts revealed that most of the enemy force was made up of disaffected South Vietnamese. If anything, Schlesinger concluded, the American policy of bombing North Vietnam only increased infiltration of North Vietnamese into the Vietcong.[25]

Finally, Schlesinger believed that "the Vietnam riddle . . . will not be solved by bad historical analogies."[26] Nothing better represented the administration's reliance on appearance instead of reality than its insistence that the Munich analogy applied to Southeast Asia. "Even the village idiot could grasp the difference" between Hitler's invasion "across old and well-established lines of national division" and the indigenous revolt of the Vietcong. Guerrilla warfare, Schlesinger noted, "is dependent on conditions and opportunities within the countries themselves."[27]

What should replace Johnson's "obsessive anti-communism" was "rational anti-communism," which was "graduated in mode and substance according to the character of the threat."[28] By defining communism as a threat dependent on the circumstances of the situation (which were not so serious in Southeast Asia), Schlesinger attempted to create a position from which one could be anticommunist and also be against escalation of U.S. involvement in Vietnam. Dissociation of the idea of communist threat created the possibility of middle ground.

The final Johnson administration argument Schlesinger questioned was that increased U.S. military pressure will shorten the war. Schlesinger dissociated the idea of "military success" into illusory and real progress toward ending the war in Vietnam by asserting that Johnson administration policy was not leading toward resolution of the conflict. Johnson's decision to escalate the bombing of North Vietnam was not inducing negotiation but was instead driving the enemy "underground," where guerrilla fighting strengthened them and weakened us.[29] The decision to send massive reinforcements of ground troops to fight a Korea-type war was also not creating a margin of superiority but was instead "lifting the stalemate to a new and more explosive level."[30]

The American "escalation machine" had not hastened the end of the war. Body counts represented only the appearance of a successful war effort. In fact, "the effect of our policy" was to "pulverize the political and institutional fabric" of South Vietnam. "In other words, our method defeats our goal," the historian lamented. A more realistic policy would include a return to Kennedy's counterinsurgency military and social programs.[31]

Schlesinger also came to differentiate between Johnson's claims that the United States was open to negotiations and the reality of American preconditions, which all but closed out negotiations. U.S. leadership was responsible for creating a favorable climate for a settlement, Schlesinger believed.[32] As the months passed and no settlement was near, Schlesinger voiced stronger doubts about the sincerity of Johnson's desire to talk with North Vietnam.[33]

By defining military success as progress toward a negotiated settlement, Schlesinger hoped to generate the belief that peace was impossible to accomplish under Johnson. In so doing, Schlesinger completed his critique against Johnson administration policy and set the stage for a "middle way out of Vietnam."

DISSOCIATION IN THE CRITIQUE OF DIRECT-ACTION PROTEST. In the months after the National Teach-In in May 1965, students and other opponents of the Vietnam war began to demonstrate their opposition through direct actions such as marching and burning draft cards. Although Schlesinger grew to oppose Johnson's Vietnam policy, he was *equally* opposed to all radical protest against the war. As early as June 1965, Schlesinger attacked a speech opposing the war given by Lewis Mumford as "an anxious blast of some inchoate sort" that generated an audience reaction which smacked of the "wild, unleashed emotionalism" of the Nuremberg rallies of Hitler's times.[34]

Schlesinger worked out his reaction against violent protest by dissociating the key idea of "protest" into apparent and real aspects. By doing so, he hoped to restore legitimacy to the progressive, pragmatic liberalism he had described in his theory of the cyclical alternations of American political consensus.

The historian proceeded by attacking what he believed to be the two fundamental premises of direct-action protest. The first premise Schlesinger attacked was that protest is communication. To Schlesinger, the belief that mass demonstration contributed ideas and messages to the public debate on Vietnam was unfounded and illusory. Schlesinger characterized direct-action protests as "the discharge of personal emotions," which provided an "emotional orgasm" and "psychic satisfaction" for the protesters but contributed nothing except hysteria and irrationality to the Vietnam controversy.[35]

For Schlesinger, real dissent was characterized by "respect for the complexities of the issue," a willingness to compromise without sacrificing principles, the acceptance of public responsibility, and, most important, "respect for the amenities of discourse."[36] It was up to the intellectual establishment, Schlesinger argued, to provide support for the values of rational debate and discussion in society. Crucially, Schlesinger viewed students as *apprentice intellectuals,* a part of a growing "political constituency" of educated and rational elites. In his characterization of antiwar protest, Schlesinger seemed to prefer the reasoned approach of the expert to what he viewed as the emotionalism of the mass public.[37]

The second premise Schlesinger attacked was that "protest results in reforms." Hopes for wholesale changes coming from mass demonstrations were also empty illusions. Schlesinger characterized calls to tear the system down as anti-Americanism that only threatened to cause violence and overreaction by flag-loving patriots.[38] The "venting of adolescent outrage" only strengthened the forces young people claimed to be fighting against. "Unless society shows unaccustomed wisdom," Schlesinger warned, "the Red Guards of Berkeley will not be an aberration but a portent" of societal repression to come.[39]

In contrast, Schlesinger argued, rational dissent *could* result in moderation in administration policy. Throughout 1966, Schlesinger maintained that the "application of reason" by courageous dissenters "in the United States Senate or in local meetings or teach-ins" could succeed in "bringing into existence a . . . serious debate on our choices in the Far East," which might affect administration actions.[40] As Schlesinger turned farther away from Johnson toward new leadership in late 1967 and 1968, he reemphasized that young people should organize as a political constituency working within existing institutions instead of a lawless mob.[41]

By dissociating the idea of "protest" into apparent and real dissent based on criteria of rationality and effectiveness, Schlesinger attempted to create a position from which young people and others in the intellectual community could protest against the Vietnam war without having to repudiate the entire American way of life. Schlesinger believed that moderation would be a safe place for members of the older intellectual "establishment." From the middle ground, liberal intellectuals like Schlesinger could attack Johnson without attacking their own institutions.

FINDING A "MIDDLE WAY" OUT OF VIETNAM.   In proposing a solution to the problem of U.S. involvement in Southeast Asia, Schlesinger carefully dissociated his proposal—a middle way out of Vietnam— from Johnson's bombing policy. In contrast to Johnson's actions, Schlesinger called for "slowing down the war" by halting the bombing of North Vietnam and the further escalation of American ground forces into South Vietnam. He also urged increasing U.S. pressure for reform in the Ky regime in the south, and holding negotiations involving the Vietcong as well as the North Vietnamese, which could lead toward free elections in South Vietnam and a new coalition government.[42]

Schlesinger's middle way contained a number of paradoxes that he hoped heroic executive leadership would solve. The major paradox involved the timing of American withdrawal from Southeast Asia. Although opposed to military escalation, Schlesinger was convinced that America should "hold the line in South Vietnam" until a settlement was reached. He feared that "Hanoi and the Vietcong would not negotiate so long as they think they can win." He also harbored doubts, lingering from his cold war upbringing, as to whether the Communists could be trusted to behave in a coalition government.[43]

Schlesinger dismissed the problem of paradox by asserting that it was "possible to slow down the war without standing still." Exactly how U.S. forces could achieve the "stalemate" that was a precondition to negotiation with a hostile enemy was never made clear. Schlesinger assumed that a good president could "find some generals" who could execute a military "holding action" in Vietnam.[44]

How continued military support for the Ky regime was to be reconciled with U.S. "pressure" for Ky to reform remained as much a mystery to Schlesinger as it had to Kennedy and Johnson. Exactly what role the United States would play in the negotiation process and postsettlement Southeast Asia was also not spelled out. It was as if Schlesinger was more concerned that a middle ground be established than about what specifics would form the basis for the middle ground.[45]

Schlesinger was sure, however, that the resolution of the Vietnam riddle required "resilient" and "forbearing" presidential leadership to foster negotiation. As the Johnson administration further "enmeshed" the country in the "grinding cogs of the escalation machine," Schlesinger came to the conclusion that new leadership was needed. He pinned his hopes for resolving the paradoxes of the middle way out of Vietnam on the emergence of a new liberal leader in 1968 to take up the standard of cool pragmatism left by John F. Kennedy.[46] In so doing, Schlesinger again followed the symbolic path charted by his reliance on the tides of national politics as a means of explaining and resolving the political crises of his time.

Assessing Schlesinger's Vietnam Rhetoric

Despite its ambiguities (or perhaps because of them), Schlesinger's middle way out of Vietnam had significant appeals for certain audiences. The arguments laid out in the persuasive campaign found some support in general public opinion. The major desires of the general public concerning Vietnam in 1966—anticommunism and ending the war as soon as possible—seemed to be fulfilled by Schlesinger's middle course. And Schlesinger's views on student demonstrations corresponded to the prevailing belief that most forms of opposition to the war were illegitimate.[47]

Schlesinger's call for moderation in the Vietnam debate also influenced the discourse within established institutions concerning American presence in Southeast Asia. By 1967, congressional debate had begun to focus on the effectiveness of U.S. military actions in Southeast Asia. For example, in a speech coauthored by Schlesinger and presented in the Senate on March 4, Robert Kennedy questioned Johnson's bombing policy. For the next year in Washington and on the presidential primary trail, the debate among policymakers tended to focus on tactics and procedures for withdrawal rather than on more fundamental issues such as the goal of U.S. foreign policy in Southeast Asia.[48]

Ultimately, however, Schlesinger's defense of his liberal frame of acceptance did not generate a "vital center" of united and enlightened liberal protest against the Vietnam War. The historian's tenuous dissociations did not appeal to a growing number of critics in the intellectual community of students, academics, and commentators who began to question purposes underlying American involvement in Southeast Asia. As the war dragged on, as moderate dissent did not result in changes in administration actions or rhetoric, protest became radicalized.

A number of critics questioned the tone and substance of Schlesinger's middle way out of Vietnam. Ronald Steel argued that Schlesinger's alternative would satisfy neither hawks nor doves who believed that "a stand has to be taken on the central issue" of "what is at stake in Vietnam." The middle course skirted "the real problem" of defining the *purpose* of U.S. foreign policy.[49] Irving Howe cautioned that Schlesinger's somewhat tepid criticism of Johnson's foreign policy was a sign of "weariness and despair" of the "intellectual opposition" that was refusing to stand up for principles.[50] Noam Chomsky asserted that "Schlesinger's 'middle course' appears to differ from the approach of the Joint Chiefs of Staff and the State Department only in tactical emphasis." The "pragmatic liberal" approach to Vietnam was flawed, Chomsky continued, because it did not "question our ends but only the likelihood of our achieving them."[51] Schlesinger's attempted dissociations, Englehardt concluded in 1981, "blurred the distinction between is and ought" in his foreign policy arguments and made him "blind to the reality of liberal culpability for the Vietnam War."[52]

As Richard Weaver wrote in describing the issue of slavery, for many people the Vietnam war increasingly became a subject about which "one has to say 'yes' or 'no,' that one has to accept an alternative to the total exclusion of the other."[53] Protest against U.S. involvement in Vietnam, radical dissenters concluded, should focus on fundamental purposes of U.S. foreign policy and not on technical aspects of military strategy.

The challenge of Vietnam seriously threatened Schlesinger's liberal perspective. Consensus no longer seemed to exist in the liberal community about definitions of liberalism and conservatism and legitimate responses to communism abroad. The predictable alternation of liberalism and conservatism failed to account for divisions within the liberal community over methods of and targets for reform. And heroic leadership brought American foreign policy not glorious triumphs but charges of adventurism and imperialism from within the liberal community itself.[54]

By 1969, Schlesinger began a sober reassessment of the relationship between liberalism and American foreign policy. The historian declared that America's failed Vietnam policy signaled "the end of the age of the superpowers." The growing power of the military-industrial complex (which Schlesinger called the "warrior class") and a messianic impulse to save the world from communism (due in part to liberal activist zeal) had led America to "lose our sense of the relation between means and ends" in Vietnam. Yet because of the rise of nationalism, Schlesinger continued, both American and Soviet influence around the world was declining even as both nations' military arsenals were rapidly expanding. In addition, Vietnam taught us "that we cannot run two crusades at once—that we cannot wage even a small war against an underdeveloped country and at the same time move creatively to meet the problems of our own land." Americans should no longer sacrifice a liberal social agenda in exchange for "trying to run the planet." Instead, the historian concluded, "we can restore our influence abroad only as we live up to our highest ideals in our national community."[55]

The Challenge of Violence, 1968–1972

By the spring of 1968, Arthur Schlesinger, Jr., began to sense that America was no longer a land of liberal political consensus. After the assassination of Martin Luther King, Jr., in April of 1968, Schlesinger, the ultimate true believer in a "vital center" of liberal values, admitted, "The ties binding our society have become brittle indeed."[56]

Once again, heroic leadership was needed to bring America together, for the nation could not "permit uncontrolled violence, from whatever source, and retain a rational society." For Schlesinger, the leader America needed in 1968 was Robert F. Kennedy. Only Kennedy could build bridges between the alienated communities within America. In a *New Republic* article in which he endorsed Robert Kennedy's bid for the White House, Schlesinger wrote that only John Kennedy's brother had the "experiencing nature" and compassion "to appeal to the reason and conscience of the young around the planet." Surely America's choice of Robert Kennedy for president would "lead our troubled land into the light of a new day."[57]

One month after Schlesinger's article was published, Robert Kennedy was assassinated in Los Angeles. The death of the promising young leader dealt yet another traumatic shock to Schlesinger's frame of acceptance.

Rhetorical Problems Generated by Violence in America

On June 5, 1968, the day Robert Kennedy lay dying in a Los Angeles hospital, Arthur Schlesinger, Jr., was in New York City, where he was to present a commencement address at the City

University. The opening two paragraphs of the address he delivered exemplified the grief he experienced during that awful summer of 1968: "The world today is asking a terrible question—a question which every citizen of this Republic should be putting to himself: what sort of people are we, we Americans? And the answer which much of the world is bound to return is that we are today the most frightening people on the planet."[58]

The speech in New York City marked the beginning of a four-year quest in which Schlesinger attempted to salvage his frame of acceptance from the shocks of prevailing political violence and unreason in America. During his quest, Schlesinger authored two books— *Violence: America in the Sixties* (1968) and *The Crisis of Confidence* (1969)—and wrote several articles and speeches on the theme of political violence. Schlesinger's campaign constituted what Shactman refers to as the "search mode" of posttrauma behavior, in which individuals respond to shock by "find[ing] the causes of our misfortune, to understand what has happened to us."[59]

The series of political assassinations during the 1960s suggested to Schlesinger "not so much a fortuitous set of aberrations as an emerging pattern of response and action—a spreading and ominous belief in the efficacy of violence and the politics of the deed."[60] "Surely we can no longer dodge the fact that violence is becoming a central factor in the American social process," Schlesinger wrote in 1969.[61]

The propensity in American society to resort to violence was being compounded by the growing feeling that "events seemed to have slipped beyond our control: we have lost our immunity to history."[62] In a "strategic moment" of "unprecedented perplexity and anxiety about their conception of their own nation and its role in the world," Schlesinger surmised, "more and more Americans . . . are beginning to wonder whether we will be able to cope in the next years—to cope all at once with the Russians, the Chinese, the French, the Africans, the Latin Americans; with the decaying cities and the blighted countryside; with the jammed freeways and the crowded airways, with the polluted water and the poisoned atmosphere, with the fury of the Blacks and the animosity of the low-income whites; with the mysterious skepticisms and irascibilities of our own children."[63]

Schlesinger labeled the combination of increased violence and increased anxiety about the future as a "crisis of confidence." Schlesinger believed that resorting to violence implied "the failure of reason" and the loss of faith among disenfranchised groups that political action was "in its essence a rational process—that is, a deliberate choice of means to achieve desired ends." The crisis of confidence had generated among some Americans a sense that there was "a larger incomprehensibility, a larger absurdity, even a larger wickedness, in our official society" that could be eliminated only by breaking away from conventions of social and political civility.[64] Thus anxiety and violence fed each other and compelled Americans "to look searchingly at ourselves and our society before hatred and violence rush us on to more evil and finally tear our nation apart."[65]

The "crisis of confidence" confronted Schlesinger's frame of acceptance with severe rhetorical problems. Once again, each component of his perspective was threatened by contradictory experiences and events. First, Schlesinger's definitions of conservatism and liberalism were challenged because both were based on assumptions of a "vital center" of reasonableness and due process that disaffected groups now saw as "a pretext for inaction and therefore a mask of injustice" and a barrier to participation in the distribution of power. The "growing cynicism about democratic institutions" and "growing defection from the democratic process" threatened to undermine what for Schlesinger was a "fighting faith" in rational political action through accommodating liberal and conservative beliefs.[66]

In addition, Schlesinger's conception of predictable alternations between conservative and liberal political eras was challenged by events that belied prediction. The decade of the 1960s, which Schlesinger had promised to be a time "of motion, of leadership, and of hope," was ending not in a "ferment of ideas" but in a nightmare of disillusionment and terror that threatened to trivialize the entire rhythm of American politics.[67] Schlesinger's belief in progress through the ebbing and flowing of liberal activism was based on the presumption that change was good, a presumption that was being severely tested almost daily. Change brought not progress but only anxiety and violent backlash.[68]

Finally, Schlesinger's belief in the need for heroic liberal leadership was challenged by the brutal carnage of political assassination itself, which threatened to rob a generation of guidance and wisdom at the top of the structure of social power. The murders of Martin Luther King and Robert Kennedy only "intensified the desperate sense among the excluded groups that some basic ugliness would rise ineluctably out of American society to strike down every leader who tried to embrace them in the promise of American life."[69]

In addition, according to Shactman, the season of political violence "also raised doubts about the legitimacy of the successors of the murdered leaders" and even "a serious doubting of authority of all levels."[70] Young people in particular, wrote Schlesinger, began to look for role models not among "the enveloping structures and hypocrisies of organized society" but in their own contemporaries and in popular culture. "The great heroes of this day," the historian observed sardonically, "are Bob Dylan and the Beatles."[71]

Schlesinger's Response to Violence

Schlesinger viewed his rhetorical response to violence in America as "in many respects a sequel" to *The Vital Center*, his 1949 work that was the foundation of much of his frame of acceptance. While admitting that some of the rhetoric concerning political violence would be "strident, extravagant, and delusive," Schlesinger hoped that no one would doubt "the reality of the ferment, or the intensity of the frustration lying behind it."[72] By the end of the decade, Schlesinger's attitude toward social unrest and protest had changed considerably from his views toward the Radical Right and Left during the halcyon days of the Kennedy administration. Yet even these changes were contained within a broader faith in the American political process born out of Schlesinger's abiding belief in the tides of national politics.

Schlesinger's responses to the challenge of violence were based on adjustments of the three components of his frame of acceptance. First, Schlesinger altered the definitions of liberalism and conservatism by locating political violence not at the fringes of American society but as part of the country's mixed "personality." The current propensity toward violence merely confirmed Reinhold Niebuhr's conception of man as part angel, part brute.[73] In his explanation of political violence, Schlesinger shifted focus from the divisions in American politics between conservatism and liberalism to the divisions between good (rationality) and evil (irrationality) in the American psyche.

Schlesinger's analysis proceeded in two steps. Initially, he established the claim that isolated acts of contemporary violence were part of a larger pattern of social misbehavior for which *all* are responsible. Schlesinger described the problem as "a contagion of political murder in the United States . . . unequalled today anywhere in the world."[74] The perpetrators of political assassination, terrorism, and violent protest were not merely "deranged and solitary individuals who are separate from the rest of us" but were individuals "stamped by our society with an instinct for hatred and a compulsion toward violence."[75] Schlesinger's claim was that everyone—even those who critiqued society—was implicated in the epidemic of violence. Those who used violence to protest violence were only "reinforcing the assault on civility and hastening the decomposition of the American social process."[76]

The next step in the two-step definitional adjustment was Schlesinger's claim that current political violence was part of a continuous tradition of American social practice. Schlesinger asserted that "the evil is in us, that it springs from some dark intolerable tension in our history and our institutions." Americans had always been "a violent people with a violent history."[77] An "impulse to destroy" and an "impulse to create" coexisted in the nation's consciousness as the result of "the mixed nature of our historical inheritance."[78]

To prove this claim, Schlesinger again turned to examples from America's past. "Self-knowledge is the indispensable prelude to self-control," Schlesinger wrote, "and self-knowledge, for a nation as well as for an individual, begins with history."[79] Schlesinger cited the experience of slavery as "a primal curse on our nation—a curse which still shadows our life."[80] While "the insensate bloodshed of the Civil War" temporarily "exhausted the national capacity for violence and left the nation emotionally and psychologically spent," the "propensity toward violence" remained "buried deep" in the nation—"in its customs, its institutions, and its psyche."[81] Now in the 1960s, violence had once more "seeped into the bloodstream of our national life."[82]

It is crucial to note that Schlesinger attributed the "downward spiral of social decomposition and moral degradation" in American society neither to frustrations of excluded groups concerning broken promises of liberal rhetoric nor to inherent evils of a capitalistic economic system. "We cannot escape that easily," he wrote. "It is not just that we were a frontier society or have become an industrial society or are a racist or capitalist society; it is something more specific than that."[83] Instead, Schlesinger adjusted his key term of "struggle" from a struggle between capitalism, with its twin political philosophies of liberalism and conservatism, and communism (the battle in the late 1940s and 1950s), to a struggle between rationality and violence (the new battle of the late 1960s and 1970s). The best way to subdue our "impulse of destruction" was to "face up to the schism in our national tradition," the schism between our "national instincts for aggression and destruction" and our "national capacity for civility and idealism."[84]

Adjusting the definitions of conservatism and liberalism while avoiding a systemic critique of capitalism allowed Schlesinger to appeal, at least implicitly, to both conservative and liberal audiences. Conservatives could support the implicit call for order, and liberals could support the implicit call for reform, in Schlesinger's analysis.

Next, Schlesinger turned to the logic of the political cycle. Rather than admit the inaccuracy of his predictions of progressive triumphs in the 1960s, Schlesinger chose to adjust his cyclical theory of American politics as a predictive mechanism to include an additional mechanism for causal explanation of the contemporary resurgence of political violence in America. While turbulent times of the past—with the exception of the Civil War—had fortunately tended to stay "within the fabric civility," the latest contagion of violence and protest in the United States had been triggered by a new development in the scene of American life.[85] Schlesinger identified this new development as "the accelerating velocity of history," defined as "the incessant and irreversible increase in the rate of social change."[86]

Schlesinger cited three ways in which the increasing velocity of history "dominates all aspects of contemporary life." First, it was "responsible for the unprecedented instability of the world" because science and technology had so altered the environment that "familiar landmarks and guideposts that had stabilized life" had disappeared. Second, it created "anxiety for the individual" because of the capacity of "the great organizations" of modern society to depersonalize and dehumanize. Third, it fostered feelings of disillusionment and powerlessness due to enhanced "electronic informational systems and electronic mechanisms of control," such as mass media, that instilled habits of instant gratification that could not be satisfied within conventional institutions.[87]

Together, these three factors had debilitated political life to the point that "the process [of technological change] was outstripping man's capacity to govern himself" and was the chief cause of the contemporary "crisis of confidence" that bred frustration and violence. The "acceleration in the velocity of history" was "plainly the dominating fact of our age," Schlesinger wrote in 1971, locking us all "into a life of permanent instability" and "political disorder" for a long time to come.[88]

For Schlesinger, two particularly violent manifestations of the accelerating velocity of history were responsible for the current surge of political upheaval and irrationality in the United States. The first manifestation was war. The fact that America had "been at war more or less continuously for a generation," most recently in Southeast Asia, had accustomed people to killing through legally sanctioned violence. The second manifestation was violence in the mass media. The rapid distribution and increased availability of violent films and television shows reinforced "aggressive and destructive impulses" and taught "the morality as well as the methods of violence."[89]

The absurdity of constant warfare and the pervasiveness of media violence contributed to "a growing sense of the dissociation between ideas and power" in society. The apparent substitution of violence for reason in more and more areas of society served to "heighten the impression of a world out of human control" and to encourage frustrated individuals to attack the rigidity of American customs and institutions through irrational and extralegal means.[90]

In his discussion of the connections between accelerating technological change and political violence, Schlesinger stopped short of arguing that the entire concept of technology as a positive value should be questioned. "It is not because of the character of the economic system" that more and more groups felt denied political participation and access to power in a technologized America. Instead, it was just that "the revolutions wrought by science and technology have gone farther here than anywhere else." American society was experiencing not the inevitable breakdown of a capitalist political economy but merely a "crisis of modernity" that would affect every nation that reached a comparable stage of development.[91] "The current American turmoil," Schlesinger concluded, "is much less the proof of decay than the price of progress."[92]

Throughout the examination of causes of the crisis of confidence, Schlesinger remained grimly optimistic about the capacity of a liberal capitalist democracy "to absorb, digest, and control the consequences of accelerated technological change."[93] "I do not accept the thesis of the inexorable decline of America," he wrote in 1970. ". . . the turmoil, confusion, even the violence may well be the birth pangs of a new epoch in the history of man."[94]

By returning to an epochal conception of historical progress, Schlesinger was able to uphold the presumption that change was good, a presumption central to his frame of acceptance. Schlesinger concluded one of his discussions of the velocity of history by quoting Ralph Waldo Emerson's optimistic belief in transcendence over crises: "If there is any period one would desire to be born in—is it not the era of revolution when the old and the new stand side by side and admit of being compared; when all the energies of man are searched by fear and hope; when the historic glories of the old can be compensated by the rich possibilities of the new era? This time like all times is a very good one if one but knows what to do with it."[95] Thus Schlesinger attempted to transcend the crisis of confidence by pronouncing the times to be promising and the problems to be "new and exhilarating, if remarkably difficult . . . for the boundless energies of American society."[96] Schlesinger's social critique was again contained within a rhetorical trajectory shaped by the tides of national politics.

Finally, Schlesinger addressed the issue of liberal leadership.

Rather than acquiescing to the growing belief that politics was irremediably corrupt and heroism a thing of the past, Schlesinger strongly reaffirmed the need for heroic political solutions to contemporary social problems. For Schlesinger, politics, while it could not "do everything to improve the state of man," was necessary to "create conditions that restrain and temper the forces of inhumanity and chaos."[97] The alternative to the existing political process was anarchy and totalitarianism. "Our process, with all its defects," said Schlesinger in a 1968 speech, "is a process of change—peaceful change—on which all decency and rationality depend."[98]

If the democratic process was to remain the paramount medium of social change in America, heroic leadership would have to arise as a salvation device to deliver that process from the forces of cynicism and violence.[99] Schlesinger's case for heroic leadership rested once again on arguments from history. In the past, Schlesinger asserted, it had been "our great leaders—Lincoln most of all" who "perceived both the destructive instinct" of the American people and "the moral necessity of transcending destruction if we are going to have any sort of rational and decent society."[100]

In making the case for heroic leadership, Schlesinger also returned to the functional and moral justification for such leadership. The functional necessity of heroic leadership was an extension of the long-standing need to *manage interests*. The interest groups that Schlesinger had so confidently believed to be part of the liberal coalition—the young, racial minorities, the poor and powerless, and the well educated—had become increasingly disaffected with the political process. Some had come to believe that political participation was beyond their reach, while others had come to believe that political participation constituted a "sell-out" to the "establishment." By 1968, Schlesinger realized that the nation was in a state of "incipient fragmentation" due to strains between races, generations, and classes. "The urgent problem of our politics," Schlesinger wrote in 1969, "is to give the presently alienated groups a feeling of membership in the national process—to include all Americans in a genuine commonwealth of reason, and opportunity."[101]

In order to draw the excluded and estranged groups back into our national life, Schlesinger continued, a "strong and purposeful Presidency" headed by a leader with the "creative political genius of the order of Jackson, Lincoln, and Roosevelt" was required.[102] Schlesinger maintained the belief that the disaffected groups in general "would prefer to preserve the process of peaceful change" and would "respond to leadership which seeks to fulfill their objectives within that process."[103] Only a leader with "the personal power to rally disparate groups behind rational policies" could manage the conflict between ever more divisive interests in American society.[104]

The moral necessity for heroic leadership was an extension of a long-standing need to *compel sacrifice*. In a time when the consensus in support of economic growth and change through democratic processes was being challenged by acts of irrationality and violence, heroic leadership was required to restore "the moral energy of American politics" and to incorporate "the grave forbodings and desperate urgencies of our time into the democratic process." Restoring faith in democratic institutions required leadership with the capacity for "intense personal identification with the victims and casualties of American society," the charisma to challenge individuals to give of themselves "on behalf of the alienated groups," and the creative relationship to the problems of the time to find innovative ways to enhance direct participation by the powerless.[105]

Schlesinger provided no concrete plan for "reaching across the barriers in our land which separate some of us from others of us" other than a vague endorsement of the direct community-action projects tried experimentally in Johnson's Great Society.[106] Again in keeping with the rhetorical trajectory, Schlesinger ultimately placed his hope in leaders who would "respect human reason and human dignity" and reject inbred impulses to violence, intolerance, or absolutism.[107] "The way to our salvation," concluded Schlesinger in 1969, was for each individual to engage in heroic acts of self-sacrifice to support the liberal causes of rationality and fairness in the face of violence and cynicism.[108]

In his call for heroic leadership, Schlesinger sharply attacked what he called the New Left for abandoning liberal faith in democracy for the "noxious rubbish" of Marcusian theories of repressive tolerance and the "fakery and fallacy" of political existentialism. The historian viewed Marcusian and existentialist strains of critique with contempt. He accused Marcusian critique of basing its hopes for liberation from the "one-dimensional society" on the erroneous utopian belief in the perfectibility of human consciousness. He charged existentialist critique with having elevated violence from a means of revolutionary change to an end in itself. Both "new creeds" constituted a dangerous "assault on rationality in politics."[109]

While critiquing strategies of the New Left, Schlesinger admitted that "pragmatic insurgencies . . . related to specific issues and specific injustices" (such as the civil rights movement) represented "a desperately needed pressure against the established complacencies of a self-righteous nation." But while understanding that "a limited amount of violence may stimulate the process of democratic change," Schlesinger warned that the Left's beliefs in its own doctrinal infallibility and the legitimacy of violence as a political end were creating "an atmosphere which destroys the process of democracy itself," an atmosphere that benefited only "those who use violence best," the political far Right.[110]

The Center Cannot Hold

In his 1968 speech following the shooting of Robert Kennedy, Schlesinger summed up the dissociation between his frame of acceptance and the radical New Left with the following peroration: "Let us strike out against the concrete and particular evils of our time. But let us not yield to that awful despair which dissolves all distinctions in thought and reason and hurtles us on to the politics of apocalypse. In the long run, any sane society must rest on freedom and reason. If we abandon this, we abandon everything."[111]

In his response to the problems of Vietnam and violence, Schlesinger evidenced his faith that ideas could be given power through state action without corrupting those ideas. In clinging to his conventional liberal frame of acceptance, Schlesinger avoided a systemic repudiation of capitalism, technology, and the political process that characterized the emerging radical critique of American society. Both Schlesinger's diagnoses of the problems and his prescriptions for solving them were contained within and constrained by a larger symbolic trajectory characterized by an abiding faith in reason, gradualism, and the political process.

Yet, by the early 1970s, more and more former members of the liberal coalition became convinced that conventional spheres of social action were inherently corrupt. Conventional liberalism was becoming less and less able to maintain any type of consensus over either means or ends.[112] Nuechterlein writes that Schlesinger and other moderate liberals may have "underestimated the degree to which a common radical sensibility had come to pervade the American left" during these turbulent years.[113]

By 1971, Schlesinger himself felt the turning away from politics occurring in the country. "An eerie quiet hangs over American politics today," he wrote. More and more former "adherents of the New Left" were "celebrating the softer line" of political thought embodied in the ecology, back-to-nature, and self-help movements. In a particularly prescient moment of reflection, Schlesinger asserted that "American politics these days . . . tends to project itself in terms of culture rather than of policy—in a conflict less of programs and measures than, in the current jargon, of 'life-styles.'" While convinced that the growing self-absorption in American society was a "transient" phase, Schlesinger did admit that the "clash of values" in the next few years would "remain largely beyond the reach both of party politics and of public policy."[114]

In a chilling bit of social commentary, Arthur Schlesinger, Jr., foreshadowed the growing obsolescence of his liberal frame of acceptance, which relied increasingly on heroic management of interests within an evaporating New Deal consensus and on heroic calls for sacrifice in a time in which America was becoming what some would label "the culture of narcissism."[115]

7

Liberalism in Retreat, 1972–1993

In the years since 1970, Arthur M. Schlesinger, Jr., has remained active as both historian and political advocate. In *The Imperial Presidency* (1973), Schlesinger examined both the constitutional origins of and growth in presidential power. While asserting that presidential power in foreign affairs had grown dangerously unchecked, culminating in the tragedy of the Vietnam war and the abuses of Watergate, Schlesinger maintained that a chief executive needed to take an active role in shaping a public consensus in support of a progressive domestic policy agenda.[1] Five years later, Schlesinger completed *Robert F. Kennedy and His Times* (1978), a biographical account of a political leader and close friend whom Schlesinger believed had embodied the consciousness and unfulfilled possibilities of the 1960s.[2] The year 1986 saw the publication of *The Cycles of American History*, a group of essays characterized by Schlesinger as "a historian's reflection on the past and the future of the American experiment."[3]

The historian also continued to participate in defining and defending American liberalism. In presidential politics, Schlesinger supported George McGovern in his failed effort in 1972 to wrest the White House from Richard Nixon.[4] Jimmy Carter's election in 1976 did not represent a liberal triumph for Schlesinger but instead meant that the White House was occupied by a conservative Democrat whom Schlesinger would characterize as another Grover Cleveland.[5] Schlesinger supported Sen. Edward Kennedy's unsuccessful bid to take the Democratic party presidential nomination away from Carter in 1980.

Schlesinger continued to draw upon his interpretation of American history as a basis for his advocacy of liberal principles and political candidates.[6] Yet by the late 1970s and early 1980s, his conventional liberal perspective was coming under increasing attack from conservatives and fellow liberals. The New Deal liberal approach was seen as no longer practical in an age of scarcity. In 1980, Morton Kondracke complained that liberal Democrats were "philosophically worn out, and the country seems to know it."[7] In an article entitled "End of the Democratic Era," Allan Mayer reported that the liberal ideals embodied in "the party of Jefferson, Jackson, and Franklin Roosevelt finds itself groping desperately for a modern identity, a new political vision that will restore its flagging spirit and rally its demoralized troops."[8] Edward Kennedy's economic keynote address at the 1980 Democratic National Convention, a speech Schlesinger undoubtedly applauded, was quickly labeled an anachronism, a last hurrah for traditional liberalism.[9] Other politicians and writers hailed 1980 as the beginning of a new conservative era in American life.[10] The decade of the 1980s saw the ascension of Ronald Reagan, a conservative president, and the erosion of public faith in liberal policies and politicians.

During the 1980s, even the word "liberal" itself took on increasingly negative associations for many Americans, becoming what Richard Weaver has called a "devil term," a "prime repellant" in the lexicon of American political discourse.[11] During the Reagan era in American politics, traditional liberals such as Arthur Schlesinger, Jr., have been faced with the ultimate threat to their ideological perspective: the threat of delegitimation.

In response to ongoing attacks against liberalism, Schlesinger has stayed the symbolic course, continuing to argue along the rhetorical trajectory generated by the tides of national politics in order to explain issues and problems and to predict future triumphs. Schlesinger's recent campaign in defense of liberalism has illustrated both the resilience and the limitations of his frame of acceptance.

The Threat of Delegitimation

Delegitimation involves the withdrawal of public and institutional support from individuals or groups with influence or authority in a community. It means the loss of communal presumptions favoring certain values, ideas, or institutions. Drawing upon the work of Weber, Parsons, and Habermas, Robert Francesconi defines legitimacy as "an on-going process of reason giving, actual and potential, which forms the basis of the right to exercise authority as well as the willingness to defer to authority."[12] In democratic societies, those who are in power must engage in reasoned rhetorical action in order to justify decisions and remain in power.

Legitimacy is maintained in two ways: by appeal to communal values and by demonstration of effectiveness in governance.[13] In each case, political leaders must devise rhetorical strategies to convince constituents that their actions are consistent with the social order, or are producing tangible benefits for the community, or both. When members of the community no longer believe that their political leadership or institutions are upholding appropriate values or are working to solve problems, they lose faith in those leaders and institutions, and a "legitimation crisis" may ensue.[14]

Public trust in both the values and effectiveness of liberal policies and politicians has rapidly diminished in the past two decades as a result of resource scarcities, uncertainty among liberals themselves, and conservative labeling. These related rhetorical problems have gravely threatened the legitimacy of Schlesinger's traditional liberal perspective.

Recognition of Resource Limits

During the 1950s, Schlesinger turned away from a structural critique of American business when he shifted the focus of his liberal agenda from quantitative to qualitative issues. Schlesinger assumed that the problems of sustaining economic growth had essentially been solved and that general prosperity plus some government intervention into the economy would solve problems of distribution. Liberalism was then to focus on concerns such as promoting civil rights and preserving individuality in a mass society.

Continued growth had become an essential feature of the liberal philosophy after World War II. Weiler writes that just as postwar capitalism required "the possibility of infinitely expanding markets and infinitely available resources," conventional postwar liberalism required "the possibility of constantly increasing standards of living" in order to avoid conflicts between goals of economic prosperity and social equality.[15]

Schlesinger's faith in the engine of economic growth was shared by mainstream conservatives and liberals alike well into the 1970s. Morris Udall summarized the consensus thinking about America's economic potential during the period from 1945 to the early 1970s: "Whatever was technically feasible would (we believed) ultimately be economically affordable; because of cheap energy, unlimited economic expansion and global industrialization seemed to be rational goals."[16] As America entered the 1970s, Shactman argues, "progress" as defined in terms of gross national product continued to be "an idea central to the American identity."[17]

According to Shactman, however, "profound changes close to the heart of modern civilization" began to occur in the 1970s as the result of "realizations about the limits of machinery, the limits of economic growth, and the limits of man imposed by the environment."[18] Americans were bombarded with events and trends that created a "psychological sense of sudden boundaries" that demanded "insistent revisions in the creed" of unlimited progress. On all fronts, the liberal ideal of progress "collided with the philosophy of limits."[19]

The liberal ideal of progress through unlimited growth was challenged on a number of fronts. Growing technological threats to human and social health from pollution and other consumer hazards made more Americans aware of the limits of technology. During the 1970s, the Arab oil embargo and subsequent increases in energy prices and supply vulnerability beckoned the coming limits of natural resources. The emergence of stagflation (simultaneously high rates of unemployment and inflation) illustrated the limits of managing a "mixed economy" through conventional fiscal and monetary policy. The constitutional crisis of Watergate confronted American society with the limits of centralized political power. And growing budget deficits placed fiscal and political limits on traditionally liberal governmental remedies to economic and social problems.[20]

With the emerging societal realization of limits, values once held in common in American society began to be questioned. Schlesinger's conception of liberalism as pragmatic and nonideological was challenged. The economic turmoil of the 1970s and the growing belief in a "zero-sum" society politicized the conflict between the liberal goals of general economic health and social equality and led the public to distrust the possibilities of affirmative government intervention. Weiler explains that "as America entered the 1970s, a time of generally declining economic expectations, serving the economic interests of minorities looked increasingly like a net loss for the majority." Critics of traditional liberal programs "used growing public opposition to social welfare spending to huge advantage" and were able to claim that the social welfare programs of the New Deal–Great Society variety were not only not "an affordable luxury in our present difficulties" but "a cause of those difficulties in the first place." The belief held by Schlesinger and other liberals that government could successfully intervene on behalf of disadvantaged groups was seen less as a practical possibility and more as an ideological obsession.[21]

Liberal Uncertainty and the Rise of "Neoliberalism"

The tumultuous events occurring in America and around the world during the 1960s and 1970s that "skewed the American sense of proportion" had a particularly disturbing impact on liberal politics.[22] Liberalism was seen as the major contributor to the problems of economic stagnation and social unrest plaguing the country. In 1977, James Nuechterlein observed that "virtually every report on the national condition includes the suggestion that the crisis of American society relates in some way, indicative if not causative, to a crisis in American liberalism." Nuechterlein also noted that a significant portion of the critique of liberalism was coming from the "mood of uncertainty" among liberals themselves. "A good deal of contemporary liberal comment," he concluded, "begins with the assumption that 'we have failed.'"[23]

During the course of the 1980 presidential campaign, in which Jimmy Carter survived the challenge from within his own party from traditional liberal Edward Kennedy only to lose in the general election to conservative Ronald Reagan, Democrats began to search for alternatives to the New Deal–style liberal message. Senator Paul Tsongas of Massachusetts summarized the plight of conventional liberal thought: "We have gone a long way on the momentum of another era, and the engine is running down. There is a very keen sense that we better come up with something new or we are just not going to survive."[24]

During the 1980s, "neoliberalism" emerged as a rival political philosophy with rhetorical strategies "designed to succeed in a society that has accepted the zero-sum assumption" of limited growth. Neoliberals attempted to distinguish themselves from traditional liberalism by stressing nonideological, innovative, and entrepreneurial themes while distancing themselves from traditional liberal notions of heroic government intervention into the political economy.[25] While neoliberals took John F. Kennedy for a role model, for them he represented an exemplar of innovative management rather than of heroic leadership. Instead of advocating more government spending to solve social ills, they stressed the issue of fiscal restraint and the attractive (though elusive) value of "fairness."[26]

Neoliberalism formed the ideological basis for the candidacy of Colorado senator Gary Hart for the Democratic presidential nomination in 1984. In the race against favored opponent Walter Mondale, Hart was characterized as "the candidate of 'new ideas,' the spokesman for a 'new generation' of Democrats who say that the New Deal has run its course."[27] According to Hart, domestic and foreign policy problems facing the nation were greatly magnified by the existence of a "vacuum of ideas and leadership" among both conservatives *and* liberals. Party leaders were obsessed with outmoded policies that "reopen[ed] all the old public debates and divisions of the past."[28] When dealing with domestic problems, Republicans responded with insensitivity and budget cutting, while Democrats too often promised to "adopt every new program on every interest agenda" and to "spend tens of billions of dollars we don't have."[29]

The real crisis of the times, Hart concluded, was that "the old, established leaders" of conventional conservatism and liberalism failed to realize that "neither the policies of the 1950s nor the policies of the 1960s will serve us in the 1980s."[30] A liberalism of "new ideas" had to be based on idealistic loyalty to "the common good" and "the national interest" in order to conquer "greed, self-interest, and division."[31]

The rejection of traditional liberalism was extended further in the presidential campaign of Michael Dukakis, who secured the Democratic party's nomination and ran against Vice President George Bush in 1988. Dukakis found considerable success in the Democratic primaries running on the neoliberal themes of fiscal responsibility and leadership through effective management. In his speech accepting the nomination, Dukakis stated that "this election is not about ideology. It's about competence." He added that "it's not about meaningless labels" such as liberal or conservative. "It's about American values. Old-fashioned values like accountability and responsibility and respect for the truth."[32] The word "liberal," according to political reporter Fred Barnes, "was all but banned from the Democratic convention."[33]

For most of the fall campaign against George Bush, Dukakis denied that he belonged in the liberal tradition. He insisted that the "L-word" in his candidacy was not "liberal, but leadership."[34] In a *Nightline* interview on October 25, when Ted Koppel asked him to define the word "liberal," Dukakis responded, "Well, I think all of us have combinations of liberal and conservative about us, Ted. I'm not a liberal."[35] Finally, on October 30, a week before the election, Dukakis shifted to embrace liberalism. "I'm a liberal in the tradition of Franklin Roosevelt and Harry Truman and John Kennedy," he told an audience in Fresno, California. Those Democratic presidents were great because they "were on the side of average families."[36] But this move occurred too late to change the outcome of the election.

George Bush defeated Michael Dukakis and succeeded Ronald Reagan in the White House. As the 1980s ended, liberalism seemed to be in full retreat.

Conservative Labeling

During the 1980s, Ronald Reagan attempted to reshape the American political landscape with his call to get government "off the backs" of the American people.[37] While the size of government actually increased during his two administrations, writes public opinion expert William Schneider, President Reagan was able to "create a powerful political coalition that brings together a variety of interests united by one thing—a distaste for big government." This coalition represented a direct contrast to the traditional liberal coalition that had been in place for fifty years. While "FDR brought together a coalition of interests who wanted something from government," the Reagan coalition "is its mirror image—groups that want less from government." This new coalition, whose key constituency was middle-class voters who want low taxes, had been held together during the 1980s by "the perception of a common threat, namely, liberalism." What "Reagan voters fear," concludes Schneider, is "that liberals will regain control of the federal government and use it, as they did in the past, to carry out an agenda that includes taxes, regulations, social reforms, and anti-military policies."[38]

Whatever its policy failings, the Reagan administration was somewhat successful during the 1980s in redefining liberalism and the Democrats as an ideology and a political party characterized by fiscal irresponsibility and moral lassitude. While liberals struggled to define themselves, Reagan conservatives took the initiative and transformed the term "liberal" into a negative label, a devil term.[39] "In the minds of too many voters," Walter Shapiro wrote after the 1988 election, "the Democrats are still the party of militant blacks, meddlesome social workers, uppity feminists, and draft-card-burning protesters."[40] Even as Americans continued to enjoy the benefits of the liberal welfare state, they associated liberalism with bad government.[41]

The transformation of "liberal" into a devil term was best illustrated during the 1988 presidential campaign, as Ronald Reagan stumped the country on behalf of Republican nominee George Bush. Reagan saw Democrat Michael Dukakis's claim that the campaign was about competence, not ideology, as a sign that the Democrats were trying to hide their true beliefs. The Democrats were "really telegraphing their greatest weakness—the very thing that worries them and their advisers the most," which was "their liberal record" in Congress.[42] "The masquerade is over," Reagan told his audience in New Orleans at the beginning of the Republican National Convention. "The stealth candidacy has to come out from cover."[43] Reagan claimed that the Democratic party that he had "once pledged loyalty to" had changed. "A party that once stood for the broad interests of America's working men and women has become a party fixated on the narrow agenda of liberal elites and special interest groups."[44] "I didn't leave my party," Reagan told an audience in Little Rock, "my party left me. It left me when it went left."[45]

Reagan drew sharp contrasts between liberalism and his own sense of conservatism. The president characterized the choice to be made in the upcoming election as "just as clear as it was in 1980 and 1984: a choice between, on the one hand, the policies of limited government, economic growth, a strong defense, and a firm foreign policy, and, on the other hand, policies of tax and spend, economic stagnation, international weakness and accommodation, and always, always, always, blame America first."[46] Reagan associated liberalism with "opposition to voluntary prayer in school, support for gun control," "left-wing judges appointed in a state like Massachusetts," and "a weak-kneed defense policy that only McGovern could love."[47] In contrast, conservatives "always, always" believed in and stood for "'I pledge allegiance to the flag of the United States.'"[48]

By defining Michael Dukakis as a typical liberal who was weak on defense, permissive in social policy, and irresponsible on economics, Reagan attempted to push liberalism to the extreme left of the political spectrum. Throughout the campaign, he asserted that "the choice this year is between the policies of liberalism or the policies of America's political mainstream."[49] "Wasn't George Bush right," Reagan told a crowd in Raleigh, North Carolina, "when he said that the opposition is over there in left field, they're out of the mainstream of American politics, and their policies can only be described by the dreaded 'L' word: liberal, liberal, liberal!"[50] By characterizing "liberal" as "the dreaded 'L' word," Reagan explicitly attempted to demonize the term and to delegitimize what it stood for.

The repeated negative references to liberalism during the fall campaign led a group of political activists and academicians, including Arthur Schlesinger, Jr., to publish a one-page advertisement in the *New York Times* that included a reaffirmation of liberal philosophy. The group expressed concern that the liberal principles of freedom, tolerance, and protection of individual rights were now being attacked by "extremists on the right and left" who have long viewed "liberalism as their greatest enemy." The group stated its goal to "reaffirm America's liberal tradition," which included the "institutional defense of decency," the fight for "freedom of individuals to attain their fullest development," and the opposition to "tyranny in all forms, past and present."[51] To Schlesinger and other liberals, the rhetorical move made by the Bush campaign to make "liberal" an explicit devil term represented the culmination of more than a decade of conservative attacks on the legitimacy of liberal principles and policies.

In Defense of Liberalism

The failure of Sen. Edward Kennedy's 1980 campaign for president and the growing chorus of attacks against traditional liberalism have led Schlesinger once more into battle in defense of his liberal perspective. Since the late 1970s, Schlesinger has written a number of editorials and popular magazine articles in an attempt to regain a sense of legitimacy for his liberal frame of acceptance.

Two items have been on Schlesinger's most recent rhetorical agenda. First, he has offered an interpretation of recent election results in order to hearten traditional liberals and refute self-congratulatory conservative and neoliberal rhetoric. Second, he has tried to reaffirm liberal values in order to maintain the faith of remaining members of the traditional liberal coalition and to attract supporters from the ranks of the uncommitted American populace.

To accomplish these goals, Schlesinger once again has adjusted all three components of his frame of acceptance to transcend the rhetorical difficulties of the times. As in other battles, Schlesinger has applied his understanding of American history to buttress his political arguments. And with the exception of a few new turns, his most recent defense of liberalism has followed a similar rhetorical path to the one he began to chart during the 1950s and has followed ever since.

Adjusting Definitions of Liberal and Conservative

Schlesinger has defended his perspective in part by returning to definitions, trying to sharpen the ideological differences between conservatism and liberalism in American politics. He began this process by reminding his audience about the true interests and values of Reaganite conservatives. Conservatives, he explained in 1981, are "sworn to two basic propositions: that government is the root of all evil, and that once we get government off our backs, our problems will solve themselves."[52] By 1988, Schlesinger observed that the Republican party under Ronald Reagan "had dedicated itself to the celebration of unfettered private enterprise as the universal panacea," believing that the "free market" was not only "a useful instrument but a mystical consecration." Unfortunately, he continued, "the Reaganite faith in free markets has tripled the national debt, transformed the United States from the world's largest creditor into the world's largest debtor, produced the largest peacetime deficits in our history, hastened the export of American jobs to foreign shores, speeded a transfer of income from the poor to the rich, increased disparities of power and opportunity in our society, and multiplied the number of Americans living in poverty."[53] The problems George Bush inherited from the Reagan administration, Schlesinger concluded in 1989, "are problems that will not solve themselves, that free markets will not solve, and that will require the intervention of government for solution."[54]

It is important to note that during the 1980s, Schlesinger chose in his definition of conservatism to reemphasize the issue of economic class, an issue that he had moved to the background in the late 1950s. The historian made this move by again referring to his view of the past. "The liberal remaking of America," he wrote in 1988, "was rooted in the understanding, firmly grounded in our history, that the rich always rule in their own interest."[55] To Schlesinger, Reagan's belief in the free market and attacks on affirmative government reflected a long-standing conservative bias in favor of big business. "For as Theodore Roosevelt perfectly understood at the turn of the century," the historian remarked, "taking government off the people's backs means putting business on the people's backs."[56] Schlesinger quoted nineteenth-century writer and philosopher Orestes Brownson, who claimed that "the men of wealth, the business men, manufacturers and merchants, bankers and brokers, are the men who exert the worst influence on government in every country. . . . They act on the beautiful maxim, 'Let the government take care of the rich, and the rich will take care of the poor,' instead of the far safer maxim, 'Let government take care of the weak, the strong can take care of themselves.'"[57]

An example of conservative class bias was the attempt by the Reagan administration to implement supply-side economics. "According to this policy," Schlesinger explained in 1981, "the business of tax policy is to allocate more money to the rich in the expectation that they will use it to produce jobs and income for the rest of us." In actuality, Reagan succeeded in "cutting taxes for the rich and social programs for the poor."[58] By 1988, conservative economic policies had resulted in "the harsh fact that the gap between rich and poor is greater today than it has been at any time since the Census Bureau started collecting data on the subject."[59] In addition, reducing economic regulation unleashed "the culture of greed" and self-interest during the 1980s, with "graft, corruption, and scandal" as the result of "the ethos of Reaganism."[60]

Perhaps the greatest tragedy of the present conservative era was that the Reagan administration's policies of increased defense spending and tax cuts for the rich produced such large budget deficits that little money was now available for affirmative government programs that could redress economic deprivation. By "contriving unprecedented budget deficits," Schlesinger asserted in 1986, Reagan "has denied liberalism flexible use of social spending for a while to come." Schlesinger thus attributed much of the growth in the federal deficit not to expanding liberal entitlement programs but to Reagan's attempt "to redraw the political map of the republic."[61]

In addition to sharpening his definition of conservatism, Schlesinger has tried to reestablish a favorable definition of liberalism and liberal values. The historian has again resorted to the strategy of dissociation concerning the term "liberal" in order to reassert traditional distinctions between political philosophies. In the context of the current political debate, he has hoped to reestablish the presumptive value of liberalism as the product and heritage of the New Deal.

Schlesinger has attempted two dissociations. First, Schlesinger has dissociated the term "liberal" into an unfavorable depiction of neoliberals and the favorable depiction of a true liberal. "Neoliberals" were not liberal in the traditional sense but were just a group of "frightened rabbits" who drew the wrong conclusion from the 1980 election that "people wanted a counter-revolution against the New Deal."[62] The essence of neoliberalism, asserted the historian in 1982, rested in the vociferous *rejection* "of the old Democratic commitment to national government as a means of attacking national problems."[63] To Schlesinger, neoliberals were in fact conservatives!

Neoliberals who claimed John F. Kennedy as their ideological predecessor were misreading history, Schlesinger argued, because they rejected Kennedy's views "on the crucial issue, which is government."[64] The true "spiritual father" of neoliberalism was President Jimmy Carter, who committed the heresy of admitting in his 1978 State of the Union message that "government cannot solve our problems."[65] Carter sinned by catering to popular opinion, which consisted in the late 1970s of "cheap prejudice against government action." To adopt Carter's neoliberal view of limited government,

Schlesinger claimed in 1980, "is to deny the heritage of the modern Democratic Party."[66] Months after Carter's defeat, Schlesinger cited the paucity of neoliberal domestic proposals as proof that the political position "is remarkably void of fresh thoughts."[67]

The "true liberal," on the other hand, quickly discerned that the 1980 election represented the repudiation not of liberalism but of an incompetent president.[68] Consequently, the 1980 election of Ronald Reagan was hardly an ideological referendum. In addition, the true liberal realized that liberalism will never successfully outflank conservatism on the Right.[69] Instead, what should be defended was the liberal tradition dating back in time from Andrew Jackson to John Kennedy. Schlesinger has reestablished Kennedy as the model *traditional* liberal, who believed "in the use of the federal government as a means of promoting the public welfare."[70] True liberals should not abandon faith in affirmative government. To abandon the means of liberalism, Schlesinger concluded in 1982, would be to abandon the ends of liberalism.[71]

In response to recent conservative attempts to vilify the term "liberal," Schlesinger has attempted a second dissociation. He has tried to distinguish between the false liberalism portrayed by conservatives and an authentic liberalism historically grounded in the values of Jackson, Roosevelt, and Kennedy. Liberals should "start by getting off the defensive about liberalism itself," Schlesinger urged in 1990. "To allow the foes of liberalism to define liberalism is political nonsense."[72] In 1988, conservatives had "distracted the electorate by putting across a caricature of liberalism and blaming liberals for everything that happened to the republic from 1961 till Ronald Reagan rode his white horse into Washington in 1981."[73]

Once again, the opponents of liberalism had misinterpreted the past. Reaganites tried "to identify liberalism with the hippie radicalism of the 1960s," explained the historian, when in fact "the attack on reason and the celebration of violence that streaked the later part of that decade was the antithesis of liberalism." Liberals should not now be blamed "for the illiberal left" of the past.[74] Conservative efforts to blame recent government failures on liberalism were also misplaced, Schlesinger reasoned, because America had not had a truly liberal national leader since 1966 when President Johnson's Great Society "vanished into the Vietnam quagmire." Schlesinger viewed Presidents Nixon, Ford, Carter, and Reagan all as conservative critics of affirmative government. "We have not had a liberal administration for more than 20 years," the historian asserted.[75]

Efforts by conservatives to draw caricatures of liberalism had "nothing to do with what Roosevelt and Truman, Kennedy and

Johnson were all about—and what Michael Dukakis is all about today," the historian continued in 1988. What liberalism truly means is a commitment to "economic opportunity, social justice, civil freedom."[76] What authentic liberals continue to believe is that today's problems must be addressed by "the resources of affirmative government" in order to correct the inequitable distribution of resources in our society.[77]

Schlesinger has admitted that the New Deal cannot be reinstated, that liberals must seek new solutions to contemporary problems. He wrote in 1990 that "the specific experience of the liberal past will be of only limited benefit in finding remedies for the future." Yet he has also insisted that "the spirit behind past policies abides and refreshes. The task which confronts us today is to apply the creativity of liberalism to the structural problems that are setting us on the course of national decline."[78]

Adjusting the Alternations Between Conservatism and Liberalism

Much as he did in the 1950s, Schlesinger has also applied his belief in the predictable alternation of liberal and conservative political epochs in his recent defense of liberalism. The historian has used his cyclical view of history both to account for conservative electoral successes during the Reagan years and to predict upcoming liberal victories in the ongoing struggle for political power in America.

Schlesinger's principal strategy has involved the adjustment of the endpoints of conservative and liberal eras in American history in order to forecast the coming of the next liberal phase. In 1980, Schlesinger believed that America was nearing the end of a conservative phase that had begun in the late 1960s. The decline of liberalism in the 1970s, he reasoned, was not caused by the realization of physical limits but was instead a *natural* part of the cycle of action and recuperation in American politics. After a season of activism in the early 1960s (spearheaded by Kennedy's New Frontier and Johnson's Great Society) that swung ominously out of control for a few violent years during the end of the decade, the American people longed for rest and recuperation. They found respite in the "me-decade" of the 1970s. Schlesinger then asserted that the time for a new public demand for liberal activism "is bound to come, and soon. Sometime in the 1980s, the dam will break, as it broke at the turn of the century, in the 1930s, and in the 1960s." "There will be a breakthrough into a new political epoch," he concluded, "a new conviction of social possibility, a new hunger for dynamism, innovation, crusading, new efforts to redeem the promise of American life."[79]

The historian interpreted the victory of Ronald Reagan in 1980 as merely a prolongation of the most recent conservative swing. Liberals could take heart that with Reagan in the White House, the failures of conservatism could be finally demonstrated to the American public. "At least we can have a full and fair test," Schlesinger concluded, "conducted without any easy alibis, of hallowed conservative positions." When Reaganomics failed, which Schlesinger believed was a certainty, Americans would turn once again to the liberal path.[80]

By the middle of the decade, Schlesinger was confronted with the fact that while Reaganomics may not have worked, Reagan was still going strong as president. The historian explained this development by once again adjusting the political cycle. In the title essay in *The Cycles of American History* (1986), Schlesinger claimed that Reagan's continuing popularity could be accounted for by the "continuing shift in national involvement, between public purpose and private interest" that had occurred throughout American history. By the 1970s, "Americans were once more, as they had been in the 1950s and 1920s, fed up with public action and disenchanted by its consequences. The compass needle now swung toward private interest and the fulfillment of self." This reaction had "reached its culmination in the age of Reagan in the 1980s."[81]

But conservatism would not triumph indefinitely in American politics. The logic of the political cycle dictated that "each phase runs its natural course," Schlesinger argued in 1987. "Problems neglected become acute, threaten to become unmanageable and demand remedy. People grow increasingly bored with selfish motives and vistas, increasingly wary of materialism and demand some larger meaning beyond themselves. They begin to ask not what their country can do for them, but what they can do for their country. This is what was happening at the end of the 1920s and the 1950s, and it is what is happening today."[82]

Schlesinger has maintained his belief in the empirical nature of his cyclical theory, which for him was confirmed with the election of John F. Kennedy back in 1960. In a clear indication of how he has been persuaded by his own view of history, Schlesinger confidently stated in 1987, "Success in prediction creates a certain presumption in favor of a hypothesis." Based on that confidence, Schlesinger forecasted that "the cyclical change now impends" in American political life. Shifting the starting point of the next phase, Schlesinger asserted that "the next phase of the cycle will not come full flood till the early 1990s. This means that the 1988 election will be a squeaker." "But, even if a Republican wins," he continued, "Reaganism is finished."[83]

While George Bush's victory over Michael Dukakis was "taken in some quarters as a refutation of the cyclical theory of American politics," Schlesinger wrote in 1989, even this disheartening result could be accounted for by his theory. Claiming that he had not guaranteed a liberal victory in 1988, Schlesinger compared the election "to a hypothetical Kennedy-Nixon contest that might have taken place exactly 30 years before, in 1958, rather than in 1960." He reasoned that "Nixon probably would have won in 1958; even 1960 was extremely close in the popular vote." The fact that Dukakis had done "considerably better that his party's nominees in 1984 and 1980" demonstrated to Schlesinger that "the national mood is changing" away from Reagan conservatism. And the Democrats, "if they keep the liberal faith," will be "the natural beneficiaries of the change."[84]

By the end of the 1980s, Schlesinger had stretched the time span of the latest political cycle from 1960 to the present in order to rationalize over twenty years of conservative dominance in presidential politics. Schlesinger accounted for this adjustment by emphasizing a new causal force behind the tides of American politics. Since 1900, he argued, America's political cycles have reflected not only swings in public attitudes or moods, but also the nature of our experiences in belonging to distinct generations with particular political interests. While he admitted in 1986 that "the division of people into generations seems arbitrary," he claimed that "epochal historical events establish boundaries between generations." Citing Karl Mannheim, Schlesinger reasoned that members of the same generation "occupy 'a common location in the historical dimension of a social process.'"[85]

Thus, the thirty-year duration of the current political cycle was due in part to the natural length of a generation. "There is nothing mystical about the thirty year cycle," he wrote in 1990. "Thirty years is the span of a generation. People tend to be formed politically by the ideals dominant in the years when they first come to political consciousness." During the twentieth century, each generation's liberal political leadership was influenced by a preceding generation. "Young people who grew up when Theodore Roosevelt and Woodrow Wilson were setting the nation's sights—Franklin Roosevelt, Eleanor Roosevelt, Harry Truman—reaffirmed the goals of their youth thirty years after in the New Deal and the Fair Deal. Young people who grew up when FDR was inspiring the country—John Kennedy, Lyndon Johnson, Hubert Humphrey, Robert Kennedy—

brought the New Deal up to date thirty years later in the New Frontier and the Great Society. In the same manner John F. Kennedy touched and formed a political generation in the 1960s."[86] This generational argument has led Schlesinger to conclude that "if the rhythm holds, the Kennedy generation's time is due in the 1990s—and Reagan's children will inaugurate a new conservative era about 2010."[87]

Adjusting the Need for Heroic Leadership

Finally, Schlesinger has reasserted the need for heroic liberal leadership by reassessing his prior belief in the "inevitability" of liberalism.[88] In 1986, he wrote that just as the cycle of American history "is not automatic, neither is it self-enforcing."[89] The swings from conservatism to liberalism that have characterized American history constitute "cycles of opportunity, not cycles of necessity. They do not dictate the future." What Schlesinger identified as the "coming phase" of liberalism in America "offers no more than an opportunity for new departures. What we do with it is up to us."[90]

Emphasizing that his cyclical view of history is suggestive rather than deterministic has allowed Schlesinger to restate his call for the emergence of liberal leaders to propel America into the next progressive political era. "It takes people to make the cycle work," he wrote in 1986. "Those who believe in public purpose must interpret events, press issues, and devise remedies." "As the national mood swings back and forth," he reiterated in 1990, new leaders tend to "arise and confront new possibilities." However, "what the leaders make of these possibilities depends on their own ideas, capacities, skills, visions."[91]

Schlesinger has also extended his functional and moral justifications for heroic leadership. Initially, Schlesinger has cited a functional need for liberal leaders to devise innovative and effective solutions to the many domestic problems plaguing the nation. In a democracy, Schlesinger wrote in 1990, "politics is about something more than the struggle for power or the manipulation of image. It is above all about the search for remedy. No amount of power and public relations will avail if, at the end of the day, policies do not work."[92] Our political leaders "must justify themselves by their effectiveness in tackling the problems of their time."[93]

Sadly, during the 1980s, neither conservative nor liberal policymakers had been able to ensure fairness and an equal chance for all to succeed in a world of limited resources.[94] Reaganomics fed the "devil-take-the-hindmost" tendencies of laissez-faire capitalism and caused much suffering among the poor.[95] New Deal Keynesian economics was inflationary and was becoming obsolete.[96] America's political leadership had "failed to convince a durable majority that one or another course will do the job" to cure the nation's economic ills.[97]

As usual, Schlesinger has been less specific in proposing liberal solutions than in listing social problems. "The national needs cry out" for liberal remedy, he asserted in 1990. Those needs include "investment in research and development and other means of increasing productivity; investment in education for a high-technology age; investment in the rehabilitation of our collapsing bridges and dams and roadways and waterways; investment in the protection of this once green planet against toxic wastes, acid rain, the depletion of the ozone layer, the greenhouse effect, and other environmental scourges; investment in the struggle for racial justice, in the rescue of our cities and in the redemption of the underclass; investment in the war against crime and the war on drugs."[98]

The historian has remained convinced that only liberal leaders with the creativity and willingness to take action could effectively address social problems such as affordable housing and crime because many of these concerns "will never be answered by analysis but only by experiment."[99] Referring again to America's liberal heritage, Schlesinger asserted that "our national tradition, after all, has been one of experiment." For Schlesinger, that tradition was embodied in President Franklin Roosevelt, who said in response to the Great Depression, " 'Take a method and try it. If it fails, admit it frankly and try another. But above all, try something.' "[100]

Schlesinger has also reemphasized another functional need for heroic liberal leadership: the need to manage interests. "The liberal movement," he admitted in 1990, "has shown a recent tendency to splinter into a variety of single-issue caucuses" and pressure groups. It was imperative for liberalism to "recapture its earlier meaning as primarily concerned with the expansion and redistribution of political and economic opportunity and not appear as a catch-all for a miscellany of cultural ideological demands." Liberal leaders "must regain a commanding national vision of the problems and prospects of the republic."[101] Only a leader with "both a conviction about the direction in which the republic must move and a capacity to convey his vision to the people" could persuade the diverse interests in American society that "the public interest is something greater than an aggregate of private claims." "People will accept painful policies," Schlesinger claimed, "so long as they perceive them as fair."[102]

Again, Schlesinger drew upon Franklin Roosevelt as the model for effective leadership. "Liberals might renew the idea of a 'concert of interests,'" the historian wrote in 1990, "so compellingly advanced by Franklin Roosevelt half a century ago." Quoting Roosevelt himself, Schlesinger continued, "'Each unit,' he said, 'must think of itself as part of a greater whole, one piece in a large design.'"[103] Only a leader who remained true to the liberal tradition of Roosevelt could generate the popular trust to transfer the pent-up energies of a nation ready for change into effective, planned management of interests.

In addition, Schlesinger has restated a moral need for heroic leadership. During the 1980s, the historian cautioned that a liberal leader must emerge soon to save the "vital center" of American values from an impending crisis of confidence potentially more threatening than the violent times of the late 1960s. The policies of Reaganomics threatened to foster class warfare and could contribute to the disintegration of the social fabric, Schlesinger wrote in 1981. Laissez-faire "entrepreneurship" in the fragile economic environment of the 1980s was a "long-odds gamble" that communicated to the poor that Reagan and other conservatives were engaged in a "withdrawal of public concern." As a result, the poor could begin to "lose faith in the justice of the social order."[104] As the cruel policies of conservatism and the watered-down policies of neoliberalism successively failed to redress the problems of distribution of wealth and opportunity, he continued in 1982, the "pervading sense of frustration and impotence" could spread to all levels of society and invite "tough right-wing Populist authoritarianism."[105] "The need for an authentic national policy is all the more urgent in the 1980s," the historian concluded in 1986. He listed divisive issues such as the widening disparities in income and opportunity; the multiplication of the poor and the underclass; the slowdown of racial justice; the mounting burden of public and private debt; and the spread of crime and violence. These and other social ills carried with them "enormous potentialities for disintegration in contemporary America."[106]

Back in 1967, Schlesinger had warned that not even the regularities of the political cycle were immune to disruption and even collapse. For example, 1932 was a "scary time" characterized by "a baffled and impotent national leadership, an apparently uncontrollable economic disintegration, [and] an increasingly angry populace moving toward ever more drastic remedies." America did not revolt or succumb to authoritarian demagoguery during the 1930s only because Franklin Roosevelt came to the fore as a leader resolute in purpose and determined to a course of pragmatic experimentation.[107] More recently, Schlesinger has soberly quoted Thurman

Arnold's admonition "Every dictatorship which we know of flowed into power like air into a vacuum because the central government, in the face of a real difficulty, declined to exercise authority."[108]

Schlesinger has claimed that today, more than ever before, America needs heroic liberal leadership to maintain popular faith in liberal values and affirmative government in the face of the selfishness and alienation caused by economic hard times and grim limitations. The historian has gone so far as to assert that traditional liberals may have "only one more chance" to demonstrate that social and economic problems can be abated through concerted human action. "If the Republicans fail today and the Democrats fail thereafter," Schlesinger speculated in 1982, "what rough beast, its hour come round at last, may be slouching toward Washington to be born?"[109] Writing in less apocalyptic terms in 1990, Schlesinger reiterated the urgency of the moment. "History has tested and vindicated liberal principles throughout this cruel century," he argued. "But liberal principles are not self-executing. The labor of democracy is unending. The challenge of American liberal democracy in the coming age of economic competition is acute."[110]

While Schlesinger has argued that Americans should look for a heroic leader who combines new ideas with the capacity to manage interests and instill faith in liberal government, he has not been forthcoming in identifying political leaders who meet such a high standard. "I have refrained from speculating about personalities who might lead a Democratic renaissance," he wrote in 1982. "Another FDR may not be immediately visible on the horizon. Yet one must remember that FDR did not become FDR until after he entered the White House."[111] In 1988, he endorsed Democrat Michael Dukakis for president, claiming that "he offers the best opportunity for fresh departures in a world of darkling change where the republic is in important ways beleaguered, dependent, and vulnerable."[112] Through heroic leadership that combines pragmatism with the ability to compel sacrifice, Schlesinger has asserted, liberal policies can once again be effective in addressing social problems, and liberal values can regain their rightful place at the core of the American consensus.

Aftermath of the 1988 Election

The defeat of Michael Dukakis confirmed for many that traditional New Deal liberalism was both obsolete and counterproductive as an ideological response to America's domestic ills. For many Americans, the brand of liberalism that emphasized the intervention of government to solve social problems had failed to recapture the significant measure of legitimacy that it had lost in recent years. Arthur Schlesinger's reliance on the inevitability of political tides did not seem to provide an answer for those who continued to question liberal values as permissive and liberal policies as anachronistic.

In short, Democrats needed to go beyond the policies and values of conventional liberalism in order to regain the White House. The unhappy state of American liberalism heading into the 1990s was aptly summarized by commentator Meg Greenfield, who concluded that the 1988 election left liberals with many "unresolved problems" to address and warned Democrats that "sooner or later, they are not only going to have to acknowledge their liberalism, they are going to have to redefine it and reclaim it."[113]

Epilogue: "A New Generation of Leadership"

As the 1992 election year approached, Arthur Schlesinger, Jr., continued to assert that the tides of American politics pointed toward the emergence of a new era of liberal dominance in American life. In a 1991 interview, Schlesinger reiterated that both the accumulation of unsolved social problems and the coming of age of a new generation of political leaders shaped and inspired by John Kennedy and the New Frontier meant that "the 1990s will give the proponents of public purpose and activist government another chance." The "generation of young men and young women who came to political maturity in the Kennedy years," he argued, would "change the national mood and direction with new bursts of innovative reform" in the liberal tradition of government activism.[114]

The beginning of the 1992 campaign season offered little to confirm Schlesinger's viewpoint. Incumbent President George Bush was riding a wave of popularity generated by America's success in the Persian Gulf war with Iraq. The Democratic party appeared to be in its usual state of disarray. Party notables such as Mario Cuomo and Bill Bradley decided not to challenge for the 1992 presidential nomination. Most of the Democrats who chose to run seemed ill suited to carry the mantle of liberal activism.

One of the Democratic challengers, Governor Bill Clinton of Arkansas, based his campaign on a search for solutions beyond conventional ideological categories. "The change I seek," Clinton stated in his speech announcing his candidacy, "and the change which we must all seek, isn't liberal or conservative. It's different and it's both."[115] Clinton was a founding member of the Democratic Leadership Council, a group of primarily Southern Democrats who organized in search of an alternative to the conventional liberalism of big government and special interest groups.[116] Clinton's message, which stressed community and responsibility, appealed to a middle-class constituency which had felt alienated from the Democratic party for twenty years.[117] Despite intense media scrutiny of his private life and strong competition from other Democrats, Clinton secured the Democratic party's presidential nomination.

At the convention in New York, Clinton's people hammered out a party platform that was pointedly moderate in tone and substance, including an admission that Americans are justifiably angry not just with Republicans but with "government itself."[118] While highlighting in his acceptance speech the negative impact of twelve years of Republican leadership on America's social ills, Clinton also called upon Democrats to recognize "that we've got some changing to do. There is not a program in government for every problem." He went on to say that the choice he offered, based on "old values" of opportunity and responsibility, "is not conservative or liberal; in many ways it's not even Republican or Democratic. It's different. It's new. And it will work." He called his approach to governing a "new covenant" and hoped through this new approach to establish in the minds of the American people the legitimacy of his party and of his own candidacy.[119]

Clinton's rejection of conventional liberalism, or at least of liberalism as an ideological label, seemed to cast him in the mold of Jimmy Carter more than of Franklin Roosevelt. Yet even while moving beyond the liberalism of the past, Clinton tried to place himself as a worthy successor within the Democratic tradition of strong, activist leadership. He did this by basing his campaign on the theme of generational change. Clinton defined the race between himself and George Bush as a choice between leadership whose ideas and values were shaped by the depression, World War II, and the cold war and a new generation of leadership born after World War II whose ideas and values were shaped by the New Frontier and the Great Society, the Vietnam war and Watergate.[120]

Clinton highlighted the generational theme in many ways. He defied conventional wisdom by choosing Al Gore, a fellow southerner and baby-boomer, as his running mate. At the press conference following Clinton's announcement, Gore emphasized that "throughout American history, each generation has passed on leadership to the next. That time has come again—the time for a new generation of leadership for the United States of America."[121] Clinton openly identified John F. Kennedy as a major source of inspiration and tried to get audiences to draw parallels between the two youthful, dynamic public leaders. A film clip showing a teenage Clinton shaking hands with President Kennedy in the Rose Garden, first shown on the night of Clinton's acceptance speech, would become a staple part of the candidate's campaign commercials during the fall.[122]

The 1992 election year was characterized by widespread public feelings of apathy, alienation, and anger toward the entire system of government, including both Congress and the chief executive. A stubborn recession, coupled with the persistence of structural economic problems such as the burgeoning federal deficit, turned public opinion against incumbents, including George Bush, and prompted the emergence of H. Ross Perot as a third-party candidate in the presidential contest. By portraying himself as the vessel of generational change in American politics, Clinton hoped to tap into public frustration with the current state of gridlock and appeal to latent hopes that new leadership with new approaches to solving problems could again make a difference. Clinton was successful, winning the election with a plurality of popular votes and in an electoral landslide over Bush and Perot.

Arthur Schlesinger, Jr., may not have agreed with Bill Clinton's reaction against liberalism as an ideological label. In many respects, however, Clinton's rhetoric seemed to contain some of Schlesinger's ideas concerning the changing tides of American politics. Clinton's message of generational change precisely matched arguments that Schlesinger had been making for years concerning political tides and generational influence.[123] In addition, while he rejected traditional New Deal liberalism, Clinton projected a willingness to lead an active government in the search for new policies that work to solve the long-neglected problems of society. In his inaugural address, President Clinton stated: "Let us resolve to make our Government a place for what Franklin Roosevelt called bold, persistent experimentation, a Government for our tomorrows, not our yesterdays."[124] Schlesinger saw such pragmatism as a central feature of the liberal tradition of active presidential leadership.

Others saw the apparent fit between Schlesinger's historical viewpoint and Clinton's successful campaign to regain the White House for the Democrats. In *Time* magazine's postelection issue, Walter Isaacson cited as the basis for understanding Clinton's victory "the old theory propounded by historians Arthur Schlesinger Sr. and Jr." that "every thirty years or so the nation turns, after a respite of conservative retrenchment, to a new era of active government, public purpose, and liberal idealism." Clinton's constant references to John Kennedy demonstrated that "the mainspring that turns the cycle is generational."[125]

Schlesinger found his own opportunity to reflect upon the significance of the 1992 election result in an essay commissioned by *Newsweek* as part of a series in which writers and academics were asked to define the importance of the World War II generation on American society. As always, he drew upon historical analogy to make the case for the emergence of a new liberal era in American politics. "How reminiscent it all is," he began, "reminiscent of 1933, of 1961—a momentous reversal of direction for the nation, an army of bright young reformers bursting to go to Washington and serve the republic, eager, after a decade of passivity and neglect, to roll up their sleeves (as the young Rex Tugwell put it 60 years ago) and make America over." As someone who "vividly recalls the excitements of 1933 and who personally partook of the excitements of 1961," Schlesinger continued, "let me offer a few thoughts to the 1993 crowd, in case anyone out there is interested."[126]

The historian then directed his remarks to those who were to become part of the new Clinton administration. "Do not lose that wonderful confidence in yourselves, in your own experience, instinct and outlook," he wrote. "Above all, don't be intimidated by the icons of the past." He advised president-elect Clinton that while "a president is president of all the people," this "does not mean that he can please all the people all the time." "In retrospect," he continued, "even Republicans concede that Franklin Roosevelt was a great president, but he was bitterly denounced—hated—in his own day." In a sober bit of advice based on a lifetime of experience, Schlesinger warned, "But do not overestimate your capacity to remold history." "The besetting illusion of the New Deal and the New Frontier," he admitted, "was that every problem had a solution."[127]

Schlesinger then stretched his conception of liberalism to include the members of the new Democratic administration as "custodians—and I trust, executors—of a great tradition. Your generation comes to power in response to the well-defined rhythm of American politics, the alteration, as Emerson said, between the Party of Memory and the Party of Hope. In your hands now lies the 20th-century legacy of Wilson, FDR, and Truman, of JFK and LBJ." While recognizing that "new problems demand new remedies," Schlesinger closed by reaffirming, as he has throughout his career, his definition of liberalism: "the spirit of concern for those Andrew Jackson called 'the humble members of society—the farmers, mechanics, and laborers'—abides. Historically, this is what the Democratic Party, at its best, has been all about. Never forget this."[128]

Arthur Schlesinger, Jr., thus viewed the outcome of the 1992 election from the perspective of the tides of national politics and explained the electoral results using a well-worn terminology born of an unwavering belief in his own historical theory. Schlesinger interpreted the 1992 election not as a narrow win by a nonideological policy wonk whom many voters saw as the least unpalatable of three alternatives but as additional confirmation of his cyclical view of American politics. While others regarded Clinton's success as proof that Democrats must shed their liberal skins in order to win the White House, Schlesinger marked Clinton's victory as the beginning of a new era of affirmative government on behalf of the people.[129]

Conclusion

As the complexity of America's social problems increased during the 1970s and 1980s, and as traditional fiscal and monetary means to cope with problems proved unsuccessful or politically unfeasible, liberal legislators and political candidates alike found it increasingly difficult to reestablish legitimacy, either through appeals to communal values or through claims that government programs were producing tangible benefits. Conservatives such as Ronald Reagan were successful in characterizing liberal values (permissiveness, softness on crime, weakness in national defense) as outside the mainstream of socially accepted values. And many Americans came to identify liberals negatively *with* government, especially with the bloated and ineffective federal bureaucracy.

In recent years, Arthur Schlesinger, Jr., has attempted to resuscitate a traditional conception of liberalism by applying the three components of his frame of acceptance along a rhetorical path or trajectory that originated with ideas he articulated in the 1950s. In so doing, he has tried to reestablish the legitimacy of liberal values, policies, and leaders.

In his latest attempt to restore legitimacy to his liberal perspective, Schlesinger has remained generally consistent in his views toward definitions of liberalism and conservatism, the inevitable course of the political cycle, and the need for heroic leadership. Some adjustments were made in order to adapt to changing times. Schlesinger moved away from his earlier focus on "qualitative liberalism" and reemphasized the economic dimension in his definitions of liberal and conservative in order to attack Reaganomics. He shifted the endpoints of the political cycle, introducing the notion of political generations as a way of accounting for the enduring popularity of conservatism during the 1980s and as a basis for forecasting the coming of the next liberal era. And he reiterated the need for liberal leadership to emerge in a time of growing economic uncertainty and building social unrest in America.

Yet while some arguments changed, Schlesinger's overall perspective toward American politics and rationale for liberalism remained remarkably consistent with what he had said decades earlier. More than anything else, Schlesinger's most recent defense of liberalism illustrates his unshakable belief in his own view of history. He has continued to maintain that affirmative government, with a heroic liberal leading the way, can point Americans toward a better life in accordance with the unfolding of the political cycle.[130]

Schlesinger's continued adherence to the tides of national politics illustrates the power of his frame of acceptance to generate a rhetorical trajectory, a constraining path of symbolic development, which provides guidance even in the face of changing circumstances. According to Kenneth Burke, "As a given historical frame of acceptance nears the point of cracking, strained by the rise of new factors it had not originally taken into account, its adherents employ its genius casuistically to extend it as far as possible."[131]

Schlesinger's defense of liberalism during the 1980s also reflects an understandable desire to maintain a degree of ideological consistency in a time of social upheaval. According to Walzer, periods when a conventional political idiom begins to lose its relevance are marked by "an increasingly disjointed and inconsistent expression of political ideas" and "a nervous insistence upon the old units and references." During times of uncertainty, "the arbitrary reassertion of the old symbolism can offer intellectual and emotional sustenance" for those who fear changes to come.[132]

For Schlesinger, the 1992 election of Bill Clinton as president marked the beginning of a new era of public activism and affirmative government. In fact, while Clinton's appeal to generational change may have provided some confirmation for Schlesinger's contention that one generation of political ideas and leaders influences the next, the 1992 campaign certainly did little to resuscitate liberalism as an ideology or "liberal" as a favorable term in the political lexicon.

Whether President Bill Clinton actually leads America into a new golden age of liberal governance remains to be seen. In his own assessment of the election, Walter Isaacson warned against a prematurely grandiose interpretation. Again picking up on Schlesinger's theory, Isaacson reminded his readers that "historical cycles are not inevitable. They depend on the strengths and frailties of those who become the repositories of the hope for change." Above all, today's political leaders must have "the backbone to convey brutal facts unflinchingly to the American people." He went on to speak of the danger of rising expectations: "With all that is at stake and with all the hope that America has invested in him, Clinton can scarcely afford to prove unequal to his task. Another failed one-term presidency would reinforce not only the notion that government cannot cope, but also the clawing anxiety that the country and its economy may be heading toward an inexorable decline."[133]

8

Conclusion

Arthur Schlesinger, Jr., has always maintained that historical understanding and insight should play an important role in defining communal values and shaping social policies in the present. In a world now characterized by the increasing velocity of history, Schlesinger wrote in 1986, "change is scary; uncharted change, demoralizing." "If the law of acceleration is not to spin out of control," he continued, "society must cherish its lifelines to the past." Fortunately, even in this modern "age of whirl," the historian concluded, "so much of the old abides."[1]

For Schlesinger, what has abided over the years has been his belief in the tides of national politics as a way of understanding the unfolding of American history past and present. This chapter offers some concluding observations about Schlesinger, the constraining influence of rhetorical trajectory, and the importance of ideological history.

Tides of National Politics as Rhetorical Trajectory

As Arthur Schlesinger, Jr., came to rely on and adapt the tides of national politics to explain a wider range of political events past and present, the cyclical theory increasingly directed him toward certain definitions of situations and toward conclusions and judgments about those situations. Burke explains that "much that we take as observations about 'reality' may be but the spinning out of possibilities implicit in our particular choice of terms."[2] Over time, Schlesinger's frame of acceptance generated a rhetorical trajectory that acted as a constraining influence upon his definitions of situations.

And just as Schlesinger's frame has directed him toward certain interpretations and judgments of situations over the years, it has also led him away from other possible interpretations and judgments. "Even if any given terminology is a *reflection* of reality," Burke writes, "by its very nature as a terminology it must be a *selection* of reality; and to this extent it must function also as a *deflection* of reality."[3] A rhetorical trajectory thus promotes not only consistency of interpretation but also a certain narrowness or limitation of responses to changing circumstances.

The concept of rhetorical trajectory aids us in understanding the symbolic choices Schlesinger has made during his unceasing efforts to define and defend liberalism. The historian has both explained events in the past and viewed the unfolding events of his own time through the interpretive lens of the "tides of national politics." As a result, Schlesinger's discourse has been characterized both by remarkable consistency in strategy and substance over time and by a limited range of responses to changing political situations.

During the 1950s, Schlesinger's response to the challenges of consensus, affluence, and power faced by liberalism was guided by his cyclical view of American history. He understood the lack of ideological struggle at home as a sign not that creative ideas among liberals and conservatives were lacking but that liberal values had become consensual American values due to the progressive movement leftward of American public opinion with the completion of each political cycle. To regain the public approval of liberal values, Schlesinger made perhaps the most significant symbolic shift of his career. He altered his own definition of liberal and conservative, substituting the concept of interests for the concept of economic class as the basis for future ideological disagreement. He made this move because he was convinced that the New Deal era of liberal activism had produced sufficient economic growth to reduce poverty and want significantly.

The historian then accounted for growing affluence in America not by an admission that New Deal economic stimulus was no longer necessary but by the assertion that New Deal–style liberal programs were in fact responsible for America's economic growth. He even went so far as to propose that since the New Deal had conquered want, liberals should abandon quantitative economic issues in favor of a new agenda stressing quality-of-life issues such as equal opportunity. His desire to defend government activism as an intrinsic part of liberalism led him to overlook a variety of reasons for America's booming economy during the 1950s and to underestimate the scope, severity, and the entrenched nature of poverty and other socioeconomic problems in America.

Schlesinger rationalized the series of Republican electoral successes in the 1950s by focusing on the alternations between public moods as a way of explaining past defeats and as a basis for predicting liberal victories to come. He prophesied that 1960 would mark a pivotal moment in American history in which a new phase of public activism would be unleashed in accordance with the changing political tides. His belief in characterological differences between conservatives and liberals and in the importance of leadership style led him to focus on the personalities of the candidates in his analysis of the 1960 presidential contest between John F. Kennedy and Richard M. Nixon. Despite the closeness of the election, Schlesinger interpreted Kennedy's victory over Nixon as the beginning of a glorious new liberal era in America and saw Kennedy as the kind of liberal hero necessary to manage divergent interests in America and to compel sacrifice for the common good.

The tides of national politics seemed to gain incontrovertible confirmation with the ascension of John F. Kennedy into the office of president. Schlesinger's participation in the Kennedy administration marked the high point of his own career and served to reinforce his belief that historical insight could guide political decisions in the present. The historian's move into government also foreshadowed an eventual breach within the political left between those who wished to work within the system and those who by the end of the decade would call to tear the system down. Now a part of the system, Schlesinger interpreted criticism of the Kennedy administration from the Left and from the Right as irrational, self-serving, and outside the "vital center" of pragmatic reform. Yet, influenced by his belief in the orderly flow of historical change, he remained confident that the American political process could handle a broad range of dissent within the democratic marketplace of ideas.

That confidence was severely tested during the next few years by an increasingly unpopular war abroad and by political violence at home. Characteristically, Schlesinger reacted to the Vietnam war by trying to find a solution compatible with his liberal sensibility. Initially, he blamed the war neither on the American military-industrial complex nor on the principles of American foreign policy. Instead, Schlesinger blamed Lyndon Johnson for not winding down American involvement as the historian believed that John Kennedy would have. At the same time, his anticommunism prevented him from calling for complete withdrawal of American forces from Southeast Asia. His belief in rationality and faith in the political process led him to chastise protest against the war as counterproductive. Underestimating the dissatisfaction with institutions that was growing within the American Left, Schlesinger urged protesters to work within the system to elect a new president, Robert F. Kennedy, who would find a middle way out of Vietnam.

The year 1968 was terrible for the nation and for Arthur Schlesinger, Jr. The Vietnam war raged on, dividing the liberal community and the Democratic party. Robert Kennedy, who represented Schlesinger's hope for the emergence of new liberal leadership, was felled by an assassin's bullet. By the end of the year, Schlesinger had begun to question his own assumptions about the rationality of political institutions and the predictability of social change. Declaring "the end of the age of the superpowers" in 1969, Schlesinger criticized America's activist foreign policy, which had lurched out of control with a failed military incursion in Southeast Asia. In the same year, he wrote of a crisis of confidence that had led many Americans to abandon their own political system in favor of apathy or violence. Because of technological changes that had increased the velocity of history, Schlesinger began to wonder whether orderly social progress was still possible.

Yet even as he grappled with the divisive issues of the Vietnam war and political unrest, Schlesinger drew upon his frame of acceptance as a way of defining situations and prescribing responses. Instead of calling for an end to the cold war or repudiating the American military, the historian suggested that American foreign policy in Vietnam and elsewhere should be based on "rational" rather than "obsessive" anticommunism. This response was based on a strategy of dissociation between appearance and reality that Schlesinger employed throughout his career, a strategy consistent with his faith in reason and in the political process.

In response to the "crisis of confidence" that characterized American society at the end of the 1960s, Schlesinger pronounced his hope that the vital center of liberal values would prevail against the forces of alienation and violence. Rather than pursuing a structural alternative to modern capitalism and technological growth, the historian restated his call for heroic leadership to bring the fragmented nation together and to work within the political system to engineer liberal social and economic reforms. Schlesinger's focus on emerging leadership as a salvation device stemmed directly from his cyclical interpretation of American history, in which liberal leaders had been instrumental in managing past crises.

During the past two decades, Schlesinger has defended traditional liberalism against the threat of delegitimation. The historian has continued to rely on the terms and assumptions of his frame of acceptance as a way of confronting the mounting problems of resource limits, liberal self-doubt, and conservative labeling. A major part of Schlesinger's recent discourse has involved the reassertion of the traditional meanings of the terms "conservative" and "liberal." The historian has attacked the Reagan administration's probusiness economic policies as an example of what conservatives value: the private accumulation of wealth at the expense of the lesser interests of society. Here Schlesinger has made a strategic return to the economic theme in distinguishing conservatism from liberalism, a theme that he had abandoned in the late 1950s for more qualitative issues. Typically, Schlesinger justified this move with references to probusiness conservatives in American history.

At the same time, Schlesinger has tried to recapture the essential meaning of liberalism from critics on the Right and revisionists on the Left. Here Schlesinger has remained true to form by identifying liberalism with a belief in affirmative government as a means of redressing social and economic inequities. Schlesinger has acknowledged that the growing budget deficit now limits the possibility for a massive infusion of government capital into the economy. He has also noted that the problems facing America today demand different solutions from those offered in the New Deal or the Great Society. Crucially, Schlesinger has blamed the Reagan administration, not the past three decades of action by the Democratically controlled Congress, for producing large deficits as a way of blocking liberal reform. While recognizing that "sometimes government intervenes too much" in the everyday lives of Americans, Schlesinger has continued to equate liberalism with the process of government action.[4] Because Schlesinger has not addressed the growing public perception that government is the *problem*, not the solution, he has had difficulty in restoring a sense of legitimacy to the traditional liberal viewpoint.

Along with the emphasis on definitions, Schlesinger has attempted in recent years to revive liberal hopes for regaining popular support and political power. He has once again explained liberal electoral defeats and predicted upcoming liberal victories through the terminological screen generated by his cyclical interpretation of American history. He has claimed that his theory warrants the persuasive force of presumption because of past successes in predicting electoral trends (particularly the 1960 presidential election). Instead of recognizing a growing public disenchantment with liberal promises of government solutions to complex problems, Schlesinger has added the concept of political generations as a way of accounting for the unusually long reign of conservative dominance in America since the end of the 1960s. He has claimed that Reaganism is finished because of the imminent emergence of a new generation of liberal political leaders whose beliefs were formed during the days of the New Frontier. Despite continuing conservative control of the presidency, Schlesinger's belief in America's political rhythms has remained unshakable. The theory the historian inherited from his father is sufficiently elastic to provide him with a way of explaining each new liberal defeat as part of the cycle.

Finally, Schlesinger has reasserted the need for heroic leadership as a necessary catalyst that will return liberalism to political favor in America. While admitting that public faith in government will be restored only through the discovery of effective remedies to societal problems, Schlesinger has stated his belief that only liberal leaders can combine reason and experimentation to make the government work again for all of the people. While recognizing the increasing fragmentation of American politics, Schlesinger has asserted that only liberal leadership can convince special interest groups and narrow factions to act together in the national interest. Once again, Schlesinger has put his faith in the emergence of a liberal leader, just as leaders have come forward in the past, as a way to transcend the challenges facing his own liberal perspective. Most recently, he has hailed the election of President Clinton in 1992 as the starting point of a new generation of liberal ascendence in accordance with the political cycle.

As the legitimacy of his liberal frame of acceptance has been threatened by a series of societal events and trends, Schlesinger has responded along a symbolic path of development generated by the tides of national politics. This framework has led him to define and judge situations in certain ways, emphasizing certain elements at the expense of others, as he has tried to uphold the status of traditional liberalism in contemporary American politics.

History the Weapon

One final way of reflecting upon Schlesinger's use of history in the service of liberal politics through the years is to consider his work and career in light of his most recent statements about the process of writing history and the significance of history in the formation of a society. In *The Disuniting of America*, his most recent book-length work published in 1991, Schlesinger discusses the rise of ethnicity and cultural conflict in American society. In one chapter, entitled

"History the Weapon," he examines the role historical understanding plays in the establishment of community identity.

He starts by revisiting the question of purpose. "Writing history," he begins, "is an old and honorable profession with distinctive standards and purposes. The historian's goals are accuracy, analysis, and objectivity in the reconstruction of the past." Then, reiterating his long-held belief in the political significance of the past, he continues, "But history is more than an academic discipline up there in the stratosphere. It also has its own role in the future of nations." For Schlesinger, "history is to the nation rather as memory is to the individual. As an individual deprived of memory becomes disoriented and lost, not knowing where he has been or where he is going, so a nation denied a conception of the past will be disabled in dealing with its present and future."[5] Schlesinger acknowledges that the invocation of history "is indispensable to nations and groups in the process of making themselves." "How else," the author asks, "can a people establish the legitimacy of its personality, the continuity of its tradition, the correctness of its course?"[6] In other words, historical understanding forms the basis for a society's political presumptions, the consensual core of values and beliefs about the shape and destiny of a community.

Because history is "a means of shaping national identity," an understanding of the past is often defined strategically in order to influence the shape of the present and the future. In such cases, Schlesinger asserts, "the writing of history then turns from a meditation into a weapon."[7] In other words, academic arguments about history can serve as the basis for political arguments from history.

The historian's task can become politicized when "the spotlight we flash into the darkness of the past is guided by our own concerns in the present." While historians "must always strive toward the unattainable ideal of objectivity," Schlesinger observes that "as we respond to contemporary urgencies, we sometimes exploit the past for nonhistorical purposes, taking from the past, or projecting upon it, what suits our own society or ideology. History thus manipulated becomes an instrument less of disinterested intellectual inquiry than of social cohesion and political purpose."[8] Here Schlesinger is describing what McGee has called ideological history.

Schlesinger goes on to identify two ways in which history may be used for political purposes in the present. In many cases, he argues, "history is invoked to justify the ruling class," to "show how noble, virtuous, and inevitable existing power arrangements are." He calls this "exculpatory history," because "it vindicates the status quo and the methods by which power is achieved and maintained." In other cases, "history is invoked to justify the victims of power, to vindicate those who reject the status quo." Schlesinger labels this "compensatory history" because it is "designed to demonstrate what Bertrand Russell called the 'superior virtue of the oppressed' by inventing or exaggerating past glories and purposes." Both kinds of ideological history, Schlesinger asserts, "use the past in order to shape the future."[9]

Much of the rest of the chapter is devoted to a discussion of ways in which ethnic and nationalistic prejudices have produced distorted and destructive views of history in a variety of times and places, in America and around the world. Schlesinger contends that while "honest history is the weapon of freedom," the production of ideologically slanted history is an abuse of history.[10] "The high purpose of history," he concludes, "is not the presentation of self nor the vindication of identity but the recognition of complexity and the search for knowledge."[11]

Ironically, even while admitting the inextricable relationship between historical understanding and political identity, Schlesinger criticizes virtually all of the ideological uses of history he identifies. This apparent contradiction reflects Schlesinger's ongoing conception of "historical insight" as a positive term and "ideology" as a negative term in his own frame of acceptance.

It is important to recognize Schlesinger's remarks in their context. Schlesinger's recent ruminations about history and politics are part of a larger argument against ethnic and cultural fragmentation in America. Even so, Schlesinger does little in this chapter to provide a clear distinction between honest and dishonest history, other than the restatement of a general and, as Schlesinger admits, unattainable ideal of objectivity. It could be argued that in a clash between the historical understandings of social movements, ethnic groups, or nations, one person or group's concrete fact may be another group's illusion.

More important, however, these most recent statements by Schlesinger can provide some insights about his own persuasive uses of history during his career. Even though Schlesinger has critiqued the use of history as a political weapon, it is clear that a hallmark of his own discourse has been the application of his own view of history in attempts to define and defend the identity and legitimacy of liberalism in American political life. For Schlesinger, history *has* become an instrument less of disinterested intellectual inquiry than of social cohesion and political purpose.

As we have seen, Schlesinger has engaged in ideological history, using arguments from history in attempts to influence the outcome of political controversies in the present. During his career, the historian has made all three of the rhetorical moves identified as characteristics of ideological history. He has begun with the notion of the tides of national politics as an explicit view of time, believing that this theory of cyclical alternation of conservatism and liberalism is strongly suggestive but not determinative of political actions during American history. He has then constructed explanation sketches of various periods in American history, especially the ages of Jackson, Roosevelt, and Kennedy, which have been grounded in his belief in political cycles. Finally, he has projected his view of history into discussions of the present and future through arguments of historical analogy and dissociation. He has employed elements of the tides of national politics to account for the successes and failures of contemporary liberal policies and politicians and to suggest at various points the coming of a new era of liberal dominance in American political life.

Throughout his career, Schlesinger has tried to establish liberalism as the more legitimate ideological viewpoint in American politics, encompassing a set of values shared by most members of society. In addition, he attempted to portray liberalism as the basis for policy responses that should be preferred when addressing contemporary problems facing American society. Schlesinger employed his own views of America's past as support for his claims concerning the presumptive value of his liberal perspective. For example, in both the 1950s and 1980s, the historian portrayed his liberal preference for government intervention in response to social or economic ills as a product of America's past, a result of a heritage of ideas and programs stemming from the Jacksonian era through the New Deal and New Frontier. By linking his advocacy of government activism in the present with past actions that had been favorably interpreted by many Americans, Schlesinger hoped to generate a presumptive belief that liberal government programs would probably work again with the guidance of liberal political leadership.

It may be noted that Schlesinger's use of history has often resembled what he has termed "exculpatory history," historical arguments presented to justify or maintain existing power arrangements.[12] A bias toward the status quo is intrinsic to Schlesinger's belief in the tides of national politics. While Schlesinger's definitions of "liberal" and "conservative" have been grounded in varying attitudes toward change, government, and the public interest, Schlesinger placed both perspectives within a "vital center" of political action. Within this vital center, political conflict is contained. Both sides maintain a respect for the political process and an elitist preference for rationality and expertise over emotion and mass participation. Schlesinger moved further toward identifying with the status quo in the 1950s, when he shifted from economic class toward a more general conception of competing interests as a basis for distinguishing liberalism from conservatism. This definitional bias was also illustrated in Schlesinger's attacks over the years against any radical group or idea that threatened the underlying stability of the democratic two-party system.

Schlesinger's conception of predictable alternations between conservative and liberal political dominance over time has also directed him toward defending existing institutions. His cyclical view of history allowed him to rationalize the weakness of liberal programs or failure of liberal politicians as part of a larger historical movement of public opinion and behavior that had less to do with the content of liberal ideas and more to do with physiological preferences for activity and rest. The desire for change was seen not principally as a product of material inequity or structural domination of one group over another, but instead as part of a naturally occurring rhythm in the body politic. And Schlesinger's ability to adjust the endpoints of the cycle whenever an election result contradicted a predicted shift in the political tides made his view of history both elastic and nonfalsifiable.

Finally, Schlesinger's constant call for the emergence of heroic liberal leadership illustrates his use of history to defend the existing political system. The reliance on heroic leaders to resolve political crises has led Schlesinger to focus more attention on the outcome of elections than on the unsolved problems of the people. As a result, Schlesinger has at times elevated the means of obtaining and keeping power for liberals over the ends of using political power for the benefit of dispossessed or marginalized groups. In Gillon's terms, Schlesinger's use of history in defense of liberalism has often favored politics over vision.[13]

This was especially illustrated by Schlesinger's relationship with John F. Kennedy. While Schlesinger viewed Kennedy's election as confirming his sense of history, the Kennedy administration produced exaggerated rhetoric and modest legislative results. Yet Schlesinger defended Kennedy as a model liberal leader whose accomplishments were tragically cut short by an assassin's bullet.

By the end of the 1960s, the inability of political leaders to cope with the problems of an unpopular war abroad and social unrest and corruption at home produced a growing public disenchantment with liberal presumptions that change was good and that government and the political process could effectively address social problems. This disillusionment has continued ever since and has produced a legitimation crisis for the liberal community.[14] Ultimately, the dwindling public support for conventional liberal values, policies, and candidates may be a political trend that Schlesinger's cyclical theory of American history may be incapable of addressing.

Final Thoughts

Over five decades of historical scholarship and political advocacy, Arthur Schlesinger, Jr., has experienced both good and bad times concerning his brand of traditional liberalism. From the heights of the New Frontier to the depths of recent presidential campaigns, Schlesinger has maintained a consistent set of political beliefs. He has believed that the course of history, while not deterministic, provides important insights and patterns of activity that can instruct human choices in the present; that liberals and conservatives have basic differences in character and interest; that social change, when regulated by reason and practicality, is basically good; that government can serve as a beneficial instrument in preserving and promoting both individual freedom and community prosperity; that dramatic changes in governmental leadership have occurred and will continue to occur periodically in this country because of alternating public moods of idealism and selfishness, public desires for activity and rest; and that the key to social progress is the emergence of heroic leaders who can persuade individuals to sacrifice individual interest for the common good and who can make government work for the people.

These beliefs have formed Schlesinger's frame of acceptance, his symbolic orientation toward the world. As we have seen, Schlesinger has shaped his beliefs into a concrete set of terms and assumptions that could be applied to a variety of situations. Throughout his career, Schlesinger has consistently referred to elements of his orientation in order to support historical and political arguments he has made in a number of persuasive contexts. Englehardt has asserted that in the face of political challenges from the Right and the Left over the years, Arthur Schlesinger, Jr., has "derived solace from his father's cyclical theory . . . in which periods of liberalism and conservatism alternated throughout American history." Schlesinger's adoption of the tides of national politics, concludes Englehardt, helps to explain why his political thought has displayed "such remarkable continuity in a time of great change."[15]

Despite Schlesinger's defiant defense of his liberal perspective, traditional liberalism continues to fade from the American political scene as members of the American public have lost faith in liberal values, policies, and politicians. Walzer explains that the "process of destruction" of a political perspective is complex and gradual, involving a "slow erosion of the old symbols, a wasting away of feelings they once evoked . . . until finally the units cease to be accepted as intellectual givens and the references cease to be meaningful."[16] This examination of Arthur Schlesinger's ideological history of American liberalism helps us to understand the gradual and ongoing delegitimation of New Deal liberalism in America.

Notes

Preface

1. John Higham, "The Construction of American History," in John Higham, ed., *The Reconstruction of American History* (New York: Harper and Row, 1962), pp. 9–10.

2. Henry Fairlie, "Books Reconsidered," review of *Robert F. Kennedy and His Times, New Republic*, September 9, 1978, p. 30.

3. Alan Brinkley, "Conflict and Consensus," review of *The Cycles of American History, New Republic*, December 1, 1986, p. 30.

4. Thomas Axworthy, "Politics on the Seesaw," review of *The Cycles of American History, Macleans*, April 6, 1987, p. 50.

5. Arthur M. Schlesinger, Jr., *The Cycles of American History* (Boston: Houghton Mifflin, 1986), pp. ix, xii.

6. Arthur Mann, "The Progressive Tradition," in *The Reconstruction of American History*, p. 174.

7. Arthur M. Schlesinger, Jr., *The Age of Jackson* (Boston: Little Brown, 1945), p. 391.

8. Dennis Wrong, "The Rhythm of Democratic Politics," in Lewis A. Coser and Irving Howe, eds., *The New Conservatives: A Critique from the Left* (New York: Quadrangle Press, 1974), pp. 90–94.

9. According to Burke, dramatism involves "a methodical inquiry into cycles or clusters of terms and their functions." Kenneth Burke, "Dramatism," in *International Encyclopedia of the Social Sciences* (New York: Macmillan, 1969), p. 445.

10. Burke argues that by considering any human discourse to be an "act" of defining a situation that implies a cycle of terms (scene, agent, agency,

act, purpose), the dramatistic critic may discover the *motives* that guided the discourse. Burke, "Dramatism," pp. 445–52.

11. Kenneth Burke, *Attitudes toward History*, 3d ed. (Berkeley: University of California Press, 1984), pp. 3–4.

12. Kenneth Burke, *A Rhetoric of Motives*, 3d ed. (Berkeley: University of California Press, 1969), pp. 20–23.

13. William H. Rueckert, *Kenneth Burke and the Drama of Human Relations*, 2d ed. (Berkeley: University of California Press, 1982), pp. 42–43.

14. Burke, *Rhetoric of Motives*, p. 43.

15. For instance, Mann has traced the influence of liberal Progressive historians on Schlesinger's interpretations of Andrew Jackson and Franklin Roosevelt. Mann, "The Progressive Tradition," in *The Reconstruction of American History*, pp. 157–79. Cunliffe has noted that Schlesinger's historical descriptions have borne a striking resemblance to contemporary events and people. Marcus Cunliffe, "Arthur Schlesinger, Jr.," in Marcus Cunliffe and Robin Winks, eds., *Pastmasters: Some Essays on American Historians* (New York: Harper and Row, 1969), pp. 345–74. Sellers, Silver, and Graham have examined Schlesinger's use of evidence in his historical accounts of Jackson, Coolidge, and Roosevelt. Charles G. Sellers, "Andrew Jackson versus the Historians," *Mississippi Valley Historical Review* 44 (1958): 615–34; Thomas B. Silver, "Coolidge and the Historians," *American Scholar* 50 (1981): 501–7; and Otis L. Graham, Jr., "Historians and the New Deal, 1944–1960," *Social Studies* 54 (1963): 133–39. Spencer has questioned Schlesinger's attempt in *The Imperial Presidency* to prove a general historical thesis concerning abuse of political power. Martin E. Spencer, "The Imperial Presidency and the Uses of Social Science," *Midwest Quarterly* 20 (1979): 281–99.

16. See Michael Wreszin, "Arthur Schlesinger, Jr., Scholar-Activist in Cold-War America, 1946–1956," *Salmagundi* 63, 4 (1984): 255–85; Marian J. Morton, *The Terrors of Ideological Politics: Liberal Historians in a Conservative Mood* (Cleveland: Case Western Reserve University Press, 1972), pp. 27–49; Carroll Englehardt, "Man in the Middle: Arthur M. Schlesinger, Jr., and Postwar American Liberalism," *South Atlantic Quarterly* 80 (1981): 119–38; James Nuechterlein, "Arthur M. Schlesinger, Jr., and the Discontents of Postwar American Liberalism," *Review of Politics* 39 (1977): 4–5; Stephen P. Depoe, " 'Qualitative Liberalism': Arthur Schlesinger, Jr., and the Persuasive Uses of Definition and History," *Communication Studies* 40 (1989): 81–96; and Stephen P. Depoe, "Arthur Schlesinger, Jr.'s 'Middle Way Out of Vietnam': Exploring the Limits of 'Technocratic Realism' as the Basis for Foreign Policy Dissent," *Western Journal of Speech Communication* 52 (1988): 148–66.

17. Burke, *Attitudes toward History*, p. 5.

18. Ibid., pp. 3–4. See also Barry Brummett, "Burkeian Transcendence and Ultimate Terms in Rhetoric by and about James Watt," *Central States Speech Journal* 33 (1982): 547–56.

19. Charles A. Beard, "Written History as an Act of Faith," *American Historical Review* 39 (1934): 219–29. For studies of the rhetorical dimensions of historical discourse, see Carl Cone, "Major Factors in the Rhetoric

of Historians," *Quarterly Journal of Speech* 33 (1947): 437–50; James R. Andrews, "The Rhetoric of History: The Constitutional Convention," *Today's Speech* 16 (1968): 23–26; Ronald H. Carpenter, "Frederick Jackson Turner and the Rhetorical Impact of the Frontier Thesis," *Quarterly Journal of Speech* 63 (1977): 117–29; Ronald H. Carpenter, "The Historical Jeremiad as Rhetorical Genre," in Karlyn Kohrs Campbell and Kathleen Jamieson, eds., *Form and Genre* (Falls Church, Va.: Speech Communication Association, 1977), pp. 103–18; E. Culpepper Clark, "Argument and Historical Analysis," in J. Robert Cox and Charles Willard, eds., *Advances in Argumentation Theory and Research* (Carbondale: Southern Illinois University Press, 1982), pp. 298–317; and Ronald H. Carpenter, "Admiral Mahan, 'Narrative Fidelity,' and the Japanese Attack on Pearl Harbor," *Quarterly Journal of Speech* 72 (1986): 290–305.

20. Richard Leo Enos, "Rhetorical Intent in Ancient Historiography: Herodotus and the Battle of Marathon," *Communication Quarterly* 24 (1976): 24.

21. Michael C. McGee, "The Fall of Wellington: A Case Study of the Relationship between Theory, Practice, and Rhetoric in History," *Quarterly Journal of Speech* 63 (1977): 28–42.

22. Some recent work has been done to explicate how historical reasoning influences public policy. Barbara Tuchman has speculated about whether or not history provides a guide to the future for our political leaders. Barbara Tuchman, *Practicing History* (New York: Alfred A. Knopf, 1981). More recently, Neustadt and May have examined ways in which recent American leaders have tried to use historical analogies and historical patterns to justify policy decisions in domestic and foreign affairs. Richard E. Neustadt and Ernest R. May, *Thinking in Time: The Uses of History for Decision-Makers* (New York: Free Press, 1986).

23. Burke has used several terms to describe the constraining influence of symbolic choice upon subsequent symbolic choice. In *Counter-Statement*, he refers to the qualitative progression of form in which one symbolic move suggests another in a dramatic unfolding of meaning. In *Permanence and Change*, he introduces piety as the desire among human beings "to round things out, to fit experiences together into a unified whole" in order to gain "a sense of what properly goes with what." In *Attitudes toward History*, he examines frames of acceptance and the tendency, due to the "Neo-Malthusian Principle," for individuals to push a perspective to its breaking point. In *The Philosophy of Literary Form*, he defines a symbol as the "dancing of an attitude" that does something for both artist and audience. In *A Grammar of Motives*, he argues that when an individual's acts are referred to a larger curve of symbolic development, "we get movement as motive." Kenneth Burke, *Counter-Statement*, 3d ed. (Berkeley: University of California Press, 1968), p. 125; Kenneth Burke, *Permanence and Change*, 4th ed. (Indianapolis: Bobbs-Merrill, 1975), pp. 74–75; Kenneth Burke, *Attitudes toward History*, 3d ed. (Berkeley: University of California Press, 1984), pp. 298–306; Kenneth Burke, *The Philosophy of Literary Form*, 3d ed. (Berkeley: University of California Press, 1973), p. 9; and Kenneth Burke, *A Grammar of Motives*, 3d ed. (Berkeley: University of California Press, 1969),

p. 32. See also Barry Brummett, "Burkeian Transcendence and Ultimate Terms in Rhetoric by and about James Watt," *Central States Speech Journal* 33 (1982): 547–56; and James Chesebro, "The Symbolic Construction of Social Realities: A Case Study in the Rhetorical Criticism of Paradox," *Communication Quarterly* 32 (1984): 164–71.

24. Leland M. Griffin, "When Dreams Collide: Rhetorical Trajectories in the Assassination of President Kennedy," *Quarterly Journal of Speech* 70 (1984): 126. Griffin uses the concept of rhetorical trajectory in an analysis of how the public rhetoric of John F. Kennedy and the private rhetoric of Lee Harvey Oswald placed them on a collision course that ended in the tragedy in Dallas.

25. George N. Dionisopoulos, Victoria J. Gallagher, Steven R. Goldzwig, and David Zarefsky, "Martin Luther King, The American Dream, and Vietnam: A Collision of Rhetorical Trajectories," *Western Journal of Speech Communication* 56 (1992): 91–107.

26. Ibid., pp. 94–95. See also Kenneth Burke, *Counter-Statement*, pp. 124–25.

27. Dionisopoulos, Gallagher, Goldzwig, and Zarefsky, "Martin Luther King," p. 95.

28. Ibid., p. 96.

29. According to Burke, the symbols we choose often act as a *terministic screen* or filter that colors our understanding and judgment of situations. A terministic screen both directs our *attention* toward certain features of a situation at the expense of others and shapes our *intention* or attitude toward elements of the situation. Kenneth Burke, *Language as Symbolic Action: Essays on Life, Literature, and Method* (Berkeley: University of California Press, 1966), pp. 44–62. For an example of a terministic screen in action, see Edward Schiappa, "The Rhetoric of Nukespeak," *Communication Monographs* 56 (1989): 253–72.

1. Origins of Schlesinger's Frame of Acceptance

1. Kenneth Burke, *Attitudes toward History*, 3d ed. (Berkeley: University of California Press, 1984), pp. 3, 25.

2. "Combative Chronicler," *Time*, December 17, 1965, p. 56. See also William V. Shannon, "Controversial Historian in the Age of Kennedy," *New York Times Magazine*, November 21, 1965, p. 133.

3. James A. Nuechterlein, "Arthur M. Schlesinger, Jr., and the Discontents of Postwar American Liberalism," *Review of Politics* 39 (January 1977): 4.

4. Marcus Cunliffe, "Arthur M. Schlesinger, Jr.," in Marcus Cunliffe and Robin Winks, eds., *Pastmasters: Some Essays on American Historians* (New York: Harper and Row, 1969), p. 345.

5. "Biography," *Current Biography*, October 1946, p. 537.

6. See Arthur M. Schlesinger, Jr., *Orestes Brownson: A Pilgrim's Progress* (Boston: Little, Brown, 1939); and Arthur M. Schlesinger, Jr., "The Problem of Richard Hildreth," *New England Quarterly* 13 (June 1940): 223–45.

7. For the association of Schlesinger, Sr., with Felix Frankfurter and his active participation in the Sacco-Vanzetti protest, see Arthur Schlesinger, Sr., *In Retrospect: The History of a Historian* (New York: Harcourt, Brace and World, 1963), pp. 127–55.

8. Cunliffe, "Arthur M. Schlesinger, Jr.," p. 349.

9. Michael Wreszin, "Arthur Schlesinger, Jr., Scholar-Activist in Cold War America: 1946–56," *Salmagundi* 63, 4 (Spring-Summer 1984): 259–60.

10. Ibid., p. 260.

11. Harvey Breit, "Talk with Mr. Schlesinger," *New York Times Book Review,* September 18, 1949, p. 19.

12. The phrase "smell the dust and sweat of battle" comes from Arthur M. Schlesinger, Jr., "The Historian and History," *Foreign Affairs* 41 (April 1963): 492.

13. For a discussion of the progressive mind-set, see John Higham, "Beyond Consensus: The Historian as Moral Critic," *American Historical Review* 67 (April 1962): 609–25; and Arthur Mann, "The Progressive Tradition," in John Higham, ed., *The Reconstruction of American History* (New York: Harper and Row, 1962), pp. 157–79.

14. Arthur Schlesinger, Sr., *The American as Reformer,* 2d ed. (New York: Atheneum, 1968), p. 96.

15. Benjamin Ginzburg, "Against Messianism," *New Republic,* February 18, 1931, pp. 15–17.

16. Higham, "Beyond Consensus," p. 612.

17. Alonzo L. Hamby, *Beyond the New Deal: Harry S. Truman and American Liberalism* (New York: Columbia University Press, 1973).

18. Norman Markowitz, *The Rise and Fall of the People's Century* (New York: Free Press, 1973).

19. Steven M. Gillon, *Politics and Vision: The ADA and American Liberalism* (New York: Oxford University Press, 1987).

20. Ibid., pp. x, vii. See also Sheldon Wolin, *Politics and Vision* (Boston: Little, Brown, 1960).

21. Burke, *Attitudes toward History,* pp. 106, 92.

22. Allen J. Matusow, "John F. Kennedy and the Intellectuals," *Wilson Quarterly* 7 (Autumn 1983): 142.

23. Arthur M. Schlesinger, Jr., *The Vital Center: The Politics of Freedom,* 2d ed. (Boston: Houghton Mifflin, 1962), p. 1. The first edition was published in 1949.

24. Ibid., pp. xxii-xxiii.

25. Ibid., p 245.

26. David Burke Griffiths, "Vital Center versus New Left: A. M. Schlesinger, Jr., and C. W. Mills," *Midwest Quarterly* 7 (Autumn 1965): 47.

27. Reinhold Niebuhr, *The Children of Light and the Children of Darkness* (New York: Charles Scribner and Sons, 1944), pp. 1–41.

28. Ibid., p. xi.

29. Schlesinger, Jr., quoted in Cunliffe, "Arthur M. Schlesinger, Jr.," p. 363.

30. Arthur M. Schlesinger, Jr., "Theology and Politics from the Social Gospel to the Cold War: The Impact of Reinhold Niebuhr," in Cushing

Strout, ed., *Intellectual History in America: From Darwin to Niebuhr,* vol. 2 (New York: Harper and Row, 1968), p. 180.

31. Griffiths, "Vital Center versus New Left," p. 47.

32. Schlesinger, Jr., *The Vital Center,* p. 255.

33. Arthur M. Schlesinger, Jr., *The Age of Jackson* (Boston: Little, Brown, 1945), p. 523.

34. For a discussion of interest-group liberalism, see Theodore J. Lowi, *The End of Liberalism: Ideology, Policy, and the Crisis of Public Authority* (New York: W. W. Norton, 1969), pp. 29–97.

35. See, for example, Arthur Schlesinger, Sr., "Extremism in American Politics," *Saturday Review,* November 27, 1965, pp. 21–25.

36. Arthur Schlesinger, Sr., *New Viewpoints in American History* (New York: Macmillan, 1923), p. 107.

37. See Schlesinger, Sr., *In Retrospect,* pp. 193–203.

38. Arthur Schlesinger, Sr., "What Then Is the American, This New Man?" *American Historical Review* 48 (January 1943): 225–44.

39. Schlesinger, Jr., quoted in Wreszin, "Arthur Schlesinger, Jr., Scholar-Activist," p. 258.

40. Schlesinger, Jr., *The Vital Center,* p. xvii.

41. Arthur M. Schlesinger, Jr., "On the Inscrutability of History," *Encounter* 27 (November 1966): 13.

42. See Schlesinger, Jr., *The Vital Center,* chaps. 2–4.

43. Ibid., pp. 40–41.

44. Ibid., pp. 39–40.

45. Ibid., p. 40.

46. Arthur M. Schlesinger, Jr., "Epilogue: The One Against the Many," in Arthur M. Schlesinger, Jr., and Morton White, eds., *Paths of American Thought* (Boston: Houghton Mifflin, 1963), pp. 532–33.

47. Schlesinger, Jr., *The Age of Jackson,* p. 163 (epigraph preceding foreword).

48. Wreszin, "Arthur Schlesinger, Jr., Scholar-Activist," pp. 257–58.

49. Schlesinger, Jr., *The Vital Center,* pp. xxi–xxii.

50. Wreszin, "Arthur Schlesinger, Jr., Scholar-Activist," pp. 257–58.

51. Schlesinger, Jr., *The Age of Jackson,* p. 251.

52. Burke, *Attitudes toward History,* pp. 3–5, 92.

53. Schlesinger, Sr., *In Retrospect,* p. 127; Arthur Schlesinger, Sr., "Tides of American Politics," *Yale Review* 29 (December 1939): 217–30.

54. Schlesinger, Sr., "Tides of American Politics," p. 219.

55. Arthur M. Schlesinger, Jr., *The Politics of Hope* (Boston: Houghton Mifflin, 1963), p. ix.

56. Arthur M. Schlesinger, Jr., "Conservative versus Liberal," *New York Times Magazine,* March 4, 1956, pp. 11, 58, 62.

57. Schlesinger, Jr., "On the Inscrutability of History," pp. 10–17.

58. Schlesinger, Jr., "Conservative versus Liberal," pp. 58–60.

59. Arthur M. Schlesinger, Jr., "One Last Chance for the Democrats," *Playboy,* November 1982, pp. 110–12.

60. Ibid., p. 252.

61. Arthur M. Schlesinger, Jr., "The New Conservatism: The Politics of Nostalgia," *Reporter*, June 16, 1955, pp. 9–12.

62. Arthur M. Schlesinger, Jr., "Not Left, Not Right, But a Vital Center," *New York Times Magazine*, April 4, 1948, pp. 7, 45–47.

63. Arthur M. Schlesinger, Jr., "Is Liberalism Dead?" *New York Times Magazine*, March 30, 1980, p. 79.

64. Arthur M. Schlesinger, Jr., "New Liberal Coalition," *Progressive*, April 1967, p. 19.

65. Schlesinger, Jr., "Not Left," p. 47.

66. Schlesinger, Sr., "Tides of American Politics," p. 220.

67. Arthur M. Schlesinger, Sr., "The Tides of National Politics," in Arthur M. Schlesinger, Sr., *Paths to the Present* (New York: Macmillan, 1949), pp. 90, 89.

68. Arthur M. Schlesinger, Jr., *The Cycles of American History* (Boston: Houghton Mifflin, 1986), p. 27.

69. Schlesinger, Jr., "Is Liberalism Dead?" pp. 79, 73.

70. Schlesinger, Sr., "The Tides of American Politics," pp. 217–30.

71. Schlesinger, Sr., "The Tides of National Politics," p. 85.

72. Schlesinger, Sr., *In Retrospect*, p. 108.

73. Schlesinger, Jr., *The Cycles of American History*, p. 30.

74. Schlesinger, Sr., "The Tides of National Politics," p. 86; and Schlesinger, Jr., "Is Liberalism Dead?" p. 79.

75. Arthur M. Schlesinger, Jr., "On Heroic Leadership and the Dilemma of Strong Men and Weak Peoples," *Encounter* 15 (December 1960): 3–11.

76. Ibid., p. 4.

77. Arthur M. Schlesinger, Jr., "The Decline of Greatness," *Saturday Evening Post*, November 1958, pp. 70–71.

78. Arthur M. Schlesinger, Jr., "Who Needs Grover Cleveland?" *New Republic*, July 7–14, 1979, pp. 14–16.

79. Schlesinger, Jr., "On Heroic Leadership," p. 5.

80. Arthur M. Schlesinger, Jr., "The Velocity of History," *Newsweek*, July 6, 1970, pp. 32–34.

81. Schlesinger, Jr., *The Vital Center*, p. 256.

82. Schlesinger, Jr., "On Heroic Leadership," p. 5.

83. According to Burke, in applying a frame of acceptance to a situation, an individual commits an act of "transcendence" whereby "he coaches his set of meanings by an 'act of will.'" The symbols chosen to bridge the contradictions of existence "contain many 'overtones'—they are 'mergers'—they are 'vessels'—they are acts of synthesis capable of infinite analysis." Burke, *Attitudes toward History*, p. 106.

2. *The Age of Jackson* and *The Age of Roosevelt:* A Foundation for Ideological History

1. "Combative Chronicler," *Time*, December 17, 1965, p. 56.

2. "The historian speaks of what has happened," wrote Aristotle in the

Poetics, while the poet or rhetorician speaks of "the kind of thing that can happen," of "what is capable of happening according to the rule of probability or necessity." Aristotle, *Poetics*, trans. Gerald F. Else (Ann Arbor: University of Michigan Press, 1967), pp. 32–33 (15161–63). While histories "should be read for their bearing upon counsels of state," Aristotle continued in the *Rhetoric*, detailed inquiries into the past "belong to Political Science, not to Rhetoric." Aristotle, *Rhetoric*, trans. Lane Cooper, 2d ed. (Englewood Cliffs, N.J.: Prentice-Hall, 1960), p. 17 (1360a35). Cicero, distinguishing between the writing of history, whose proper aim was truth, and the use of elegy for propaganda, spoke of a "great responsibility" of a writer of history to "not dare to tell anything but the truth" and to "make bold to tell the whole truth." Cicero, *De Oratore*, trans. E. W. Sutton, Loeb ed. 3d ed. (Cambridge, Mass.: Harvard University Press, 1959), p. 245 (II, xv, 62).

3. See, for example, Leopold von Ranke, *Gescluchten der romanischen und germanischen Volker*, vols. 33–34 (Leipzig, 1824), p. 7, in R. G. Collingwood, *The Idea of History*, 5th ed. (New York: Oxford University Press, 1962), p. 130. See also Matthew A. Fitzsimons, Charles E. Nowell, and Alfred G. Pundt, eds., *The Development of Historiography* (Harrisburg, Pa.: Stackpole, 1954).

4. According to North, even classical Greek teachers and politicians saw the virtue of embellishing historical discourse with the stylistic devices of *narratio*. Helen F. North, "Rhetoric and Historiography," *Quarterly Journal of Speech* 42 (October 1956): 234–42. See also Richard Leo Enos, "Rhetorical Intent in Ancient Historiography: Herodotus and the Battle of Marathon," *Communication Quarterly* 24 (Winter 1976): 24–31.

5. Charles A. Beard, "Written History as an Act of Faith," *American Historical Review* 39 (January 1934): 220–21. See also R. G. Collingwood, *The Idea of History*, 5th ed. (New York: Oxford University Press, 1962).

6. See Carl Cone, "Major Factors in the Rhetoric of Historians," *Quarterly Journal of Speech* 33 (December 1947): 437–50; James A. Andrews, "The Rhetoric of History: The Constitutional Convention," *Today's Speech* 16 (November 1968): 23–26; and Ronald H. Carpenter, "Frederick Jackson Turner and the Rhetorical Impact of the Frontier Thesis," *Quarterly Journal of Speech* 63 (April 1977): 117–29.

7. Kenneth Burke, *Philosophy of Literary Form*, 3d ed. (Berkeley: University of California Press, 1973), p. 1.

8. Michael C. McGee, "The Fall of Wellington: A Case Study of the Relationship Between Theory, Practice, and Rhetoric in History," *Quarterly Journal of Speech* 63 (February 1977): 28.

9. Ibid., pp. 28, 31.

10. Beard, "Written History," pp. 319–29; J. H. Hexter, "Historiography: The Rhetoric of History," in *International Encyclopedia of the Social Sciences* (New York: Macmillan, 1969), pp. 368–93; and Hayden White, *Metahistory: The Historical Imagination in Nineteenth-Century Europe* (Baltimore: Johns Hopkins University Press, 1973).

11. Kenneth Burke, *Attitudes toward History*, 3d ed. (Berkeley: University of California Press, 1984), p. 5.

12. Carl Hempel, "The Function of General Laws in History," *Journal of*

Philosophy 39 (1942): 35–48; and David Zarefsky, "Causal Argument Among Historians: The Case of the American Civil War," *Southern Speech Communication Journal* 15 (1980): 187–205.

13. For a description of the functions of grounds and claims in argument, see Stephen Toulmin, Richard Rieke, and Allan Janik, *An Introduction to Reasoning* (New York: Macmillan, 1979), pp. 21–42.

14. For a discussion of distinctions between technical and public argument, see G. Thomas Goodnight, "The Personal, Technical, and Public Spheres of Argument: A Speculative Inquiry into the Art of Public Deliberation," *Journal of the American Forensic Association* 18 (1982): 214–27.

15. In 1828, Whately defined presumption as "a preoccupation of the ground." A statement that carries presumption is assumed to "stand good till some sufficient reason is adduced against it." Richard Whately, *Elements of Rhetoric* (Carbondale: Southern Illinois University Press, 1963), p. 112.

16. G. Thomas Goodnight, "The Liberal and the Conservative Presumption: On Political Philosophy and the Foundation of Public Argument," in *Proceedings of the [First] Summer Conference on Argumentation* (Falls Church, Va.: Speech Communication Association, 1980), pp. 304–37.

17. McGee, "Fall of Wellington," p. 41.

18. Carpenter, "Frederick Jackson Turner," p. 128.

19. Arthur M. Schlesinger, Jr., "On the Inscrutability of History," *Encounter* 27 (November 1966): 10.

20. Arthur M. Schlesinger, Jr., *The Age of Jackson* (Boston: Little, Brown, 1945), pp. ix, x.

21. Arthur M. Schlesinger, Jr., "The Thread of History: Freedom or Fatality?" *Reporter*, December 15, 1955, pp. 45–47.

22. Ibid., p. 45.

23. Schlesinger, Jr., "On the Inscrutability of History," p. 11.

24. Ibid.

25. Schlesinger, Jr., quoted in *Conversations with Henry Brandon* (Boston: Houghton Mifflin, 1968), pp. 53–54.

26. Hempel, "The Function of General Laws in History," p. 42.

27. Schlesinger, Jr., quoted in *Conversations*, p. 44.

28. Ibid., p. 45.

29. Schlesinger, Jr., "The Thread of History," p. 47.

30. Arthur M. Schlesinger, Jr., "Epilogue: The One against the Many," in Arthur Schlesinger, Jr., and Morton White, eds., *Paths of American Thought* (Boston: Houghton Mifflin, 1963), pp. 531–38.

31. Schlesinger, Jr., *The Age of Jackson*, pp. 12, 26, 29, 307, 316, 505–19, 87.

32. Ibid., pp. 83–84.

33. Ibid., p. 84.

34. Ibid., pp. 159–89, 384–86.

35. Other historians have given leaders of Jackson's time similarly mixed reviews. Robert Remini applauds Van Buren's ability to blend a belief in Jeffersonian agrarianism with a keen sense of political organization, while Benson charges that Van Buren was no friend of the common man. Pessen

points out that nearly all of the leading politicians of the era—Whigs and Democrats—came from similar upper-middle-class economic and social backgrounds and hence could equally sympathize with (or exploit) the commoners. Van Deusen asserts that Whigs, while possibly afflicted with a "certain smug consciousness of superiority," were men of equal and even more far-reaching vision than their Democratic counterparts. See Robert Remini, *Martin Van Buren and the Making of the Democratic Party*, 2d ed. (New York: W. W. Norton, 1954); Lee Benson, *The Concept of Jacksonian Democracy: New York as a Test Case* (New York: Atheneum, 1969); Edward Pessen, *Jacksonian America: Society, Personality, and Politics* (Homewood, Ill.: Dorsey Press, 1969); and Glyndon Van Deusen, *The Jacksonian Era, 1828–48* (New York: Harper and Row, 1959).

36. Arthur M. Schlesinger, Jr., *The Coming of the New Deal* (Boston: Houghton Mifflin, 1959), pp. 19, 17.

37. Ibid., pp. 456–70, 27–84, 87–176.

38. Ibid., p. 533. In contrast, Leuchtenburg argues that political compromises and the purposeful maintenance of overlapping bureaucracies were the major contributors to the conceptual fuzziness of the New Deal. See William Leuchtenburg, *Franklin D. Roosevelt and the New Deal* (New York: Harper and Row, 1963).

39. Schlesinger, Jr., *The Coming of the New Deal*, pp. 528, 533.

40. Schlesinger, Jr., *The Age of Jackson*, p. 391.

41. Ibid., pp. 391, 305.

42. Ibid., p. 305.

43. Charles Sellers, in an article entitled "Andrew Jackson versus the Historians," notes that "Andrew Jackson was intimately identified with the full flowering of American democracy; and as long as democracy remains preeminently the distinguishing feature of our society, the period and symbol of its triumph will remain controversial." Marvin Meyers, in his attempt to describe a "Jacksonian persuasion," explains that while commentators and scholars agree that "the second quarter of the nineteenth century is properly remembered as an Age of Jackson," "here agreement ends." Edward Pessen completely rejects the Jacksonian democracy concept and has argued that 1825–45 was neither the age of Jackson nor the age of the common man but an "age of materialism and opportunism." "Jacksonian Democracy," Pessen concludes, "gave power not to Tom, Dick, and Harry, but to the shrewd, ambitious, wealthy, and able politicians who knew best how to flatter them." Common men were pawns, not kings, in Pessen's view of nineteenth-century America. Benson, upon examining voting patterns and party policies in New York from 1816 to 1844, finds that "the Whigs come closer than the Democrats to satisfying the requirements of historians in search of nineteenth-century precursors to twentieth-century New Dealers." Benson also asserts that "the superficial analogies drawn between the parties [Jeffersonians-Democrats, Federalists-Whigs] have warped American historiography." Glyndon Van Deusen takes a more equivocal stance towards how Jackson fits into a tradition of liberal reform. "Jacksonian Democracy," Van Deusen concludes, ". . . joined an apprecia-

tion of the common man, and a desire to serve his needs and aspirations with an inadequate concept of the economic methods by which liberty and equality might be achieved and maintained on behalf of the masses of mankind." See Charles Sellers, Jr., "Andrew Jackson versus the Historians," *Mississippi Valley Historical Review* 44 (1958): 615–16; Marvin Meyers, *The Jacksonian Persuasion: Politics and Belief,* 2d ed. (Stanford, Calif.: Stanford University Press, 1960), p. 5; Pessen, pp. 324–25; Benson, pp. 104, 63; Van Deusen, pp. xi–xii.

44. See Arthur M. Schlesinger, Jr., *The Crisis of the Old Order* (Boston: Houghton Mifflin, 1957).

45. Schlesinger, Jr., *The Coming of the New Deal,* pp. 1–3.

46. Ibid., pp. 95, 22.

47. Ibid., p. 558.

48. Schlesinger, Jr., *The Age of Jackson,* p. 39.

49. Ibid., p. 522.

50. Ibid., p. 43.

51. Martin Van Buren, *Inquiry into the Origin and Course of Political Parties in the United States* (New York, 1867), pp. 171–72, quoted in Schlesinger, Jr., *The Age of Jackson,* p. 43.

52. Schlesinger, Jr., *The Age of Jackson,* p. 43. John William Ward uses a similar rhetorical approach in *Jackson: Symbol for an Age.* Ward identifies three dominant ideas that recur in the rhetoric of and about Andrew Jackson—Nature, Providence, and Will—and argues that "these general concepts are the structural underpinnings of the ideology of the society of early-nineteenth-century America, for which Andrew Jackson is one *symbol.*" In the minds of many Americans, Ward asserts, Andrew Jackson epitomized everything an American *should be.* Jackson tamed nature without destroying its essential innocence and piety. Jackson had God on his side in his political battles. Jackson had an iron will tempered with compassion. In short, Jackson was more paradigm than person, even *in his own time.* Ward concludes that Jackson's power as a shaping force in American history was largely *symbolic;* the symbolic figure of Andrew Jackson was *not* "the creation of Jackson . . . or of the Democratic Party" but a "creation of the times" and a source of information *about* the times. See John William Ward, *Andrew Jackson: Symbol for an Age* (New York: Oxford University Press, 1962), pp. 10, 213.

Other historians have described Jackson in harsher terms. Pessen describes Jackson alternatively as a political opportunist who flip-flopped on more than one issue on behalf of more than one interest. Van Deusen argues that Old Hickory did not have a "well-thought-out philosophy of party or of government" except a "belief in the worth (and voting strength) of the common man," which he could not reconcile with a belief in limited government. See Pessen, pp. 347–51; Van Deusen, pp. 36–37.

53. Schlesinger, Jr., *The Coming of the New Deal,* pp. 550–51.

54. Ibid., pp. 553, 557, 588.

55. Ibid., p. 551.

56. Schlesinger, Jr., *The Coming of the New Deal,* pp. 581–88. In contrast,

Leuchtenburg's account of interest-group liberalism springs from a power-broker state created by economic stagnation and resource maldistribution. See Leuchtenburg, *Franklin D. Roosevelt and the New Deal.*

57. Schlesinger, Jr., "On the Inscrutability of History," p. 17.

58. Pessen, p. vii.

59. Sellers, p. 626.

60. Hammond complained that Schlesinger's "Manichean naivete with respect to all things Jacksonian and the sordidness of all things opposed" rendered the historian's biases all too transparent. With biting sarcasm, Hammond noted: "Mr. Schlesinger's vocabulary purrs over his friends. The landscapes at the Hermitage and Kinderhook smile in a fashion not noticeable where Whigs and Federalists live. The Jacksonian leaders have a 'pervading insight,' their wrath is 'magnificent,' one or another of them is 'handsome,' 'grave,' 'masterly,' 'erudite,' 'thoughtful,' 'quiet,' 'intelligent,' 'brilliant,' etc., etc., and the old hero himself is touchingly fond of children. The opposition is a sorry outfit. They are Bank 'lackeys,' they 'roar' and 'snarl,' they deal in 'hullabaloo,' they are 'phony,' they have 'fantasies,' they work 'backstairs,' their best minds are 'opaque,' and one gets the impression that Mr. Schlesinger never thinks of them as loving little children at all." Bray Hammond, "Public Policy and National Banks," review, *Journal of Economic History* 6 (May 1946): 79–84.

61. Thomas B. Silver, "Coolidge and the Historians," *American Scholar* 50 (Autumn 1981): 501–17.

62. "Portrait," book review, *Time,* October 22, 1945, pp. 103–106.

63. Esmund Wright, "The Age of Roosevelt," review, *History Today* 7 (November 1957): 775.

64. Gerald W. Johnson, "FDR: A Political Portrait," review, *Atlantic Monthly* 199 (March 1957): 69.

65. James A. Nuechterlein, "Arthur M. Schlesinger, Jr., and the Discontents of Postwar American Liberalism," *Review of Politics* 39 (January 1977): 4–5.

66. Marcus Cunliffe, "Arthur Schlesinger, Jr.," in Marcus Cunliffe and Robin Winks, eds., *Pastmasters: Some Essays on American Historians* (New York: Harper and Row, 1969), pp. 353–58, 367–68.

67. John Higham, "The Construction of American History," in John Higham, ed., *The Reconstruction of American History* (New York: Harper and Row, 1962), pp. 9–10.

3. From the New Deal to Camelot: Ideological History in Action

1. Michael Wreszin, "Arthur Schlesinger, Jr., Scholar-Activist in Cold War America, 1946–56," *Salmagundi* 63, 4 (Spring-Summer 1984): 261.

2. Carroll Englehardt, "Man in the Middle: Arthur M. Schlesinger, Jr., and Postwar American Liberalism," *South Atlantic Quarterly* 80 (April 1981): 121–22.

3. Wrezsin, "Arthur Schlesinger, Jr., Scholar-Activist," p. 261.

4. Ibid., p. 267.

5. Ralph de Toledano, "Junior's Misses," *American Mercury* 77 (November 1953): 5.

6. Allen J. Matusow, "John F. Kennedy and the Intellectuals," *Wilson Quarterly* 7 (Autumn 1983): 141.

7. Arthur M. Schlesinger, Jr., "Where Does the Liberal Go from Here?" *New York Times Magazine*, August 4, 1957, p. 7.

8. Arthur Schlesinger, Jr., *The Age of Jackson* (Boston: Little, Brown, 1945), p. 163.

9. Arthur M. Schlesinger, Jr., *The Vital Center: The Politics of Freedom*, 2d ed. (Boston: Houghton Mifflin, 1962), p. 9.

10. Ibid., p. 245.

11. Allen J. Matusow, *The Unraveling of America: A History of Liberalism in the 1960s* (New York: Harper and Row, 1984), p. 5.

12. James A. Nuechterlein, "Arthur M. Schlesinger, Jr., and the Discontents of Postwar American Liberalism," *Review of Politics* 39 (January 1977): 12.

13. Daniel Bell, *The End of Ideology* (Glencoe, Ill.: Free Press, 1960), p. 110.

14. Schlesinger, Jr., *The Age of Jackson*, pp. 30–44; and Arthur M. Schlesinger, Jr., *The Crisis of the Old Order* (Boston: Houghton Mifflin, 1957), pp. 49–89.

15. Matusow, *The Unraveling of America*, p. xiii.

16. Louis Hartz, quoted in Garry Wills, *Nixon Agonistes* (Boston: Houghton Mifflin, 1969), p. 559.

17. Matusow, *The Unraveling of America*, p. 6.

18. Ibid., pp. 8–9.

19. Nuechterlein, "Arthur M. Schlesinger, Jr.," p. 15.

20. William L. O'Neill, *Coming Apart: An Informal History of America in the 1960s*, 2d ed. (New York: Quadrangle Press, 1978), p. 7; Matusow, *The Unraveling of America*, p. xiii.

21. O'Neill, "Coming Apart," p. 7.

22. Englehardt, "Man in the Middle," p. 135.

23. According to Dionisopolous and Goldzwig, "The rhetorical act of drawing 'lessons from history' is grounded in the 'processes of oversimplification and analogical extension.'" "The ability to 'coach' attitudes," they continue, "frame conceptualizations, and adopt analogical models or templates is crucial for constructing the narratives of cultural history." George N. Dionisopolous and Steven R. Goldzwig, "'The Meaning of Vietnam': Political Rhetoric as Revisionist Cultural History," *Quarterly Journal of Speech* 78 (1992): 75.

24. Bruce E. Gronbeck, "Argument from History-1 and Argument from History-2: Uses of the Past in Public Deliberations," in Donn W. Parson, ed., *Argument in Controversy: Proceedings of the Seventh SCA/AFA Conference on Argumentation* (Annandale, Va.: Speech Communication Association, 1991), p. 97.

25. Zarefsky has noted that "to choose a definition is to plead a cause."

An advocate who names an object or idea in a certain way can influence attitudes about that object or idea. David Zarefsky, Carol Miller-Tutzauer, and Frank Tutzauer, "Reagan's Safety Net for the Truly Needy: The Rhetorical Uses of Definition," *Central States Speech Journal* 35 (1984): 113. See also Charles L. Stevenson, *Ethics and Language* (New Haven: Yale University Press, 1944), pp. 206–26.

26. Chaim Perelman and L. Olbrechts-Tyteca, *The New Rhetoric: A Treatise on Argumentation,* trans. John Wilkinson and Purcell Weaver (Notre Dame, Ind.: University of Notre Dame Press, 1969), pp. 411–15. The strategic use of definition through dissociation has been illustrated in recent studies of Ronald Reagan's "safety net" approach to social programs and Lyndon Johnson's "War on Poverty." David Zarefsky, Carol Miller-Tutzauer, and Frank Tutzauer, "Reagan's Safety Net for the Truly Needy: The Rhetorical Uses of Definition," *Central States Speech Journal* 35 (1984): 113–19; and David Zarefsky, *President Johnson's War on Poverty: Rhetoric and History* (University: University of Alabama Press, 1986).

27. Perelman and Olbrechts-Tyteca, "New Rhetoric," pp. 444–50.

28. Michael C. McGee, "The 'Ideograph': A Link Between Rhetoric and Ideology," *Quarterly Journal of Speech* 66 (1980): 1–16; and Celeste M. Condit, "Democracy and Civil Rights: The Universalizing Influence of Public Argumentation," *Communication Monographs* 54 (1987): 1–18.

29. Arthur M. Schlesinger, Jr., "Stevenson and the American Liberal Dilemma," *Twentieth Century* 153 (January 1953): 29.

30. Arthur M. Schlesinger, Jr., "Eisenhower Won't Succeed," *New Republic,* April 5, 1954, p. 8.

31. Ibid.

32. Schlesinger, Jr., "Stevenson and the American Liberal Dilemma," pp. 28–29.

33. Arthur M. Schlesinger, Jr., "Liberalism in America: A Note for Europeans," *Perspectives, U.S.A.* 14 (Winter 1956), in Arthur M. Schlesinger, Jr., *The Politics of Hope* (Boston: Houghton Mifflin, 1963), p. 63.

34. Arthur M. Schlesinger, Jr., "Liberalism," *Saturday Review,* June 8, 1957, p. 37.

35. Arthur M. Schlesinger, Jr., "The New Conservatism in America: A Liberal Comment," *Confluence* 2 (December 1953): 61; and Arthur M. Schlesinger, Jr., "The New Conservatism: The Politics of Nostalgia," *Reporter,* June 16, 1955, p. 9.

36. Schlesinger, Jr., "The New Conservatism: The Politics of Nostalgia," p. 12.

37. Arthur M. Schlesinger, Jr., "A Democratic View of Republicans," *New York Times Magazine,* July 17, 1960, p. 7.

38. Schlesinger, Jr., "Eisenhower Won't Succeed," p. 9.

39. Schlesinger, Jr., "A Democratic View," p. 7.

40. Schlesinger, Jr., "Eisenhower Won't Succeed," p. 9.

41. Arthur M. Schlesinger, Jr., "The New Mood in Politics," *Esquire,* January 1960, p. 60.

42. Schlesinger, Jr., "A Democratic View," p. 48.

43. Schlesinger, Jr., "Eisenhower Won't Succeed," p. 9.

44. Ibid.; and Arthur M. Schlesinger, Jr., *Kennedy or Nixon: Does it Make a Difference?* (New York: Macmillan, 1960), p. 47.

45. Schlesinger, Jr., "Where Does the Liberal Go from Here?" p. 7.

46. Ibid., p. 36.

47. Ibid. By 1963, Schlesinger asserted that the New Deal was "a response to pent-up frustrations and needs" in American society "which would have produced an activist, practical mood had there been no depression at all." Arthur M. Schlesinger, Jr., "Sources of the New Deal," in Arthur M. Schlesinger, Jr., and Morton White, eds., *Paths of American Thought* (Boston: Houghton Mifflin, 1963), pp. 391, 375.

48. As early as 1949, Schlesinger asserted that "Mr. and Mrs. Average Citizen are a good deal better off today than they were ten years ago." The New Deal's success had generated agreement that "it is the responsibility of Government to put a floor under our economy." As a result, America had "a true prosperity which, with wise public policy, we can maintain for an indefinite period to come." Arthur M. Schlesinger, Jr., and Seymour Harris, "Are We Richer Today?" *Ladies Home Journal*, September 1949, pp. 2, 42, 108, 110.

49. Arthur M. Schlesinger, Jr., "The Future of Liberalism: The Challenge of Abundance," *Reporter*, May 3, 1956, p. 9.

50. Arthur M. Schlesinger, Jr., "The New Mood in Politics," p. 60.

51. Schlesinger, Jr., "Where Does the Liberal Go from Here?" p. 36.

52. Arthur M. Schlesinger, Jr., "The Shape of National Politics to Come" (memorandum for private circulation, copy in the Northwestern University library, Evanston, Ill., 1959), p. 17.

53. Schlesinger, Jr., "The New Mood in Politics," p. 60; and Schlesinger, Jr., "The Shape," pp. 11–15.

54. Schlesinger, Jr., "The Shape," pp. 15–16.

55. Burke has called the strategy of terminological "circumference," in which "the quality of the context in which a subject is placed will affect the quality of the subject placed in that context." Kenneth Burke, *A Grammar of Motives*, 3d ed. (Berkeley: University of California Press, 1969), pp. 77–85.

56. Schlesinger, Jr., "Stevenson," p. 25.

57. Schlesinger, Jr., "Where Does the Liberal Go from Here?" p. 36.

58. Schlesinger, Jr., "The Shape," p. 1.

59. Schlesinger, Jr., "The New Mood in Politics," p. 58.

60. Ibid., p. 59.

61. Ibid.

62. Schlesinger, Jr., "The Shape," pp. 2–3.

63. Ibid., p. 1.

64. Schlesinger, Jr., "The New Mood in Politics," p. 58.

65. Schlesinger, Jr., "The Shape," p. 7.

66. Ibid., pp. 4–5.

67. Ibid., p. 22.

68. Ibid., p. 7.

69. Schlesinger, Jr., "The New Mood in Politics," p. 59.

70. Schlesinger, Jr., "The Shape," p. 7.

71. Schlesinger, Jr., "The Future of Liberalism," p. 10.

72. Schlesinger, Jr., "Eisenhower Won't Succeed," p. 9.
73. Schlesinger, Jr., "The Shape," p. 10.
74. Ibid., p. 11.
75. Schlesinger, Jr., "Eisenhower Won't Succeed," p. 9.
76. Ibid., p. 12.
77. Arthur M. Schlesinger, Jr., "The Case for Kennedy," *New York Times Magazine*, November 6, 1960, p. 19; and Arthur M. Schlesinger, Jr., "Right Man for the Big Job," *New York Times Magazine*, April 3, 1960, pp. 120–21.
78. Schlesinger, Jr., "Right Man for the Big Job," p. 120.
79. Ibid.
80. Ibid.
81. Schlesinger, Jr., "The New Mood in Politics," p. 60.
82. Kenneth Burke suggests that one way of charting the course of a frame of acceptance is to select out of the various discourses a *representative anecdote*, a case of symbolic action "summational in character . . . wherein human relations grandly converge," which can be analyzed as a key to unlocking the whole rhetoric of an individual or movement. From the study of a representative anecdote, the critic may discover whether the frame of acceptance has overcome the rhetorical burdens erected by a given situation. Burke, *A Grammar of Motives*, pp. 323–25.
83. Arthur M. Schlesinger, Jr., *A Thousand Days: John F. Kennedy in the White House* (Boston: Houghton Mifflin, 1965), pp. 77–78.
84. Ibid., pp. 16–18, 23–24.
85. Ibid., pp. 27–30, 68–70.
86. Ibid., pp. 72–74, 76.
87. Schlesinger, Jr., *Kennedy or Nixon*, foreword.
88. Schlesinger, Jr., *A Thousand Days*, p. 64.
89. Schlesinger, Jr., *Kennedy or Nixon*, p. 2.
90. Ibid., pp. 35–50.
91. Nuechterlein, "Arthur M. Schlesinger, Jr.," p. 22.
92. Schlesinger, Jr., *Kennedy or Nixon*, pp. 2–18.
93. Ibid., pp. 18–34.
94. Ibid., p. 51.
95. Arthur M. Schlesinger, Jr., *The Politics of Hope* (Boston: Houghton Mifflin, 1963), p. xii.
96. Schlesinger, Jr., *A Thousand Days*, pp. 75–76.
97. Marian J. Morton, "Arthur M. Schlesinger, Jr., and the Search for the Vital Center," in Marian J. Morton, *The Terrors of Ideological Politics: Liberal Historians in a Conservative Mood* (Cleveland: Case Western Reserve University Press, 1972), p. 41.
98. Schlesinger, Jr., *A Thousand Days*, p. 104.
99. Arthur M. Schlesinger, Jr., *The Politics of Hope* (Boston: Houghton Mifflin, 1963), p. xii.
100. Kenneth Burke, *Counter-Statement*, 3d ed. (Berkeley: University of California Press, 1968), pp. 124–25.
101. Leland M. Griffin, "Where Dreams Collide: Rhetorical Trajectories in the Assassination of President Kennedy," *Quarterly Journal of Speech* 70 (1984): 127.

102. Kenneth Burke, *Language as Symbolic Action* (Berkeley: University of California Press, 1966), pp. 101, 44–62.
103. Schlesinger, Jr., *A Thousand Days*, pp. 206–7.

4. The Tides of National Politics and the Rhetoric of Dawnism

1. John Kenneth Galbraith, *Who Needs the Democrats?—and What It Takes to Be Needed* (Garden City, N.Y.: Doubleday, 1970), pp. 64–66.
2. John F. Kennedy, "The Democratic National Convention Acceptance Address," *Vital Speeches* 26 (August 1, 1960): 611.
3. Kathleen Jamieson, *Packaging the Presidency: A History and Criticism of Presidential Campaign Advertising* (New York: Oxford University Press, 1984), p. 124.
4. Allen J. Matusow, *The Unraveling of America: A History of Liberalism in the 1960s* (New York: Harper and Row, 1984), pp. ix–29.
5. Carroll Englehardt, "Man in the Middle: Arthur M. Schlesinger, Jr., and Postwar American Liberalism," *South Atlantic Quarterly* 80 (1981): 119.
6. Arthur M. Schlesinger, Jr., *A Thousand Days: John F. Kennedy in the White House* (Boston: Houghton Mifflin, 1965), pp. 17–19.
7. Henry Fairlie, *The Kennedy Promise: The Politics of Expectation* (Garden City, N.Y.: Doubleday, 1973), pp. 17–20.
8. John F. Kennedy, in U.S. Congress, Senate, Committee of Commerce, Subcommittee on Communications, *Freedom of Communications*, 87th Cong., 1st sess., Senate Report No. 994, Part 1 of 2 (Washington, D.C.: U.S. Government Printing Office, 1961), p. 282.
9. Kennedy, in *Freedom of Communications*, p. 498.
10. Ritter writes that Kennedy's "new frontier" message resembled the jeremiad form in that it included a warning of impending disaster and a hope for redemption or salvation. Kurt W. Ritter, "American Political Rhetoric and the Jeremiad Tradition: Presidential Nomination Acceptance Addresses, 1960–76," *Central States Speech Journal* 31 (1980): 153–71.
11. Kennedy, in *Freedom of Communications*, p. 524.
12. Ibid., p. 604.
13. Ibid., p. 244.
14. John F. Kennedy, "A Time of Decision: A Challenging Agenda," *Vital Speeches* 26 (July 15, 1960): 583.
15. "The Democratic National Convention," p. 611.
16. John F. Kennedy, in *Public Papers of the Presidents of the United States, 1961* (Washington, D.C.: U.S. Government Printing Office, 1962), p. 3.
17. *Freedom of Communications*, p. 133.
18. Herbert S. Parmet, *JFK: The Presidency of John F. Kennedy*, 2d ed. (New York: Penguin Books, 1984), pp. 83–99, 237–76.
19. Kennedy, in *Freedom of Communications*, pp. 389, 464.
20. *Public Papers, 1961*, p. 19.

21. Ibid., pp. 727–28.

22. Ibid., p. 22; and John F. Kennedy, in *Public Papers of the Presidents of the United States, 1962* (Washington, D.C.: U.S. Government Printing Office, 1963), p. 15.

23. *Public Papers, 1962*, p. 806.

24. Arthur M. Schlesinger, Jr., *The Age of Jackson* (Boston: Little, Brown, 1945), p. 390.

25. See Arthur M. Schlesinger, Jr., "The New Mood in Politics," *Esquire*, January 1960, pp. 58–60.

26. *Freedom of Communications*, p. 104.

27. Ibid., p. 359.

28. "The Democratic National Convention," p. 612.

29. *Freedom of Communications*, p. 113.

30. Arthur M. Schlesinger, Jr., *Kennedy or Nixon: Does It Make Any Difference?* (New York: Macmillan, 1960).

31. *Public Papers, 1961*, p. 1.

32. Ibid., pp. 19, 22.

33. Arthur M. Schlesinger, Jr., "The Shape of National Politics to Come" (memorandum for private circulation, copy in the Northwestern University library, Evanston, Ill., 1959), p. 23.

34. "The Democratic National Convention," p. 611.

35. *Freedom of Communications*, p. 167.

36. Ibid., p. 733.

37. Ibid., p. 753.

38. Ibid., p. 52.

39. Ibid., p. 119.

40. Ibid., p. 402.

41. Ibid., p. 813.

42. *Public Papers, 1961*, p. 1.

43. *Public Papers, 1962*, p. 15.

44. John F. Kennedy, in *Public Papers of the Presidents of the United States, 1963* (Washington, D.C.: U.S. Government Printing Office, 1964), pp. 889–90.

45. *Public Papers, 1962*, pp. 315–16.

46. Schlesinger, Jr., "The New Mood in Politics," p. 60.

47. According to Brummett, the strategy of transcendence occurs "when one redefines some action as part of a new, higher context." In the "renaming of unacceptable experiences," an advocate "transcends contexts in which they seem undesirable and redefines them as something more acceptable." Barry Brummett, "Burkean Transcendence and Ultimate Terms by and about James Watt," *Central States Speech Journal* 33 (1982): 78.

48. "The Democratic National Convention," p. 611.

49. *Freedom of Communications*, pp. 95–96.

50. For other examples, see *Freedom of Communications*, pp. 147–48, 240, 319, 496–97, 549.

51. *Freedom of Communications*, p. 769.

52. Ibid., p. 311.

53. Ibid., p. 632.

54. T.R.B., "Sail On!" editorial, *New Republic*, March 27, 1961, p. 2.
55. "JFK on the First Hundred Days," *Newsweek*, May 8, 1961, p. 23.
56. *Public Papers, 1961,* p. 341.
57. Ibid., pp. 305–6.
58. Ibid., pp. 725–27.
59. *Public Papers, 1963,* pp. 735–38.
60. *Public Papers, 1962,* p. 422.
61. Ibid., pp. 471–73.
62. *Freedom of Communications,* pp. 95, 448.
63. Ibid., p. 775.
64. Ibid., p. 442.
65. Ibid., p. 452.
66. Ibid., p. 911.
67. *Public Papers, 1961,* pp. 2–3.
68. Ibid., p. 306.
69. See, for example, Fairlie, *The Kennedy Promise,* pp. 209–34.
70. Schlesinger, Jr., "The Shape," pp. 1–23.
71. The following comment made in 1985 by Senator Joseph Biden, who would stage a brief candidacy for the Democratic presidential nomination three years later, illustrates the enduring legacy of dawnism in liberal rhetoric: "1988 is going to be like 1960. We're going to have in the White House a popular President with a set of failed policies. Back then, the message from John Kennedy was a simple one. . . . He said, 'We can do better. We have to get the country moving again.'" Biden, quoted in Paul Taylor, "The Democratic Center Finds There's Strength in Numbers," *Washington Post Weekly Edition,* November 25, 1985, p. 13. According to Jefferson Morley, the promise of "new ideas" has been "the most enduring tactic of Democratic Presidential candidates" for a generation. One of the chief sources of the liberals' affection for "new ideas," concludes Morley, has been Arthur Schlesinger, Jr. The historian's articulation of a new "qualitative liberalism" in the late 1950s, argues Morley, was the source of much of what has occurred in liberal rhetoric since 1960. Jefferson Morley, "The Old Idea of 'New Ideas,'" *New Republic,* May 27, 1985, pp. 14–15.
72. Galbraith, "Who Needs the Democrats?" pp. 65–66. The War on Poverty is a good example of the Johnson administration's efforts to engineer social change through the identification of a crisis and the promise of transcendence. See David Zarefsky, "President Johnson's War on Poverty: The Rhetoric of Three 'Establishment' Movements," *Communication Monographs* 44 (1977): 352–73.
73. Galbraith, "Who Needs the Democrats?" p. 66. See also David Zarefsky, "The Impasse of the Liberal Argument: Speculation on American Politics in the Late 1960s," in David Zarefsky, Malcolm Sillars, and Jack Rhodes, eds., *Argument in Transition: Proceedings of the Third Summer Conference on Argumentation* (Annandale, Va.: Speech Communication Association, 1983), pp. 365–79.
74. Galbraith, "Who Needs the Democrats?" p. 65.
75. David Zarefsky, *President Johnson's War on Poverty: Rhetoric and History* (University: University of Alabama Press, 1986), pp. 202–8, 203.

76. Fairlie argues that Kennedy's alarmist rhetoric generated a "politics of expectation" in American life. And the progression from the "politics of expectation" to "the politics of crisis" to "the politics of confrontation" was "all but unavoidable." In the "strenuous climate" created by the Kennedy discourse, problems were magnified into crises, and solutions were sought in confrontations that demanded sacrifice. Kennedy led his audiences to "expect too much of their political institutions and of their political leaders." As a result, the American public developed an unduly elevated "sense of national purpose and [of] the activity of the Presidency that accompanies it." Fairlie, *The Kennedy Promise*, pp. 13–15, 11.

77. David Burner and Thomas R. West, *The Torch Is Passed: The Kennedy Brothers and American Liberalism* (New York: Atheneum, 1984), pp. 3–13, 250–71.

5. In the Halls of Power, 1961–1965

1. Arthur M. Schlesinger, Jr., "Right Man for the Big Job," *New York Times Magazine*, April 3, 1960, pp. 120–21.

2. Arthur M. Schlesinger, Jr., *A Thousand Days: John F. Kennedy in the White House* (Boston: Houghton Mifflin, 1965), pp. 142–43, 206.

3. Ibid., p. 162.

4. Columnist Henry Taylor once warned of "the risks in general from the Schlesinger mentality operating in abundance at the policy level." *Time* magazine characterized Schlesinger as a harmless onlooker who "serves as President Kennedy's court philosopher, instant historian, vice-president in charge of sparkling conversation, memo composer and occasional speechwriter." See "Moonlight Writer," *Time*, June 29, 1962, p. 12.

5. See, for example, the following four pieces by Schlesinger: "The Historian and History," *Foreign Affairs* 41 (April 1963): 491–97; "The Historian as Artist," *Atlantic Monthly*, July 1963, pp. 34–41; "On the Writing of Contemporary History," *Atlantic Monthly*, March 1967, pp. 69–74; and "The Historian as Participant," *Daedalus* 100 (Spring 1971): 339–58.

6. Arthur M. Schlesinger, Jr., *The Politics of Hope* (Boston: Houghton Mifflin, 1963), pp. 126–82.

7. Schlesinger, Jr., *A Thousand Days*, pp. 109, 744.

8. James A. Nuechterlein, "Arthur M. Schlesinger, Jr., and the Discontents of Postwar American Liberalism," *Review of Politics* 39 (January 1977): 3–40.

9. Schlesinger, Jr., "The Historian and History," pp. 491–95.

10. Ibid., pp. 496–97.

11. Ibid., pp. 494–95.

12. Arthur M. Schlesinger, Jr., "The New Mood in Politics," *Esquire*, January 1960, pp. 58, 59.

13. See Allen J. Matusow, *The Unraveling of America: A History of Liberalism in the 1960s* (New York: Harper and Row, 1984), pp. 60–96; and Jim Heath, *Decade of Disillusionment* (Bloomington: Indiana University Press, 1975), pp. 69–73, 109–17.

14. See, for example, Oscar Gass, "The New Frontier Fulfilled," *Commentary* 32 (December 1961): 461–73. For a look at the Radical Right, see Willie Morris, "Houston's Superpatriots," *Harper's*, October 1961, pp. 48–56. For a discussion of the New Left, see Leland M. Griffin, "The Rhetorical Structure of the 'New Left' Movement, Part I," *Quarterly Journal of Speech* 50 (April 1964): 113–35.

15. Arthur M. Schlesinger, Jr., "The 'Threat' of the Radical Right," *New York Times Magazine*, June 17, 1962, pp. 10, 58.

16. Ibid., pp. 55–58.

17. Ibid., p. 8.

18. Ibid., p. 58.

19. Arthur M. Schlesinger, Jr., "The Administration and the Left," *New Statesman*, February 8, 1963, p. 185.

20. Ibid., pp. 185–86.

21. Ibid., p. 185.

22. Schlesinger quoted anarchist Paul Goodman's "programme" in an attempt to parody the insipid agenda of the New Left: "An occasional fist fight, a better orgasm, friendly games, a job of useful work, initiating enterprises, deciding real issues in manageable meetings, and being moved by things that are beautiful, curious, and wonderful." See "The Administration and the Left," p. 185.

23. Schlesinger, Jr., "The Administration and the Left," p. 186.

24. Ibid.

25. Schlesinger, Jr., "The 'Threat' of the Radical Right," p. 10.

26. Arthur M. Schlesinger, Jr., "A Eulogy: John Fitzgerald Kennedy," *Saturday Evening Post*, December 14, 1963, p. 33.

27. Tom Shactman, *Decade of Shocks: Dallas to Watergate, 1963–74* (New York: Poseidon Press, 1983), p. 45.

28. Ibid., pp. 60–61.

29. William V. Shannon, "Controversial Historian of the Age of Kennedy," *New York Times Magazine*, November 21, 1965, p. 132.

30. Schlesinger, Jr., *A Thousand Days*, pp. x–xi.

31. George P. Hunt, "Schlesinger and John F. Kennedy," *Life*, July 16, 1965, p. 5.

32. Schlesinger, Jr., *A Thousand Days*, p. ix.

33. Ibid., pp. 62–63.

34. Ibid., p. xi.

35. Schlesinger evaluated the book's "real value and purpose" in the preface to his series of excerpts published in *Life* magazine: "I think that the things President Kennedy stood for are a great national resource. As much as can be told about his Presidency, as soon as possible, will help not only future historians, but the country." Hunt, "Schlesinger and John F. Kennedy," p. 5.

36. Schlesinger, Jr., *A Thousand Days*, pp. 623, 726.

37. Ibid., p. 120.

38. Ibid., p. 677.

39. Ibid., p. 213.

40. Ibid., pp. 713–14, 1030–31.

41. Ibid., pp. 586, 681.

42. Ibid., p. 710.

43. Ibid., pp. 719–21, 714.

44. Ibid., pp. 114, 714.

45. Ibid., pp. 644–47.

46. Schlesinger cites Kennedy's commencement address at American University in 1963 as an example of Kennedy's emphasis on diversity in his foreign policy rhetoric. See *A Thousand Days*, pp. 298–99, 899–902.

47. *A Thousand Days*, pp. 755–56.

48. Ibid., p. 1021.

49. Ibid., p. 1024.

50. Ibid., p. 1028.

51. Ibid., pp. 1030–31.

52. Ibid., p. 1031.

53. See, for example, the following reviews: "The Taste of Memory," editorial, *Nation*, August 2, 1965, pp. 49–50; "Of Many Things," editorial, *America*, August 7, 1965, p. 124; "Bitter Pen of Arthur M.," review, *National Review*, August 10, 1965, p. 680; Meg Greenfield, "Byzantium on the Potomac," review, *Reporter*, August 12, 1965, pp. 10–12; "Trials of an Instant Author," *Time*, August 27, 1965, p. 31; and "Peephole Journalism," review, *Commonweal*, September 3, 1965, p. 613.

54. Cong. William Widnall, "Remarks," *Congressional Record*, 89th Cong., 1st sess., July 26, 1965, pp. H18122–23.

55. Max Freedman, "Idealism Spurs Kennedy Authors," *Washington (D.C.) Evening Star*, August 9, 1965, cited by Senator George McGovern, *Congressional Record*, 89th Cong., 1st sess., August 11, 1965, pp. S20084–85.

56. Shannon, "Controversial Historian," p. 30.

6. Vietnam and Violence, 1965–1972

1. "The Superstars," *Newsweek*, October 17, 1966, p. 68; and "Swinging Soothsayer," *Time*, March 3, 1967, p. 27.

2. See, for example, William V. Shannon, "Controversial Historian of the Age of Kennedy," *New York Times Magazine*, November 21, 1965, p. 30.

3. Schlesinger defended the limited increase in American ground forces to ensure South Vietnamese stability and said that he "understood" that the Johnson administration was trying to force North Vietnam to the bargaining table. "Principal Participants," *New York Times*, May 16, 1965, p. 62.

4. In his presentation at the Washington teach-in, Schlesinger expressed his belief that "a deep, moving, and impressive" national concern was responsible for the meeting. The historian also remarked that he believed that the academic world and the American people would conduct a discussion of Vietnam based on reason. "Principal Participants," p. 62.

5. Arthur M. Schlesinger, Jr., "On the Inscrutability of History," *Encounter* 27 (November 1966): 10–17.

6. A quick account of Schlesinger's activities during 1966, for example,

demonstrates his prominence in the public debate over Vietnam. The year 1966 was perhaps the most prolific in Schlesinger's career. On January 14, he participated in a public roundtable discussion in New York City called "The Theatre for Ideas." In attendance were such glamorous intellectuals as Susan Sontag, Irving Howe, and Norman Mailer. On February 5, he gave a speech at Providence College in which he called U.S. involvement in Vietnam a "tragedy." On April 13, in a taped interview broadcast on a Princeton University radio station, he referred to U.S. support of the Ky government as "gullible." On May 9, one week after receiving the Pulitzer Prize in biography for A *Thousand Days*, he announced on the CBS interview program "Face the Nation" that Johnson was relying too much on bad advice from his staff and cabinet (particularly Secretary of State Rusk). On May 15, Schlesinger addressed the Roosevelt Day ADA Dinner in Newark, New Jersey, and chastised critics of Johnson for being hysterical and irrational. On June 7, in a commencement address at the New School for Social Research, Schlesinger warned against the use of staid historical analogies in the Vietnam debate.

Schlesinger grew more critical of Johnson in the later months of 1966. In the August 9 issue of *Look*, Schlesinger responded to the question "What Should We Do Now in Vietnam?" by sharply criticizing the widening of the war and calling for negotiation now. On the WNBC radio talk show of August 13, Schlesinger charged that Johnson was paying "lip service" to negotiations. August 13 also saw the publication in the *Saturday Evening Post* of a Schlesinger piece warning that radical student protest was a sign that "McCarthyism Is Threatening Us Again." On September 18, the *New York Times Magazine* printed Schlesinger's ten-page "Middle Way Out of Vietnam." The October 19 headline of the *New York Herald-Tribune* proclaimed Schlesinger's opinion: "Vietnam Is Johnson's War." At his first public lecture as Albert Schweitzer Professor of Humanities at the City University of New York on October 25, Schlesinger defined the proper roles of intellectual and student in protesting Vietnam policy. And in November, *Encounter* published Schlesinger's "On the Inscrutability of History," an explanation of the use of history as insight.

7. Arthur M. Schlesinger, Jr., *A Thousand Days: John F. Kennedy in the White House* (Boston: Houghton Mifflin, 1965), pp. 981–98, 320–42, 532–50.

8. Although few critics questioned American purpose in Vietnam during the 1960s, their voices were heard by many in the intellectual community. Prior to Schlesinger's entry into the Vietnam debate, the agenda for dissenting opinions had not yet been firmly set, and discussion of culpability often included the role of the Kennedy administration in U.S. involvement. See Charles Kadushin, *The American Intellectual Elite* (Boston: Little, Brown, 1973), pp. 123–219; and Hans Morgenthau's response in "What Should We Do Now?" *Look*, August 9, 1966, pp. 24–25.

9. "Principal Participants," p. 62.

10. See "On the Inscrutability of History," pp. 10–17; and Arthur M. Schlesinger, Jr., "McCarthyism Is Threatening Us Again," *Saturday Evening Post*, August 13, 1966, p. 14.

11. Arthur M. Schlesinger, Jr., "Remarks on U.S. Foreign Policy, March 8, 1967," in *The Bitter Heritage: Vietnam and American Democracy, 1941–1968*, 3d ed. (Greenwich, Conn.: Fawcett, 1968), p. ix. See also Arthur M. Schlesinger, Jr., "What Should We Do Now?" *Look*, August 9, 1966, p. 31.

12. Arthur M. Schlesinger, Jr., "A Middle Way Out of Vietnam," *New York Times Magazine*, September 18, 1966, p. 117.

13. According to Schlesinger, the administration's definition of America's commitment was based on the claims that the provisions of the SEATO treaty legally bound the United States to support militarily any government under attack, that the history of military involvement, and the U.S. foreign policy, determined by questions of "right" and "wrong," was morally justified in pursuing foreign policy goals of containment of communism, self-determination, and a negotiated settlement in Southeast Asia. See *Bitter Heritage*, pp. xviii, 21–31.

14. Ibid., p. 30.

15. Schlesinger, Jr., "A Middle Way Out of Vietnam," p. 47.

16. Schlesinger, Jr., *Bitter Heritage*, pp. 47, 43.

17. Schlesinger, Jr., "A Middle Way Out of Vietnam," p. 47.

18. Schlesinger in fact admitted that "moderate critics of the Administration's policy *do not question* its acclaimed purposes" (emphasis added). "What Should We Do Now?" p. 31.

19. Schlesinger, Jr., *Bitter Heritage*, p. 21.

20. The administration's definition of the Communist threat, Schlesinger argued, was based on perceptions that Chinese communism controlled all Communist factions in Asia and was actively involved in North Vietnamese actions; that the North Vietnamese were in turn responsible for instigating rebellion by the Vietcong; and that the lessons of history revealed that compromise with the enemy would be seen as appeasement and weakness.

21. Arthur M. Schlesinger, Jr., "Liberal Anti-Communism Revisited," *Commentary* 44 (September 1967): 68–71.

22. Schlesinger, Jr., *Bitter Heritage*, pp. 78–79.

23. Schlesinger, Jr., "A Middle Way Out of Vietnam," p. 114.

24. Ibid., p. 47. See also "Schlesinger Denies China Is the Issue in Vietnam," *New York Times*, February 1, 1967, p. 6.

25. Schlesinger, Jr., *Bitter Heritage*, p. 54.

26. Ibid., p. 81.

27. Schlesinger, Jr., "A Middle Way Out of Vietnam," p. 115.

28. Schlesinger, Jr., "Liberal Anti-Communism Revisited," p. 69.

29. The administration's definition of military success, according to Schlesinger, rested on arguments that bombing North Vietnam would sufficiently increase the "quotient of pain" so that the North Vietnamese would negotiate; that gradual escalation of ground forces in South Vietnam was necessary to ensure cooperation by the Vietcong; and that, while the United States was willing to negotiate at any time, the North Vietnamese should be blamed for failure to reach an agreement. See Schlesinger, Jr., "A Middle Way Out of Vietnam," p. 111; and "A Talk-In on Vietnam," *New York Times Magazine*, February 6, 1966, p. 76.

30. Schlesinger, Jr., "A Middle Way Out of Vietnam," p. 111.

31. According to Schlesinger, the United States had "lost our understanding of the uses of power," which implied above all "precision in its application." Ibid., pp. 111–13.

32. Ibid., p. 120. See also "Schlesinger Backs Talks with Vietcong," *New York Times*, August 14, 1966, p. 18.

33. In April 1966, Schlesinger called Johnson "gullible." In May, Johnson "had the right instincts" but listened too much to his advisers and "lacked confidence in his own judgment." In August, Johnson was "paying lip service" to negotiations. By March 1967, it was clear to Schlesinger that Johnson was not really interested in negotiating. See "Schlesinger Finds Johnson Gullible," *New York Times*, April 14, 1966, p. 36; Richard Eder, "Rusk Sure Ky Won't Delay Vote and Shift to Civil Rule," *New York Times*, May 9, 1966, p. 3; "Schlesinger Backs Talks," p. 18; Hedrick Smith, "Schlesinger Charges U.S. Wants No Peace Talks Now," *New York Times*, March 9, 1967, p. 1; and Peter Grose, "Schlesinger Asks Shift on Vietnam," *New York Times*, October 9, 1967, p. 3.

34. Harry Gilroy, "Two in Arts Chided by Schlesinger," *New York Times*, June 8, 1965, p. 46.

35. "A Talk-In on Vietnam," p. 79; Schlesinger, Jr., "McCarthyism Is Threatening Us Again," p. 13.

36. See "Two in Arts," p. 46; Michael T. Kaufman, "Schlesinger Sees a Role for Ideas," *New York Times*, October 26, 1966, p. 94.

37. See "McCarthyism Is Threatening Us Again," p. 13; and Kaufman, "Schlesinger Sees a Role for Ideas," p. 94.

38. Schlesinger, Jr., "McCarthyism Is Threatening Us Again," p. 13.

39. Kaufman, "Schlesinger Sees a Role for Ideas," p. 94.

40. Schlesinger, Jr., "McCarthyism Is Threatening Us Again," p. 13; and "A Talk-In on Vietnam," p. 79.

41. Marjorie Hunter, "McCarthy Backed by Board of ADA," *New York Times*, February 11, 1968, p. 39.

42. Schlesinger, Jr., "A Middle Way Out of Vietnam," pp. 117–19.

43. "What Should We Do Now?" p. 31. In January 1966, Schlesinger remarked, "The purpose of American policy must be a withdrawal with honor. That is, a withdrawal that will not abandon friends who've committed themselves in the expectation of our support against some kind of repression or massacre. I don't think anyone here in this room should delude himself as to what a Vietcong victory, a communist South Vietnam, would mean." "A Talk-In on Vietnam," p. 76. In this statement, Schlesinger revealed a fundamental hatred of communism that guided all of his arguments on the Vietnam issue.

44. See Schlesinger, Jr., "A Middle Way Out of Vietnam," p. 117; and "What Should We Do Now?" p. 31.

45. Ronald Steel, "The Cool Way Out," review, *Book Week*, March 5, 1967, p. 19. Schlesinger admitted that "of course we cannot see now the shape of negotiation; all we can do is define its limits. For one can rarely forecast the details of a political settlement." Schlesinger, Jr., *Bitter Heritage*, p. 118.

46. Schlesinger, Jr., "A Middle Way Out of Vietnam," p. 120. See also Arthur M. Schlesinger, Jr., "Why I Am For Kennedy," *New Republic*, May 4, 1968, pp. 19–23. As we will see in the next section, the assassination of Robert Kennedy dealt another shock to Schlesinger's frame of acceptance.

47. Seymour Martin Lipset, "The President, the Polls, and Vietnam," *Trans/Action* (September-October 1966): 20.

48. Arthur M. Schlesinger, Jr., *Robert F. Kennedy and His Times* (Boston: Houghton Mifflin, 1978), pp. 724–42, 771–77; Leslie Gelb, *The Irony of Vietnam: The System Worked* (Washington, D.C.: Brookings, 1979), pp. 216–18.

49. Steel, "Cool Way Out," p. 19. Arguing from origins and first principles is preferred by Weaver as the sounder kind of argument because it is grounded in something that transcends the situation. Richard M. Weaver, *The Ethics of Rhetoric* (South Bend, Ind.: Regnery/Gateway, 1953), pp. 56, 85–114.

50. Irving Howe, "A New Turn at Arthur's," review, *New York Review of Books*, February 23, 1967, pp. 13–14.

51. Noam Chomsky, "*The Bitter Heritage*—A Review," *Ramparts* 5 (April 1967), reprinted in Chomsky, *American Power and the New Mandarins* (New York: Pantheon, 1969), pp. 304, 296.

52. Carroll Englehardt, "Man in the Middle: Arthur M. Schlesinger, Jr., and Postwar American Liberalism," *South Atlantic Quarterly* 80 (Spring 1981): 131, 138.

53. Weaver, *Ethics of Rhetoric*, p. 105.

54. See Marian J. Morton, "Arthur Schlesinger, Jr., and the Search for the Vital Center," in Morton, *The Terrors of Ideological Politics: Liberal Historians in a Conservative Mood* (Cleveland: Case Western Reserve University Press, 1972), pp. 27–49.

55. Arthur M. Schlesinger, Jr., "Vietnam and the End of the Age of the Superpowers," *Harper's*, March 1969, pp. 41–49.

56. The assassination of King "showed" Schlesinger "how far white America has yet to go to make up for centuries of injustice toward our non-white citizens, how much more must be done to open full membership in our national community to the excluded groups, and how little time remains." Schlesinger, Jr., "Why I Am for Kennedy," p. 21.

57. Schlesinger cited George McGovern's description of Robert Kennedy as a man having "the absolute personal honesty of Woodrow Wilson, the stirring passion for leadership of Andrew Jackson, and the profound acquaintance with personal tragedy of Abraham Lincoln." Schlesinger, Jr., "Why I Am for Kennedy," p. 23.

58. Arthur Schlesinger, Jr., "America, 1968: The Politics of Violence," *Harper's*, August 1968, p. 19.

59. Tom Shactman, *Decade of Shocks: Dallas to Watergate, 1963–1974* (New York: Poseidon Press, 1983), p. 63.

60. Arthur M. Schlesinger, Jr., "The Dark Heart of American History," *Saturday Review*, October 19, 1968, p. 20.

61. Arthur M. Schlesinger, Jr., *The Crisis of Confidence: Ideas, Power, and Violence in America* (Boston: Houghton Mifflin, 1969), p. 3. "How

fragile the membranes of our civilization are," Schlesinger concluded, "stretched so thin over a nation so disparate in its composition, so tense in its interior relationships, so cunningly enmeshed in underground fears and antagonisms, so entrapped by history in the ethos of violence." Schlesinger, Jr., "America, 1968," p. 20.

62. Schlesinger, Jr., *Crisis of Confidence*, p. ix.

63. Arthur M. Schlesinger, Jr., "America and the World: A New Fix?" *Vogue*, February 1, 1969, p. 184.

64. Schlesinger, Jr., *Crisis of Confidence*, pp. 32–36.

65. Schlesinger, Jr., "America, 1968," p. 19.

66. Ibid., p. 21.

67. Arthur M. Schlesinger, Jr., "The New Mood in Politics," *Esquire*, January 1960, p. 60.

68. "Change is always scary," Schlesinger admitted in 1970; ". . . uncharted, uncontrolled change can be deeply demoralizing." See Arthur M. Schlesinger, Jr., "The Velocity of History," *Newsweek*, July 6, 1970, p. 33.

69. Arthur M. Schlesinger, Jr., "The 1968 Election: An Historical Perspective," *Vital Speeches*, December 15, 1968, p. 151. The speech cited here was delivered by Schlesinger as part of the Alf Landon annual lecture series on the campus of Kansas State University.

70. Shactman, *Decade of Shocks*, p. 62.

71. Schlesinger, Jr., *Crisis of Confidence*, pp. 234–35.

72. Arthur M. Schlesinger, Jr., "*The Vital Center* Reconsidered," *Encounter*, September 1970, p. 89. Assessing the seriousness of the threat to his liberal frame of acceptance in the foreword of *The Crisis of Confidence*, Schlesinger referred to the warning John Kennedy had made in 1961: "Before my term is ended, we shall have to test anew whether a nation organized and governed such as ours can endure. The outcome is by no means certain." Schlesinger, Jr., *Crisis of Confidence*, pp. xii, xiii.

73. Schlesinger, Jr., "*The Vital Center* Reconsidered," p. 89.

74. Schlesinger, Jr., "The Dark Heart," pp. 21–22.

75. Schlesinger, Jr., *Crisis of Confidence*, p. 9.

76. Schlesinger, Jr., "America, 1968," p. 20.

77. Ibid., p. 20.

78. Schlesinger, Jr., *Crisis of Confidence*, pp. 10, xi.

79. Schlesinger, Jr., "The Dark Heart," p. 21.

80. The "institutionalization of violence in the slavery system" illustrated America's concrete "capacity for sin" and also "shaped our national unconscious." As early as 1838, Abraham Lincoln "named internal violence as the supreme threat to American political institutions." See Schlesinger, Jr., *Crisis of Confidence*, pp. 10–16.

81. Schlesinger, Jr., "The Dark Heart," p. 21.

82. Schlesinger, Jr., "America, 1968," p. 20.

83. Schlesinger, Jr., "The Dark Heart," p. 22.

84. Ibid., p. 81; and Schlesinger, Jr., *Crisis of Confidence*, p. xi.

85. Schlesinger, Jr., *Crisis of Confidence*, p. 7.

86. Schlesinger, Jr., "The Velocity of History," p. 32. Schlesinger had referred to this concept, borrowed from Henry Adams, in *The Vital Center*

(1949): "The velocity of life has entered a new phase. With it has become [sic] the imperative need for a social structure to contain that velocity." Arthur M. Schlesinger, Jr., *The Vital Center: The Politics of Freedom*, 2d ed. (Boston: Houghton Mifflin, 1962), p. 3.

87. Ibid., p. 33.

88. Arthur M. Schlesinger, Jr., "Politics, 1971," *Vogue*, February 1, 1971, p. 139.

89. Schlesinger, Jr., *Crisis of Confidence*, pp. 25–32.

90. Ibid., pp. 52–53.

91 Schlesinger, Jr., "The Velocity of History," p. 33.

92. Schlesinger, Jr., "*The Vital Center* Reconsidered," p. 91.

93. Ibid., p. 92.

94. Schlesinger, Jr., "The Velocity of History," p. 34.

95. Ibid., p. 33.

96. Schlesinger, Jr., "America and the World," p. 239.

97. Schlesinger, Jr., *Crisis of Confidence*, pp. 243, 238.

98. Schlesinger, Jr., "America, 1968," p. 20.

99. Schlesinger, Jr., *Crisis of Confidence*, p. 243.

100. Schlesinger, Jr., "America, 1968," p. 20.

101. Schlesinger, Jr., *Crisis of Confidence*, p. 239.

102. Schlesinger, Jr., "The 1968 Election," p. 154.

103. Schlesinger, Jr., *Crisis of Confidence*, p. 252.

104. Ibid., p. 285.

105. Only a leader with "the ability to perceive the world from the viewpoint of its casualties and victims" and the skill to translate that perspective into a vision of communal sacrifice could transcend the current "crisis of confidence." See Schlesinger, Jr., *Crisis of Confidence*, pp. 283–98.

106. Ibid., p. 299.

107. Schlesinger, Jr., "America, 1968," p. 24.

108. Schlesinger exhorted his readers by quoting the martyred Robert F. Kennedy's call for heroic sacrifice: "Few will have the greatness to bend history itself, but each of us can work to change a small portion of events, and in the total of all those acts will be written the history of this generation. . . . Each time a man stands for an ideal, or acts to improve the lot of others, or strikes out against injustice, he sends forth a ripple of hope, and crossing each other from a million different centers of energy and daring those ripples build a current that can sweep down the mightiest wall of oppression." See Schlesinger, Jr., *Crisis of Confidence*, pp. 299–300.

109. Schlesinger, Jr., "America, 1968," pp. 21–23.

110. Ibid., p. 23.

111. Ibid., p. 24.

112. William Pfaff, "The Decline of Liberal Politics," *Commentary* 48 (October 1969): 45–51.

113. James A. Nuechterlein, "Arthur M. Schlesinger, Jr., and the Discontents of Postwar American Liberalism," *Review of Politics* 39 (January 1977): 29.

114. Schlesinger, Jr., "Politics, 1971," pp. 138–39.

115. The above phrase is taken from Christopher Lasch, *The Culture of*

Narcissism: American Life in an Age of Diminishing Expectations (New York: W. W. Norton, 1979).

7. Liberalism in Retreat, 1972–1993

1. Calls to subordinate the executive branch to Congress in all areas of governance, Schlesinger argued, ran the risk of "creating a generation of weak Presidents in an age when the turbulence of race, poverty, inflation, crime and urban decay was straining the delicate bonds of national cohesion and demanding, quite as much as in the 1930s, a strong domestic Presidency to hold the country together." Arthur M. Schlesinger, Jr., *The Imperial Presidency* (Boston: Houghton Mifflin, 1973), p. 403. For representative reviews of this work, see Walter Mondale, "Shadows of Watergate," *Psychology Today*, March 1974, pp. 92, 94; John Pierson, "The President as an Emperor," *Wall Street Journal*, January 29, 1974, p. 18; and Michael Novak, "The Presidency and Professor Schlesinger," *Commentary* 54 (February 1974): 74–78.

2. Schlesinger felt it necessary to "declare an interest" and a bias in the foreword. "I was a great admirer and devoted friend of Robert Kennedy." He hoped that his sympathy with his subject "would illumine" rather than distort the story of a life that "tells us a great deal about the American ordeal in the middle decades of the twentieth century." Arthur M. Schlesinger, Jr., *Robert F. Kennedy and His Times* (Boston: Houghton Mifflin, 1978), p. xv. Critics derided the effort as an apologia on behalf of the Kennedy administration. For example, see Henry Fairlie, "Books Considered," *New Republic*, September 9, 1978, pp. 30–34; Marshall Frady, "The Transformation of Bobby Kennedy," *New York Review of Books*, October 12, 1978, pp. 42–51; Paul Gray, "Re-Creation of the Way It Was," *Time*, September 4, 1978, pp. 74–75; and Michael Nelson, "Scholar-Politicians and Sheriffs," *Virginia Quarterly Review* 55 (1979): 329–37.

3. Arthur M. Schlesinger, Jr., *The Cycles of American History* (Boston: Houghton Mifflin, 1986), p. ix.

4. Arthur M. Schlesinger, Jr., "The Case for George McGovern," *New Republic*, February 26, 1972, pp. 15–17.

5. Arthur M. Schlesinger, Jr., "Who Needs Grover Cleveland?" *New Republic*, July 7–14, 1979, pp. 14–16.

6. A wonderful example of using history in the service of politics can be found in a 1978 speech delivered by Schlesinger in commemoration of the forty-fifth anniversary of the beginning of the New Deal. Schlesinger asserted that "the spirit of the New Deal, if it could only be released again, would considerably improve our national capacity to deal with the problems that presently assail us." While he admitted that specific New Deal policies should not be resurrected, Schlesinger called upon liberals to recapture its "unifying vision," grounded in a "remarkable intellectual vitality" and willingness to experiment with new reforms; an abiding "concern for ordinary human beings"; and a "readiness to act," to use the powers of the

federal government to serve the national welfare. What liberalism needed most, Schlesinger concluded, was a national leader such as Franklin Roosevelt who understood that "politics is ultimately an educational process" and who "had a power to convey to others both a sense of the past and a vision of the future." Arthur M. Schlesinger, Jr., "If F.D.R. Were President," *Washington Post*, March 12, 1978, pp. C-1, C-5.

7. Morton Kondracke, "Frayed Hopes," *New Republic*, August 16, 1980, p. 12.

8. Allan J. Mayer, "End of the Democratic Era?" *Newsweek*, August 18, 1980, p. 21.

9. Edward Kennedy, "Principles of the Democratic Party," *Vital Speeches* 46 (September 1, 1980): 714–16. See also Stephen P. Depoe, "Requiem for Liberalism: The Therapeutic and Deliberative Functions of Nostalgic Appeals in Edward Kennedy's Address to the 1980 Democratic National Convention," *Southern Communication Journal* 55 (1990): 175–90.

10. Mayer, "End of the Democratic Era?" p. 25.

11. Richard Weaver, *The Ethics of Rhetoric* (South Bend, Ind.: Regnery/Gateway, 1953), p. 222.

12. Robert A. Francesconi, "James Hunt, the Wilmington 10, and Institutional Legitimacy," *Quarterly Journal of Speech* 68 (1982): 49.

13. Ibid., pp. 49–52.

14. See Jurgen Habermas, *Legitimation Crisis*, trans. Thomas McCarthy (Boston: Beacon Press, 1975).

15. Michael Weiler, "The Rhetoric of Neo-Liberalism," *Quarterly Journal of Speech* 70 (November 1984): 371.

16. Udall, quoted in Tom Shactman, *Decade of Shocks: Dallas to Watergate, 1963–1974* (New York: Poseidon Press, 1983), p. 263.

17. "We had already accepted the magnificent bribe" of technological growth, writes Shactman, but "we did not fully understand the price we might soon have to pay." Ibid., pp. 203–205.

18. Lance Morrow, "Rediscovering America," *Time*, July 7, 1980, p. 29.

19. Ibid., p. 29.

20. Shactman, *Decade of Shocks*, pp. 201–35.

21. Weiler, "Rhetoric of Neo-Liberalism," pp. 366–68.

22. Morrow, "Rediscovering America," p. 29. Davis notes that what Americans experienced during the 1960s was "perhaps the most wide-ranging, sustained, and profound assault on the native belief concerning the 'natural' and the 'proper' that has ever been visited on a people over so short a time." Fred Davis, *Yearning for Yesterday: A Sociology of Nostalgia* (New York: Macmillan, 1979), pp. 105–106.

23. James A. Nuechterlein, "Arthur M. Schlesinger, Jr., and the Discontents of Postwar American Liberalism," *Review of Politics* 39 (January 1977): 3.

24. Tsongas, quoted in Mayer, "End of the Democratic Era?" p. 21.

25. Weiler, "Rhetoric of Neo-Liberalism," p. 367.

26. See Steven V. Roberts, "ADA Debates Role of Liberalism in a Year of Losses and Budget Cuts," *New York Times*, July 15, 1980, p. A-14.

27. George Lardner, Jr., "Gary Hart: He Cherishes Ideas, But Can He Lead a Nation?" *Washington Post Weekly Edition*, February 13, 1984, p. 8.

28. Gary Hart, *A New Democracy: A Democratic Vision for the 1980s and Beyond* (New York: Quill, 1983), p. 8.

29. Gary Hart, "Let Us Choose a New Path," speech text, *New York Times*, February 23, 1984, p. 13.

30. Ibid.

31. Gary Hart, "Text of Speech Prepared for Delivery to the Democratic Delegates," *New York Times*, July 19, 1984, p. 6.

32. Michael Dukakis, "Transcript of the Speech Accepting the Democrats' Nomination," *New York Times*, July 22, 1988, p. A-10.

33. Barnes quoted in Fred Siegel, "What Liberals Haven't Learned and Why," *Commonweal*, January 13, 1989, p. 18.

34. Andrew Rosenthal, "Dukakis Insists That His 'L Word' Is 'Leadership,'" *New York Times*, August 16, 1988, p. A-16.

35. Alexander Cockburn, "The L-Word in Crisis," *New Statesman*, November 4, 1988, p. 14.

36. Robin Toner, "Dukakis Asserts He Is a 'Liberal,' But in Old Tradition of His Party," *New York Times*, October 31, 1988, pp. A-1, B-4.

37. Michael Barone, *Our Country: The Shaping of America from Roosevelt to Reagan* (New York: Free Press, 1990), pp. 599–670.

38. William Schneider, "Tough Liberals Win, Weak Liberals Lose," *New Republic*, December 5, 1988, p. 13.

39. In September 1988, a *New York Times*/CBS News poll found that the proportion of adult Americans calling themselves liberal had dropped to 15 percent, the lowest level since the poll began tracking the trend in 1976. Toner, "Dukakis Asserts He Is a 'Liberal,'" p. B-4.

40. Walter Shapiro, "Are the Democrats Cursed?" *Time*, November 21, 1988, p. 58.

41. Michael Kinsley, "Hypocrisy and the L-Word," *Time*, August 1, 1988, p. 23.

42. Ronald W. Reagan, in *Public Papers of the Presidents of the United States, 1988* (Washington, D.C.: U.S. Government Printing Office, 1989), p. 1074.

43. *Public Papers, 1988*, p. 1075.

44. Ibid.

45. Ibid., p. 1396.

46. Ibid., p. 1075.

47. Ibid., p. 1396.

48. Ibid., p. 1362.

49. Ibid., p. 1075.

50. Ibid., p. 1362.

51. "A Reaffirmation of Principle," *New York Times*, October 26, 1988, p. A-21.

52. Arthur M. Schlesinger, Jr., "Neo-Conservatism and the Class Struggle," *Wall Street Journal*, June 2, 1981, p. 30.

53. Arthur M. Schlesinger, Jr., "Dukakis for President," *Atlantic Monthly*, October 1988, pp. 69, 75.

54. Arthur M. Schlesinger, Jr., "How Goes the Cycle Now?" *Wall Street Journal*, January 4, 1989, p. A-8.

55. Arthur M. Schlesinger, Jr., "Hurrah for the L-Word," *Wall Street Journal*, October 21, 1988, p. A-14.

56. Schlesinger, Jr., "Dukakis," p. 76.

57. Schlesinger, Jr., "Neo-Conservatism," p. 30.

58. Ibid.

59. Schlesinger, Jr., "Hurrah for the L-Word," p. A-14.

60. Schlesinger, Jr., "Dukakis," p. 76.

61. Arthur M. Schlesinger, Jr., *The Cycles of American History* (Boston: Houghton Mifflin, 1986), p. 37.

62. Arthur M. Schlesinger, Jr., "One Last Chance for the Democrats," *Playboy*, November 1982, p. 112.

63. Arthur M. Schlesinger, Jr., "American Politics on a Darkling Plain," *Wall Street Journal*, March 17, 1982, p. 28.

64. Schlesinger, Jr., "One Last Chance," p. 112.

65. Schlesinger, Jr., "Darkling Plain," p. 28.

66. Arthur M. Schlesinger, Jr., "The Great Carter Mystery," *New Republic*, April 12, 1980, p. 21.

67. Schlesinger, Jr., "Darkling Plain," p. 28.

68. Arthur M. Schlesinger, Jr., "Requiem for Neo-Liberalism," review of Gary Hart's *A New Democracy, New Republic*, June 6, 1983, p. 28.

69. Schlesinger, Jr., "One Last Chance," p. 252.

70. Arthur M. Schlesinger, Jr., "The End of an Era?" *Wall Street Journal*, November 20, 1980, p. 26.

71. Schlesinger, Jr., "One Last Chance," pp. 252–53.

72. Arthur M. Schlesinger, Jr., "The Liberal Opportunity," *American Prospect*, Spring 1990, p. 13.

73. Schlesinger, Jr., "Hurrah for the L-Word," p. A-14.

74. Schlesinger, Jr., "The Liberal Opportunity," p. 13.

75. Schlesinger, Jr., "Hurrah for the L-Word," p. A-14.

76. Ibid.

77. Schlesinger, Jr., "How Goes the Cycle Now?" p. A-8.

78. Schlesinger, Jr., "The Liberal Opportunity," p. 15.

79. Arthur Schlesinger, Jr., "Is Liberalism Dead?" *New York Times Magazine*, March 30, 1980, p. 79.

80. Schlesinger, Jr., "End of an Era?" p. 26.

81. Schlesinger, Jr., *The Cycles of American History*, pp. 27, 32.

82. Arthur M. Schlesinger, Jr., "America's Political Cycle Turns Again," *Wall Street Journal*, December 10, 1987, p. 28.

83. Ibid.

84. Schlesinger, Jr., "How Goes the Cycle Now?" p. A-8.

85. Schlesinger, Jr., *The Cycles of American History*, pp. 29, 30.

86. Schlesinger, Jr., "The Liberal Opportunity," p. 11.

87. Schlesinger, Jr., "How Goes the Cycle Now?" p. A-8.

88. Schlesinger, Jr., "Is Liberalism Dead?" p. 79.

89. Schlesinger, Jr., *The Cycles of American History*, p. 45.

90. Schlesinger, Jr., "The Liberal Opportunity," p. 11.

91. Ibid.

92. Ibid., p. 15.

93. Schlesinger, Jr., "One Last Chance," p. 248.

94. Arthur M. Schlesinger, Jr., "Time for Constitutional Change?" *Wall Street Journal*, December 24, 1982, p. 4.

95. Schlesinger, Jr., "Neo-Conservatism," p. 30.

96. Schlesinger, Jr., "Darkling Plain," p. 28.

97. Schlesinger, Jr., "Time for Constitutional Change?" p. 4.

98. He added that he found "no incompatibility between social liberalism and tough law enforcement." Schlesinger, Jr., "The Liberal Opportunity," p. 15.

99. Schlesinger, Jr., "The Liberal Opportunity," p. 16.

100. Schlesinger, Jr., "One Last Chance," p. 254.

101. Schlesinger, Jr., "The Liberal Opportunity," pp. 16–17.

102. Schlesinger, Jr., "One Last Chance," pp. 254, 252.

103. Schlesinger, Jr., "The Liberal Opportunity," p. 17.

104. Schlesinger, Jr., "Neo-Conservatism," p. 30.

105. Schlesinger, Jr., "One Last Chance," p. 252. This statement serves as a chilling forecast of the meteoric rise of David Duke and the popularity of H. Ross Perot during the 1990s.

106. Schlesinger, Jr., *The Cycles of American History*, p. 46.

107. Arthur M. Schlesinger, Jr., "New Liberal Coalition," *Progressive*, April 1967, p. 19.

108. Arthur M. Schlesinger, Jr., "The Revolution That Never Was," *Wall Street Journal*, October 24, 1979, p. 22.

109. Schlesinger, Jr., "One Last Chance," p. 254.

110. Schlesinger, Jr., "The Liberal Opportunity," p. 18.

111. Schlesinger, Jr., "One Last Chance," p. 254.

112. Schlesinger, Jr., "Dukakis for President," p. 78.

113. Meg Greenfield, "Tongue-Tied Liberals," *Newsweek*, October 31, 1988, p. 82.

114. "The Tide Is Turning: A New Political Cycle in the 1990s," interview with Arthur M. Schlesinger, Jr., *Challenge*, November-December 1991, p. 11.

115. Robin Toner, "Arkansas' Clinton Enters the '92 Race for President," *New York Times*, October 4, 1991, p. A-10.

116. Robin Toner, "1992 Ticket Puts Council of Moderates to Stiff Test," *New York Times*, July 15, 1992, p. A-7.

117. Leslie H. Gelb, "Wonks versus Liberals," *New York Times*, July 16, 1992, p. A-25.

118. David E. Rosenbaum, "Democratic Platform Shows Shift in Party's Focus," *New York Times*, July 14, 1992, p. A-9.

119. "Transcript of Speech by Clinton Accepting Democratic Nomination," *New York Times*, July 17, 1992, p. A-14.

120. Howard Fineman, "Sixties Coming of Age," *Newsweek*, July 20, 1992, pp. 32–35.

121. "Excerpts from Clinton's and Gore's Remarks on the Ticket," *New York Times*, July 10, 1992, p. A-16. See also R. W. Apple, Jr., "Behind Clinton's Choice," *New York Times*, July 10, 1992, pp. A-1, A-18.

122. William Grimes, "Film Tribute to Clinton Focuses on Simple Values," *New York Times*, July 17, 1992, p. A-11.

123. Both Clinton and Gore were influenced by a book written by Strauss and Howe on recurring cycles of generational patterns in American history. Maureen Dowd, "Two Baby Boomers on One Ticket, But Will it Work?" *New York Times*, July 13, 1992, pp. A-1, B-6. See also William Strauss and Neil Howe, *Generations: The History of America's Future, 1584–2069* (New York: Morrow, 1991).

124. "An 'American Renewal': Transcript of the Address by President Clinton," *New York Times*, January 21, 1993, p. A-11.

125. Walter Isaacson, "A Time for Courage," *Time*, November 16, 1992, pp. 26–28.

126. Arthur M. Schlesinger, Jr., "Memo to the 1993 Crowd: Believe in Yourselves," *Newsweek*, January 11, 1993, p. 39.

127. Ibid.

128. Ibid.

129. See also Arthur M. Schlesinger, Jr., "The Turn of the Cycle," *New Yorker*, November 16, 1992, pp. 46–54.

130. Carroll Englehardt, "Man in the Middle: Arthur M. Schlesinger, Jr., and Postwar American Liberalism," *South Atlantic Quarterly* 60 (Spring 1981): 132, 120.

131. Kenneth Burke, *Attitudes toward History*, 3d ed. (Berkeley: University of California Press, 1984), p. 23.

132. Michael Walzer, "On the Role of Symbolism in Political Thought," *Political Science Quarterly* 82 (June 1967): 198.

133. Isaacson, "A Time for Courage," pp. 27, 28.

8. Conclusion

1. Arthur M. Schlesinger, Jr., *The Cycles of American History* (Boston: Houghton Mifflin, 1986), p. xi.

2. Kenneth Burke, *Language as Symbolic Action* (Berkeley: University of California Press, 1966), p. 46.

3. Ibid., p. 45.

4. Arthur M. Schlesinger, Jr., "Dukakis for President," *Atlantic Monthly*, October 1988, p. 76.

5. Arthur M. Schlesinger, Jr., *The Disuniting of America* (New York: W. W. Norton, 1991), pp. 44–45.

6. Ibid., p. 48.

7. Ibid., p. 46.

8. Ibid., pp. 45–46.

9. Ibid., pp. 48–50.

10. Ibid., p. 52.

11. Ibid., p. 72.

12. The use of historical argument to establish or reinforce presumptions carries a danger that alternative views or voices may be overlooked or ignored in a public debate or controversy. According to Cox, the rhetorical privileging of the past either can help to foster a "cultural memory" by preserving the essential values of a community or can seduce audiences with "the lure of nostalgia—the retreat into the past as escape or resignation." The memory of an individual or society, warns Cox, is "susceptible to reification; the telling of the stories may also sustain a vision in the interests of power and manipulation." J. Robert Cox, *Cultural Memory and Public Argument*, 1987 Van Zelst Lecture in Communication (Evanston, Ill.: Northwestern University School of Speech, 1987), p. 6.

13. Steven M. Gillon, *Politics and Vision: The ADA and American Liberalism* (New York: Oxford University Press, 1987), pp. x, 243.

14. See Alonzo B. Hamby, *Liberalism and Its Challengers: FDR to Reagan* (New York: Oxford University Press, 1985), pp. 339–54; and E. J. Dionne, *Why Americans Hate Politics* (New York: Simon and Schuster, 1991).

15. Carroll Englehardt, "Man in the Middle: Arthur M. Schlesinger, Jr., and Postwar American Liberalism," *South Atlantic Quarterly* 60 (Spring 1981): 132, 120.

16. Michael Walzer, "On the Role of Symbolism in Political Thought," *Political Science Quarterly* 82 (June 1967): 198.

Bibliography

Books

Aristotle. *Poetics*. Translated by Gerald F. Else. Ann Arbor: University of Michigan Press, 1967.

———. *Rhetoric*. Translated by Lane Cooper. Englewood Cliffs, N.J.: Prentice-Hall, 1960.

Bell, Daniel. *The End of Ideology*. Glencoe, Ill.: Free Press, 1960.

Benson, Lee. *The Concept of Jacksonian Democracy: New York as a Test Case*. 6th ed. New York: Atheneum, 1969.

Burke, Kenneth. *Attitudes toward History*. 2d ed. Los Altos, Calif.: Hermes Publications, 1959.

———. *Counter-Statement*. 3d ed. Berkeley: University of California Press, 1968.

———. *A Grammar of Motives*. 2d ed. Berkeley: University of California Press, 1962.

———. *Language as Symbolic Action*. Berkeley: University of California Press, 1966.

———. *Permanence and Change: An Anatomy of Purpose*. 4th ed. Indianapolis: Bobbs-Merrill, 1975.

———. *The Philosophy of Literary Form*. 3d ed. Berkeley: University of California Press, 1973.

———. *A Rhetoric of Motives*. 3d ed. Berkeley: University of California Press, 1969.

Burner, David, and West, Thomas R. *The Torch Is Passed: The Kennedy Brothers and American Liberalism*. New York: Atheneum, 1984.

Chomsky, Noam. *American Power and the New Mandarins.* New York: Pantheon, 1969.

Cicero. *De Oratore.* Translated by E. W. Sutton. Loeb ed. 3d ed. Cambridge, Mass.: Harvard University Press, 1959.

Collingwood, R. G. *The Idea of History.* 5th ed. New York: Oxford University Press, 1962.

Croce, Benedetto. *History as the Story of Liberty.* Translated by Sylvia S. Sprigge. London: Allen and Unwin, 1941.

Davis, Fred. *Yearning for Yesterday: A Sociology of Nostalgia.* New York: Macmillan, 1970.

Edelman, Murray. *Politics as Symbolic Action.* New York: Academic Press, 1971.

———. *The Symbolic Uses of Politics.* Urbana: University of Illinois Press, 1964.

Fairlie, Henry. *The Kennedy Promise: The Politics of Expectation.* Garden City, N.Y.: Doubleday, 1973.

Fitzsimons, Matthew A., Nowell, Charles E., and Pundt, Alfred G., eds. *The Development of Historiography.* Harrisburg, Pa.: Stackpole, 1954.

Galbraith, John Kenneth. *Who Needs the Democrats? And What It Takes to be Needed.* Garden City, N.Y.: Doubleday, 1970.

Gay, Peter. *Style in History.* New York: Basic Books, 1974.

Gelb, Leslie. *The Irony of Vietnam: The System Worked.* Washington, D.C.: Brookings, 1979.

Gillon, Steven. *Politics and Vision: The ADA and American Liberalism.* New York: Oxford University Press, 1987.

Habermas, Jurgen. *Knowledge and Human Interests.* Translated by Jeremy Shapiro. Boston: Beacon Press, 1971.

Hamby, Alonzo J. *Beyond the New Deal: Harry S. Truman and American Liberalism.* New York: Columbia University Press, 1973.

———. *Liberalism and Its Challengers: FDR to Reagan.* New York: Oxford University Press, 1985.

Hart, Gary. *A New Democracy: A Democratic Vision for the 1980s and Beyond.* New York: Quill, 1983.

Heath, Jim. *Decade of Disillusionment.* Bloomington: Indiana University Press, 1975.

Higham, John, ed. *The Reconstruction of American History.* New York: Harper and Row, 1962.

Jamieson, Kathleen. *Packaging the Presidency: A History and Criticism of Presidential Campaign Advertising.* New York: Oxford University Press, 1984.

Kadushin, Charles. *The American Intellectual Elite.* Boston: Little, Brown, 1974.

Lasch, Christopher. *The Culture of Narcissism: American Life in an Age of Diminishing Expectations.* New York: W. W. Norton, 1979.

———. *The New Radicalism in America, 1889–1963: The Intellectual as Social Type.* New York: Knopf, 1966.

Leuchtenburg, William. *Franklin D. Roosevelt and the New Deal.* New York: Harper and Row, 1963.

————. *In the Shadow of FDR: From Harry Truman to Ronald Reagan.* Ithaca, N.Y.: Cornell University Press, 1983.

Lowi, Theodore J. *The End of Liberalism: Ideology, Policy, and the Crisis of Public Authority.* New York: W. W. Norton, 1969.

Markowitz, Norman. *The Rise and Fall of the People's Century.* New York: Free Press, 1973.

Matusow, Allen J. *The Unraveling of America: A History of Liberalism in the 1960s.* New York: Harper and Row, 1984.

Meyers, Marvin. *The Jacksonian Persuasion: Politics and Belief.* 2d ed. Stanford, Calif.: Stanford University Press, 1960.

Morton, Marian J. *The Terrors of Ideological Politics: Liberal Historians in a Conservative Mood.* Cleveland: Case Western Reserve University Press, 1972.

Niebuhr, Reinhold. *The Children of Light and the Children of Darkness.* New York: Charles Scribner and Sons, 1944.

O'Neill, William L. *Coming Apart: An Informal History of America in the 1960's.* 2d ed. New York: Quadrangle Press, 1978.

Parmet, Herbert S. *JFK: The Presidency of John F. Kennedy.* 2d ed. New York: Penguin Books, 1984.

Perelman, Chaim, and Olbrechts-Tyteca, L. *The New Rhetoric: A Treatise on Argumentation.* Translated by John Wilkinson and Purcell Weaver. Notre Dame: University of Notre Dame Press, 1969.

Pessen, Edward. *Jacksonian America: Society, Personality, and Politics.* Homewood, Ill.: Dorsey Press, 1969.

Public Papers of the Presidents of the United States, 1961. Washington, D.C.: U.S. Government Printing Office, 1962.

Public Papers of the Presidents of the United States, 1962. Washington, D.C.: U.S. Government Printing Office, 1963.

Public Papers of the Presidents of the United States, 1963. Washington, D.C.: U.S. Government Printing Office, 1964.

Remini, Robert. *Martin Van Buren and the Making of the Democratic Party.* 2d ed. New York: W. W. Norton, 1954.

Rueckert, William H. *Critical Responses to Kenneth Burke.* Minneapolis: University of Minnesota Press, 1969.

————. *Kenneth Burke and the Drama of Human Relations.* 2d ed. Berkeley: University of California Press, 1983.

Schlesinger, Arthur M., Jr. *The Age of Jackson.* Boston: Little, Brown, 1945.

————. *The Bitter Heritage: Vietnam and American Democracy.* 3d ed. Boston: Houghton Mifflin, 1968.

————. *The Coming of the New Deal.* Boston: Houghton Mifflin, 1959.

————. *The Crisis of Confidence: Ideas, Power, and Violence in America.* Boston: Houghton Mifflin, 1969.

————. *The Crisis of the Old Order.* Boston: Houghton Mifflin, 1957.

————. *The Cycles of American History.* Boston: Houghton Mifflin, 1986.

————. *The Disuniting of America.* New York: W. W. Norton, 1991.

————. *The Imperial Presidency.* Boston: Houghton Mifflin, 1973.

————. *Kennedy or Nixon: Does It Make Any Difference?* New York: Macmillan, 1960.

————. *Orestes Brownson: A Pilgrim's Progress.* Boston: Little, Brown, 1939.

————. *The Politics of Hope.* Boston: Houghton Mifflin, 1963.

————. *The Politics of Upheaval.* Boston: Houghton Mifflin, 1960.

————. *Robert F. Kennedy and His Times.* Boston: Houghton Mifflin, 1978.

————. *The Shape of National Politics to Come.* Memorandum for private circulation, 1959. (Copy in the Northwestern University Library, Evanston, Ill.)

————. *A Thousand Days: John F. Kennedy in the White House.* Boston: Houghton Mifflin, 1965.

————. *The Vital Center: The Politics of Freedom.* 2d ed. Boston: Houghton Mifflin, 1962.

Schlesinger, Arthur M., Jr., and White, Morton, eds. *Paths of American Thought.* Boston: Houghton Mifflin, 1963.

Schlesinger, Arthur, Sr. *The American as Reformer.* 2d ed. New York: Atheneum, 1968.

————. *In Retrospect: History of a Historian.* New York: Harcourt, Brace and World, 1963.

————. *New Viewpoints in American History.* New York: Macmillan, 1923.

————. *Paths to the Present.* 2d ed. Boston: Houghton-Mifflin, 1964.

Shactman, Tom. *Decade of Shocks: Dallas to Watergate, 1963–1974.* New York: Poseidon Press, 1983.

Stevenson, Charles L. *Ethics and Language.* New Haven, Conn.: Yale University Press, 1944.

Stewart, Charles, Smith, Craig, and Denton, Robert E. *Persuasion and Social Movements.* Prospect Heights, Ill.: Waveland Press, 1984.

Strauss, William, and Howe, Neil. *Generations: The History of America's Future, 1584–2069.* New York: Morrow, 1991.

U.S. Congress. Senate. Committee on Commerce. Subcommittee on Communications. *Freedom of Communications, Part I.* 87th Cong., 1st sess. Senate Report No. 994. Washington, D.C.: U.S. Government Printing Office, 1961.

Van Deusen, Glyndon. *The Jacksonian Era, 1828–48.* New York: Harper and Row, 1959.

Ward, John William. *Andrew Jackson: Symbol for an Age.* New York: Oxford University Press, 1962.

Weaver, Richard M. *The Ethics of Rhetoric.* South Bend, Ind.: Regnery/Gateway, 1953.

Whately, Richard. *Elements of Rhetoric (1828).* Carbondale: Southern Illinois University Press, 1963.

White, Hayden. *Metahistory: The Historical Imagination in Nineteenth-Century Europe.* 3d ed. Baltimore: Johns Hopkins University Press, 1980.

Wills, Garry. *The Kennedy Imprisonment: A Meditation on Power.* Boston: Little, Brown, 1983.

————. *Nixon Agonistes.* Boston: Houghton Mifflin, 1970.

Wolin, Sheldon. *Politics and Vision.* Boston: Little, Brown, 1960.

Zarefsky, David. *President Johnson's War on Poverty: Rhetoric and History.* University: University of Alabama Press, 1986.

Articles

Ahlstrom, Sydney E. "Mr. Schlesinger's Vital Center." *Religion in Life* 19, 2 (1950): 205–12.

"An 'American Renewal': Transcript of the Address by President Clinton." *New York Times,* January 21, 1992, p. A-11.

Andrews, James A. "The Rhetoric of History: The Constitutional Convention." *Today's Speech* 16 (November 1968): 13–16.

Apple, R. W., Jr. "Behind Clinton's Choice." *New York Times,* July 10, 1992, pp. A-10, A-18.

Beard, Charles A. "Written History as an Act of Faith." *American Historical Review* 39 (January 1934): 219–29.

Bernstein, Barton J. Introduction to Barton J. Bernstein, ed., *Towards a New Past,* pp. v–xiii. New York: Pantheon, 1968.

"Biography." *Current Biography,* October 1946, pp. 537–38.

"Bitter Pen of Arthur M." Review of *A Thousand Days. National Review,* August 10, 1965, pp. 680–81.

Brandon, Henry. "Schlesinger at the White House: An Historian's Inside View of Kennedy at Work." *Harper's,* July 1964, pp. 57–60.

Breit, Harvey. "Talk with Mr. Schlesinger." *New York Times Book Review,* September 18, 1949, p. 19.

Brummett, Barry. "Burkeian Transcendence and Ultimate Terms in Rhetoric by and about James Watt." *Central States Speech Journal* 33 (Winter 1982): 547–56.

Burke, Kenneth. "Definition of Man." *Hudson Review* 16 (Winter 1963–64): 491–514.

———. "Dramatism." In *International Encyclopedia of the Social Sciences,* pp. 445–52. New York: Macmillan, 1969.

Carpenter, Ronald H. "Frederick Jackson Turner and the Rhetorical Impact of the Frontier Thesis." *Quarterly Journal of Speech* 63 (April 1977): 117–29.

———. "The Historical Jeremiad as Rhetorical Genre." In Karlyn Kohrs Campbell and Kathleen Hall Jamieson, eds., *Form and Genre,* pp. 103–18. Falls Church, Va.: Speech Communication Association, 1977.

Cogley, John. "Follow the Bouncing Ball." *Commonweal,* August 23, 1957, p. 522.

"Combative Chronicler." *Time,* December 17, 1965, pp. 54–60.

Cone, Carl B. "Major Factors in the Rhetoric of Historians." *Quarterly Journal of Speech* 33 (December 1947): 437–50.

Cunliffe, Marcus. "Arthur Schlesinger, Jr." In Marcus Cunliffe and Robin W. Winks, eds., *Pastmasters: Some Essays on American Historians,* pp. 345–74, 468–72. New York: Harper and Row, 1969.

Daniels, Johnathan. "Ready to Be Radical." Review of *The Vital Center. Saturday Review of Literature,* September 10, 1949, pp. 11–12.

Davis, T. N. "Of Many Things." Review of *A Thousand Days. America,* August 7, 1965, p. 124.

Decter, Midge. "Kennedyism." *Commentary* 49 (January 1970): 19–27.

————. "Kennedyism Again." *Commentary* 66 (December 1978): 23–29.

de Toledano, Ralph. "Junior's Misses." *American Mercury* 77 (November 1953): 5–14.

Dionisopoulos, George N., Gallagher, Victoria J., Goldzwig, Steven P., and Zarefsky, David. "Martin Luther King, The American Dream, and Vietnam: A Collision of Rhetorical Trajectories." *Western Journal of Speech Communication* 56 (1992): 91–107.

Dowd, Maureen. "Two Baby Boomers on One Ticket, But Will it Work?" *New York Times*, July 13, 1992, pp. A-1, B-6.

"The Election and After (Discussion)." *New York Times Book Review*, August 16, 1984, pp. 33–38.

Englehardt, Carroll. "Man in the Middle: Arthur M. Schlesinger, Jr., and Postwar American Liberalism." *South Atlantic Quarterly* 80 (Spring 1981): 119–38.

Enos, Richard L. "Rhetorical Intent of Ancient Historiography: Herodotus and the Battle of Marathon." *Communication Quarterly* 24 (Winter 1976): 24–31.

"Excerpts from Clinton's and Gore's Remarks on the Ticket." *New York Times*, July 10, 1992, p. A-16.

Fairlie, Henry. "Books Reconsidered." Review of *Robert F. Kennedy and His Times. New Republic*, September 9, 1978, pp. 30–34.

Fineman, Howard. "Sixties Coming of Age." *Newsweek*, July 20, 1992, pp. 32–35.

Frady, Marshall. "The Transformation of Bobby Kennedy." Review of *Robert F. Kennedy and His Times. New York Review of Books*, October 12, 1978, pp. 42–51.

Francesconi, Robert A. "James Hunt, the Wilmington 10, and Institutional Legitimacy." *Quarterly Journal of Speech* 68 (1982): 47–59.

Gass, Oscar. "The New Frontier Fulfilled." *Commentary* 32 (December 1961): 461–73.

Gelb, Leslie. "Wonks versus Liberals." *New York Times*, July 16, 1992, p. A-25.

Ginzburg, Benjamin. "Against Messianism." *New Republic*, February 18, 1931, pp. 15–17.

Goodman, Walter. "Schlesinger's Case for Robert Kennedy." Review of *Robert F. Kennedy and His Times. New Leader*, October 9, 1978, pp. 16–17.

Goodnight, G. Thomas. "The Liberal and Conservative Presumptions: On Political Philosophy and the Foundation of Public Argument." In *Proceedings of the [First] Summer Conference on Argumentation*, pp. 304–37. Falls Church, Va.: Speech Communication Association, 1980.

————. "The Personal, Technical, and Public Spheres of Argument: A Speculative Inquiry into the Art of Public Deliberation." *Journal of the American Forensic Association* 18 (Spring 1982): 214–27.

Graham, Otis L., Jr. "Historians and the New Deal, 1944–60." *Social Studies* 54 (April 1963): 133–39.

Greeley, Andrew M. "Robert Kennedy and His Times." *Critic*, November 1978, pp. 2–8.

Greenfield, Meg. "Byzantium on the Potomac." Review of *A Thousand Days*. *Reporter*, August 12, 1965, pp. 10–14.

Griffin, Leland M. "The Rhetorical Structure of the 'New Left' Movement, Part I." *Quarterly Journal of Speech* 50 (April 1964): 113–35.

———. "When Dreams Collide: Rhetorical Trajectories in the Assassination of President Kennedy." *Quarterly Journal of Speech* 70 (May 1984): 111–31.

Griffiths, David Burke. "Vital Center versus New Left: A. M. Schlesinger, Jr., and C. W. Mills." *Midwest Quarterly* 7 (Autumn 1965): 43–50.

Grimes, William. "Film Tribute to Clinton Focuses on Simple Values." *New York Times*, July 17, 1992, p. A-11.

Habermas, Jurgen. "The Public Sphere: An Encyclopedia Article." Translated by Sara and Frank Lennox. *New German Critique* 3 (1974): 49–55.

Hammond, Bray. "Public Policy and National Banks." Review of *The Age of Jackson*. *Journal of Economic History* 6 (1946): 79–84.

Hart, Gary. "Let Us Choose a New Path." *New York Times*, February 23, 1984, p. 13.

———. "Text of Speech Prepared for Delivery to the Democratic Delegates." *New York Times*, July 19, 1984, p. 6.

Hempel, Carl. "The Function of General Laws in History." *Journal of Philosophy* 39 (1943): 35–48.

Hexter, J. H. "Historiography: The Rhetoric of History." In *International Encyclopedia of the Social Sciences*, pp. 368–93. New York: Macmillan, 1968.

Higham, John. "Behind Consensus: The Historian as a Moral Critic." *American Historical Review* 67 (April 1962): 609–25.

———. "The Construction of American History." In John Higham, ed., *The Reconstruction of American History*, pp. 9–24. New York: Harper and Row, 1962.

Holland, Virginia. "Kenneth Burke's Dramatistic Approach in Speech Criticism." *Quarterly Journal of Speech* 61 (December 1955): 352–58.

Hook, Sidney. "The Technique of Mystification." *Partisan Review* 4 (December 1937): 57–62.

Howe, Irving. "A New Turn at Arthur's." Review of *The Bitter Heritage*. *New York Review of Books*, February 23, 1967, pp. 13–14.

Hunt, George P. "Schlesinger and John F. Kennedy." *Life*, July 16, 1965, p. 5.

Isaacson, Walter. "A Time for Courage." *Time*, November 16, 1992, pp. 26–29.

Jasinski, James. "James Madison and the American Public Sphere." Paper presented at the 1984 Central States Speech Association Convention, Chicago, Illinois, April 1984.

Johnson, Gerald W. "FDR: A Political Portrait." *Atlantic Monthly*, March 1957, pp. 69–72.

Kennedy, Edward. "Principles of the Democratic Party." *Vital Speeches* 46 (September 1, 1980): 714–16.

———. "The Voyage That Is America." *Vital Speeches* 46 (February 15, 1980): 260–63.

Kennedy, John F. "The Democratic National Convention Acceptance Address." *Vital Speeches* 26 (August 1, 1960): 610–12.

———. "A Time of Decision: A Challenging Agenda." *Vital Speeches* 26 (July 15, 1960): 580–83.

Keyserling, Leon. "Eggheads and Politics." *New Republic*, October 27, 1958, pp. 13–17.

Kondracke, Morton. "The Dream Is Dead." *New Republic*, August 23, 1980, pp. 6–8.

Lipset, Seymour Martin. "The President, the Polls, and Vietnam." *Trans/Action*, September-October 1966, pp. 19–24.

McGee, Michael C. "The Fall of Wellington: A Case Study of the Relationship Between Theory, Practice, and Rhetoric in History." *Quarterly Journal of Speech* 63 (February 1977): 28–42.

———. "The 'Ideograph': A Link Between Rhetoric and Ideology." *Quarterly Journal of Speech* 66 (February 1980): 1–16.

———. "In Search of 'The People': A Rhetorical Alternative." *Quarterly Journal of Speech* 61 (October 1975): 235–49.

McGee, Michael C., and Martin, Martha Anne. "Public Knowledge and Ideological Argumentation." *Communication Monographs* 50 (March 1983): 47–65.

McGrory, Mary. "A Democrat Who Won't Move Right." *Washington Post Weekly Report*, November 26, 1984, p. 25.

Mann, Arthur. "The Progressive Tradition." In John Higham, ed., *The Reconstruction of American History*, pp. 157–79. New York: Harper and Row, 1962.

Matusow, Allen J. "John F. Kennedy and the Intellectuals." *Wilson Quarterly* 7 (Autumn 1983): 140–53.

Mayer, Allan J. "End of the Democratic Era?" *Time*, August 18, 1980, pp. 21–25.

"Moonlight Writer." *Time*, June 29, 1962, p. 12.

Morgenthau, Hans. "What Should We Do Now (about Vietnam)?" *Look*, August 9, 1966, pp. 24–25.

Morley, Jefferson. "The Old Idea of 'New Ideas.'" *New Republic*, May 27, 1985, pp. 14–15.

Morris, Willie. "Houston's Superpatriots." *Harper's*, October 1961, pp. 48–56.

Morrow, Lance. "Rediscovering America." *Time*, July 7, 1980, pp. 21–29.

Morton, Marian J. "Arthur Schlesinger, Jr., and the Search for the Vital Center." In Marian J. Morton, *The Terrors of Ideological Politics: Liberal Historians in a Conservative Mood*, pp. 345–74. Cleveland: Case Western Reserve University Press, 1972.

Nelson, Michael. "Scholar-Politicians and Sheriffs." Review of *Robert F. Kennedy and His Times*. *Virginia Quarterly Review* 55 (Spring 1979): 329–37.

North, Helen F. "Rhetoric and Historiography." *Quarterly Journal of Speech* 42 (October 1956): 234–42.

Nuechterlein, James A. "Arthur M. Schlesinger, Jr., and the Discontents of

Postwar American Liberalism." *Review of Politics* 39 (January 1977): 3–40.

"The Old Deal." Review of *The Age of Jackson*. *Time*, October 22, 1945, pp. 103–106.

"On Writing History: A Conversation with Professor Arthur Schlesinger, Jr." In *Conversations with Henry Brandon*, pp. 40–54. Boston: Houghton Mifflin, 1968.

"Peephole Journalism." Review of *A Thousand Days*. *Commonweal*, September 3, 1965, p. 613.

Pfaff, William. "The Decline of Liberal Politics." *Commentary* 48 (October 1969): 45–51.

"Portrait." *Saturday Review of Literature*, September 24, 1945, pp. 10–11.

Radosh, Ronald. "Schlesinger and Kennedy: Historian in the Service of Power." *Nation*, August 6, 1977, pp. 104–109.

Railsback, Celeste Condit. "The Contemporary American Abortion Controversy: Stages in the Argument." *Quarterly Journal of Speech* 70 (November 1984): 410–24.

Rosenbaum, David E. "Democratic Platform Shows Shift in Party's Focus." *New York Times*, July 14, 1992, p. A-9.

Rosenberg, John. "If FDR Were Alive Today . . ." *Nation*, April 15, 1978, pp. 420–21.

Schlesinger, Arthur M., Jr. "The Administration and the Left." *New Statesman*, February 8, 1963, pp. 185–86.

———. "America, 1968: The Politics of Violence." *Harper's*, August 1968, pp. 19–24.

———. "America and the World: A New Fix?" *Vogue*, February 1, 1969, pp. 184–85, 239.

———. "American Politics on a Darkling Plain." *Wall Street Journal*, March 16, 1982, p. 28.

———. "Are We Richer Today?" With Seymour E. Harris. *Ladies' Home Journal*, September 1949, pp. 42, 108–13.

———. "The Case for Kennedy." *New York Times Magazine*, November 6, 1960, pp. 19, 113–16.

———. "A Century of FDR." *Signature*, January 1982, pp. 40–43, 60–62.

———. "Conservative versus Liberal—A Debate." *New York Times Magazine*, March 4, 1956, pp. 11, 58–62.

———. "The Dark Heart of American History." *Saturday Review*, October 19, 1968, pp. 20–23, 81.

———. "The Decline-and-Fall Mood." *Wall Street Journal*, June 5, 1979, p. 2.

———. "The Decline of Greatness." *Saturday Evening Post*, November 1, 1958, pp. 25, 68–71.

———. "A Democratic View of Republicans." *New York Times Magazine*, July 17, 1960, pp. 7, 48.

———. "Eisenhower Won't Succeed." *New Republic*, April 5, 1954, pp. 8–12.

———. "The End of an Era?" *Wall Street Journal*, November 20, 1980, p. 26.

———. "Epilogue: The One Against the Many." In Arthur M. Schlesinger,

Jr., and Morton White, eds., *Paths of American Thought*, pp. 531–38. Boston: Houghton Mifflin, 1963.

———. "A Eulogy: John Fitzgerald Kennedy." *Saturday Evening Post*, December 14, 1963, pp. 32–33.

———. "The Future of Liberalism: The Challenge of Abundance." *Reporter*, May 3, 1956, pp. 8–11.

———. "The Great Carter Mystery." *New Republic*, April 12, 1980, pp. 1, 18–21.

———. "The Historian and History." *Foreign Affairs* 41 (April 1963): 491–97.

———. "The Historian as Artist." *Atlantic Monthly*, July 1963, pp. 35–41.

———. "The Historian as Participant." *Daedalus* 100, 2 (Spring 1971): 339–58.

———. "Is Liberalism Dead?" *New York Times*, March 30, 1980, pp. 42, 70–79.

———. "Legacy of Andrew Jackson." *American Mercury* 64 (February 1947): 168–73.

———. "Liberal Anti-communism Revisited." *Commentary* 44 (September 1967): 68–71.

———. "Liberalism." *Saturday Review*, June 8, 1957, pp. 11–12, 37.

———. "Liberalism in America: A Note for Europeans." *Perspectives, U.S.A.* 14 (Winter 1956). Reprinted in Arthur M. Schlesinger, Jr., *The Politics of Hope*, pp. 63–80. Boston: Houghton Mifflin, 1963.

———. "The Liberal Opportunity." *American Prospect*, Spring 1990, pp. 10–18.

———. "McCarthyism Is Threatening Us Again." *Saturday Evening Post*, August 13, 1966, pp. 10–11.

———. "Memo to the 1993 Crowd: Believe in Yourselves." *Newsweek*, January 11, 1993, p. 39.

———. "A Middle Way Out of Vietnam." *New York Times Magazine*, September 18, 1966, pp. 47–48, 111–20.

———. "Neo-Conservatism and the Class Struggle." *Wall Street Journal*, June 2, 1981, p. 30.

———. "The New Conservatism: The Politics of Nostalgia." *Reporter*, June 16, 1955, pp. 9–12.

———. "The New Conservatism in America: A Liberal Comment." *Confluence* 2 (December 1953): 61–71.

———. "New Liberal Coalition." *Progressive*, April 1967, pp. 15–19.

———. "The New Mood in Politics." *Esquire*, January 1960, pp. 58–60.

———. "The 1968 Election: An Historical Perspective." *Vital Speeches*, December 15, 1968, pp. 148–54.

———. "Not Left, Not Right, But a Vital Center." *New York Times Magazine*, April 4, 1948, pp. 7, 44–47.

———. "One Last Chance for the Democrats." *Playboy*, November 1982, pp. 110, 112, 246–54.

———. "On Heroic Leadership and the Dilemma of Strong Men and Weak Peoples." *Encounter* 15 (December 1960): 3–11.

———. "On the Inscrutability of History." *Encounter*, November 1966, pp. 10–17.

———. "On the Writing of Contemporary History." *Atlantic Monthly*, March 1967, pp. 69–74.

———. "Our Country and Our Culture." *Partisan Review* 19 (September 1952): 590–93.

———. "Politics, 1971." *Vogue*, February 1, 1971, pp. 139–40.

———. "The Problem of Richard Hildreth." *New England Quarterly* 13 (June 1940): 223–45.

———. "Reply to Englehardt." *South Atlantic Quarterly* 80 (Spring 1981): 139–42.

———. "The Revolution That Never Was." *Wall Street Journal*, October 24, 1979, p. 22.

———. "Right Man for the Big Job." *New York Times Magazine*, April 3, 1960, pp. 120–21.

———. "Sources of the New Deal." In Arthur M. Schlesinger, Jr., and Morton White, eds., *Paths of American Thought*, pp. 372–91. Boston: Houghton Mifflin, 1963.

———. "Stevenson and the American Liberal Dilemma." *Twentieth Century* 153 (January 1953): 24–29.

———. "Theology and Politics from the Social Gospel to the Cold War: The Impact of Reinhold Niebuhr." In Cushing Strout, ed., *Intellectual History in America: From Darwin to Niebuhr*, vol. 2, pp. 158–81. New York: Harper and Row, 1968.

———. "The Thread of History: Freedom of Fatality" (Review). *Reporter*, December 15, 1955, pp. 45–47.

———. "The 'Threat' of the Radical Right." *New York Times Magazine*, June 17, 1962, pp. 10, 55–58.

———. "Time for Constitutional Change." *Wall Street Journal*, December 24, 1982, p. 4.

———. "The Turn of the Cycle." *New Yorker*, November 16, 1992, pp. 46–54.

———. "The Velocity of History." *Time*, July 6, 1970, pp. 32–34.

———. "Vietnam and the End of the Age of the Superpowers." *Harper's*, March 1969, pp. 41–49.

———. "*The Vital Center* Reconsidered." *Encounter*, September 1970, pp. 89–93.

———. "What Should We Do Now (about Vietnam)?" *Look*, August 9, 1966, p. 31.

———. "Where Does the Liberal Go from Here?" *New York Times Magazine*, August 4, 1957, pp. 7, 36–38.

———. "Who Needs Grover Cleveland?" *New Republic*, July 7–14, 1979, pp. 14–16.

———. "Why I Am for Kennedy." *New Republic*, May 4, 1968, pp. 19–23.

Sellers, Charles G., Jr. "Andrew Jackson versus the Historians." *Mississippi Valley Historical Review* 44 (1958): 615–34.

Shannon, William V. "Controversial Historian of the Age of Kennedy." *New York Times Magazine*, November 21, 1965, pp. 30–31, 132–36.

Shribman, David. "A Closer Look at the Hart Generation." *New York Times Magazine*, May 27, 1984, pp. 32–35, 59–62.

Sievers, Rodney M. "Adlai E. Stevenson and the Crisis of Liberalism." *Midwest Quarterly* 14 (January 1973): 135–49.

Silver, Thomas B. "Coolidge and the Historians." *American Scholar* 50 (Autumn 1981): 501–17.

Smith, Gaddis. "The Shadow of John Foster Dulles." *Foreign Affairs* 52 (1974): 403.

Spencer, Martin E. "*The Imperial Presidency* and the Uses of Social Science." *Midwest Quarterly* 20 (Spring 1979): 281–99.

Steel, Ronald. "The Cool Way Out." Review of *The Bitter Heritage*. *Book Week*, March 5, 1967, p. 194.

"The Superstars." *Newsweek*, October 17, 1966, p. 68.

Swados, Harvey. "Does America Deserve a New Frontier?" In Harvey Swados, *A Radical at Large: American Essays*, pp. 277–306. London: Rupert Hart-Davis, 1968.

Taft, John. "The Once and Future Mandarin." *New Republic*, November 26, 1977, pp. 16–19.

"A Talk-In on Vietnam." *New York Times Magazine*, February 6, 1966, pp. 12–13, 72–79.

"The Taste of Memory." Review of *A Thousand Days*. *Nation*, August 2, 1965, pp. 49–50.

Taylor, Paul. "The Democratic Center Finds There's Strength in Numbers." *Washington Post Weekly Edition*, November 25, 1985, pp. 12–13.

"The Tide Is Turning: A New Political Cycle in the 1990s." Interview with Arthur M. Schlesinger, Jr. *Challenge*, November-December 1991, pp. 9–14.

Toner, Robin. "Arkansas' Clinton Enters the '92 Race for President." *New York Times*, October 4, 1991, p. A-10.

———. "1992 Ticket Puts Council of Moderates to Stiff Test." *New York Times*, July 15, 1992, p. A-7.

"Transcript of Speech by Clinton Accepting Democratic Nomination." *New York Times*, July 17, 1992, p. A-14.

"Trials of an Instant Author." Review of *A Thousand Days*. *Time*, August 27, 1965, p. 31.

Walzer, Michael. "On the Role of Symbolism in Political Thought." *Political Science Quarterly* 82 (June 1967): 191–204.

Weaver, Richard. "The Middle of the Road and Where It Leads." *Human Events* 13 (March 24, 1956): n.p.

Weiler, Michael. "The Rhetoric of Neo-Liberalism." *Quarterly Journal of Speech* 70 (November 1984): 362–78.

Williams, William A. "Schlesinger: Right Crisis, Wrong Order." Review of *Crisis of the Old Order*. *Nation*, March 23, 1957, pp. 257–60.

Wills, Garry. "Fierce in His Loyalties and Enemies." Review of *Robert F. Kennedy and His Times*. *New York Times Book Review*, November 12, 1978, pp. 7, 54–56.

Windt, Theodore. "The Presidency and Speeches on International Crises: Repeating the Rhetorical Past." In Theodore Windt and Beth Ingold, eds.,

Essays in Presidential Rhetoric, pp. 61–70. Dubuque, Iowa: Kendall/Hunt, 1983.

Witcover, Jules. "Robert Kennedy 'Might Have Changed History.'" Review of *Robert F. Kennedy and His Times. Progressive,* November 1978, pp. 53–55.

Woodward, C. Vann. "The Crisis of the Old Order." *Saturday Review,* March 2, 1957, pp. 11–12.

Wreszin, Michael. "Arthur Schlesinger, Jr., Scholar-Activist in Cold War America, 1946–1956." *Salmagundi* 63, 4 (Spring-Summer 1984): 255–85.

Wright, Esmund. "The Age of Roosevelt." *History Today* 7 (November 1957): 775.

Wrong, Dennis. "How Critical Is Our Condition?" *Dissent* 28 (Fall 1981): 414–24.

———. "The Rhythm of Democratic Politics." In Lewis A. Coser and Irving Howe, eds., *The New Conservatives: A Critique from the Left,* pp. 90–106. New York: Quadrangle, 1974.

Zarefsky, David. "Causal Argument Among Historians: The Case of the American Civil War." *Southern Speech Communication Journal* 15 (Winter 1980): 187–205.

———. "The Impasse of the Liberal Argument: Speculation on American Politics in the Late 1960's." In David Zarefsky, Malcolm Sillars, and Jack Rhodes, eds., *Argument in Transition: Proceedings of the Third Summer Conference on Argumentation,* pp. 365–79. Annandale, Va.: Speech Communication Association, 1983.

———. "President Johnson's War on Poverty: The Rhetoric of Three 'Establishment' Movements." *Communication Monographs* 44 (November 1977): 352–73.

Index

Parsons, Talcott, 100
Perelman, Chaim, 35
Perot, H. Ross, 120
Pessen, Edward, 27
The Politics of Upheaval (1960), 16
Presumption, 29, 44, 90, 94, 112, 131,
133, 134; role in shaping community
identity, xii, 18–19; definition of, 18,
145 (n. 15); and legitimation, 100–101

Radical Right. *See* Conservatism
Reagan, Ronald, 100, 103, 104, 108, 109,
110, 112, 114; attacks liberalism in
1988 campaign, 105–6
Representative anecdote, 44, 152 (n. 82).
See also Dramatism
Resource limits, 59, 101–3
Rhetorical trajectory, 32, 48, 75, 77, 94,
96, 100, 123, 125–26; definition of,
xiii–xiv. *See also* Dramatism
Robert F. Kennedy and His Times
(1978), 99; reviews of, 165 (n. 2)
Roosevelt, Franklin D. (FDR), 3, 13, 14,
25, 27, 34, 41, 42, 65, 66, 69, 95, 100,
104, 105, 110, 113, 116, 117, 119, 120,
121, 133; death of, 4; as model leader,
9–10, 115–16; as administrator, 23–
24; personality of, 24, 26–27; as poli-
tician, 26; as compared to John F.
Kennedy, 71, 72
Roosevelt, Theodore, 42, 108, 113
Rueckert, William, xi
Rusk, Dean, 74, 81

Schlesinger, Arthur M., Jr.: political activities of, ix, 5, 31–32, 44–46, 50,
78–79, 99, 158–59 (n. 6); influence on
American liberalism, ix–x, x, 29–30,
49; on how the past influences the
present, x, 19–20, 63–64, 125, 131;
writings shaped by liberal ideology, x,
28, 29, 138 (n. 15); on "tides of
national politics," x, 10–14, 21, 26–
27, 40–42, 48, 64, 91, 94, 118; formative years of, 1–3; on academic
versus political life, 2, 3, 19, 62;
career at Harvard, 5, 16; on postwar
world, 5; influenced by Niebuhr, 5–6,
on inevitability of social conflict, 6–
7, 32–33, 65, 68, 92; influenced by
his father, 7–8; on communism, 7,
67, 81, 82, 127–28, 161 (n. 43); prefers
empiricism over ideology, 8, 9; on

"doughface progressivism," 8; influenced by FDR, 9–10; on importance
of strong leadership, 9–10, 34, 69;
frame of acceptance of, 10–14; on
importance of "vital center" of reasoned discourse, 11–12, 68, 75–76, 86,
89, 97, 127, 133; on increasing velocity of history, 14, 80–81, 92–94,
125, 163–64 (n. 86); public vocabulary
of, 14, 132; prefers historical understanding over determinism, 20–21,
132; on age of Jackson, 22–23, 24,
25–26; on age of Roosevelt, 23, 24–
25, 26–27; on relationship between
political elites and public, 27, 84;
treatment of Coolidge critiqued, 28;
public persona transformed to liberal
spokesman, 31, 75, 77; defines 1950s
consensus as liberal consensus, 37,
126; responds to New Conservatism,
37–38; defines liberal and conservative interests, 38–39, 107–8, 129;
redirects liberal agenda to qualitative
issues, 39–40, 101, 126–27; explains
electoral defeats as part of political
cycle, 40–41, 111–13, 127; predicts
new liberal era in 1960s, 41–42, 64,
127; states need for leadership in
1960s, 42–44; analyzes Kennedy's and
Nixon's personalities, 46–47; stresses
importance of 1960 election, 47–48,
53–54; activities in Kennedy administration, 61–62; defends role of
historian as participant, 62–64; responds to Radical Right, 65–66;
responds to New Left, 66–68, 96–97;
on assassination of John F. Kennedy,
68, 74; assassination as challenge to
frame of acceptance, 69; decides to
write memoirs of Kennedy administration, 69–70; *A Thousand Days* as
defense of his liberal frame, 70–71;
portrays Kennedy as representative
liberal facing legislative obstacles,
71–72; portrays Kennedy as heroic
leader, 72–74; growing opposition to
war in Vietnam, 78–79; sees history
as inscrutable, 80; criticizes Johnson
administration Vietnam policy, 80–
83; defends Kennedy's Vietnam
record, 81; criticizes direct action
protest against Vietnam war,
83–85; defines "middle way out of

Vietnam," 85–86; "middle way" critiqued, 86–87; declares "end of the age of superpowers," 87–88, 128; on presidential candidacy of Robert F. Kennedy, 88; describes "crisis of confidence" in American society, 89–90; depicts pattern and tradition of violence in America, 91–92; sees growing instability in political cycle, 92–93; maintains presumption that change is good, 94; reaffirms need for heroic leadership, 94–96, 114–17; comments that America is turning away from politics, 97–98; liberal faith in economic growth and government intervention challenged during 1970s and 1980s, 103–7; upset by negative references to liberalism, 106–7; attacks Reaganomics, 108–9, 114–15, 116; attacks neo-liberalism, 109, 116; accuses conservatives of misinterpreting past, 110; identifies true meaning of liberalism, 110–111; restates faith in political tides, 112, 124; states importance of political generations, 113–14, 129–30; endorses Michael Dukakis for president in 1988, 117; predicts new liberal era in 1990s, 118; reflects upon importance of 1992 election, 120–22, 123–24, 130; tries to restore legitimacy to liberal perspective, 122–23; clarifies purpose of writing history, 131; has written "exculpatory history," 132–35. *See also* Tides of national politics

Schlesinger, Arthur M., Sr.: as father, 2; as academician, 2; as progressive historian, 3; on "middle zone" of political action, 7; as supporter of FDR, 9; and "tides of national politics," 10, 12, 13

Schneider, William, 105

Sellers, Charles, 27

Shactman, Tom, 69, 70, 102

Shannon, William, 75

"The Shape of National Politics to Come" (1959), 42, 44, 50

Shapiro, Walter, 105

Shocks, societal, 69, 166 (n. 22); responses to, 70, 75, 89

Silver, Thomas, 28

Steel, Ronald, 87

Stevenson, Adlai, ix, 31, 37, 41, 44–45, 46, 73

A Thousand Days: John F. Kennedy in the White House (1965), 48, 65, 70–74, 76, 79; reviews of, 74–75

Tides of national politics, x, xii, xiii, xiv, 14, 15, 21, 30, 32, 36, 50, 51, 60, 77, 86, 91, 100, 118, 125, 126, 130, 133; importance of in American politics, x–xi; origins of, 10; and definitions of liberal and conservative, 10–11; and predictable alternations of liberal and conservative epochs, 12–13, 33, 53; psychological causes of, 12; moves public opinion progressively leftward, 13; and need for heroic leadership, 13–14, 34, 114–15; and possibilities of transcendence, 14–15; as explanation sketch, 21, 24; and age of Jackson, 22–23, 24, 25–26, 33; and age of Roosevelt, 23–24, 24–25, 26–27, 33; as reason for liberal political defeats in 1950s, 40–41; as impetus for liberal era in 1960s, 41–42, 53, 54, 64; vindicated by 1960 election, 48, 112, 127; as rhetorical trajectory, 48, 124, 125; critique of, 75–76; challenged by Vietnam war, 79–80; challenged by growing violence, 90–91; influenced by generational factor, 113–14; cited to explain outcome of 1992 election, 120, 121–22; accounts for consistency in Schlesinger's discourse, 126, 135; biased toward status quo, 133–35. *See also* Schlesinger, Arthur M., Jr.

Totalitarianism, 6, 8, 20, 33, 95; as threat to progressive liberalism, 3–4, 25

Transcendence, 5, 14, 51, 55, 56, 57, 59, 107, 143 (n. 83), 154 (n. 47). *See also* Dramatism

Truman, Harry S., 4, 5, 41, 104, 110, 113, 121

Tsongas, Paul, 103

Turner, Frederick Jackson, 2, 3

Van Buren, Martin, 22, 24, 26

Vietnam War, xi, 59, 76, 77, 78–88, 119, 127; as threat to Schlesinger's frame of acceptance, 79–80, 86. *See also* Johnson, Lyndon B.

Violence: growing amount of in American society, 88–89; and crisis of confidence, 89–90; as threat to Schlesinger's frame of acceptance, 90–91

The Vital Center (1949, 1962), 5, 8, 9, 32, 67, 91

Wallace, Henry, 4, 8, 23
Walzer, Michael, 123, 135–36

Weaver, Richard, 87, 100
Weber, Max, 100
Webster, Daniel, 22, 24
Weiler, Michael, 101, 102
Wilson, Woodrow, 113, 121
Wreszin, Michael, 31
Wright, Esmond, 29
Wrong, Dennis, x

Zarefsky, xiii–xiv, 59–60

About the Author

Stephen P. Depoe is Associate Professor of Communication, University of Cincinnati. He received his bachelor's degree from Emporia State University and his masters and doctorate from Northwestern University.

About the Series

STUDIES IN RHETORIC AND COMMUNICATION
General Editors:
E. Culpepper Clark, Raymie E. McKerrow, and David Zarefsky

The University of Alabama Press has established this series to publish major new works in the general area of rhetoric and communication, including books treating the symbolic manifestations of political discourse, argument as social knowledge, the impact of machine technology on patterns of communication behavior, and other topics related to the nature of impact of symbolic communication. We actively solicit studies involving historical, critical, or theoretical analyses of human discourse.